MIGHTY FITZ

Reasons to Believe: New Voices in American Fiction
Creative Conversations: The Writer's Complete Guide to
Conducting Interviews
Dharma Lion: A Biography of Allen Ginsberg
Crossroads: The Life and Music of Eric Clapton
There but for Fortune: The Life of Phil Ochs
Francis Ford Coppola: A Filmmaker's Life

MIGHTY FITZ

THE SINKING OF THE *EDMUND FITZGERALD*

—— MICHAEL SCHUMACHER ——

BLOOMSBURY

Public Library

Copyright © 2005 by Michael Schumacher

Published by Bloomsbury Publishing, New York and London
Distributed to the trade by Holtzbrinck Publishers

Title page painting by Doris Sampson (dorissampsonartist@hotmail.com),
reprinted by permission.

All papers used by Bloomsbury Publishing are natural, recyclable products
made from wood grown in well-managed forests. The manufacturing processes
conform to the environmental regulations of the country of origin.

Library of Congress Cataloging-in-Publication Data

Schumacher, Michael.
    Mighty fitz : the sinking of the *Edmund Fitzgerald* / Michael Schumacher.
        p.   cm.
    Includes bibliographical references and index.
    ISBN–13: 978–1–58234–647–2 (hardcover)
    ISBN–10: 1–58234–647–X (hardcover)
    1. *Edmund Fitzgerald* (Ship). 2.   Shipwrecks—Superior, Lake. I. Title.
G530. E26S38 2005
917.74'90443—dc22   2005009768

363.123

First U.S. Edition 2005

1 3 5 7 9 10 8 6 4 2

Typeset by Westchester Book Group
Printed in the United States of America by Quebecor World Fairfield

To the crew of the *Edmund Fitzgerald*

and

to Gordon Lightfoot

for giving us a song to remember them by

CONTENTS

PREFACE

THE LIGHT FROM THE SURFACE OF LAKE SUPERIOR FADED SLOWLY, UNTIL the water was as black as night.

Bruce Fuoco drifted downward through the frigid water, suspended by a harness connected to a ship on the surface, and protected from the icy cold by a diving suit that looked as if it had been made for *Star Wars*. Hundreds of feet below him, broken in two sections and resting exactly where it had fallen nearly two decades earlier, was the object of Fuoco's mission: the wreckage of the S.S. *Edmund Fitzgerald*.

The *Fitzgerald*, often called the *Titanic* of the Great Lakes, was not only the most famous freshwater shipwreck; it was also the biggest mystery in Great Lakes history. The ship had captured national headlines when it sank without warning in the teeth of a terrible storm in the early evening hours of November 10, 1975. No Mayday had been transmitted, no lifeboats launched. The *Fitzgerald* simply plunged to the bottom of the lake and disappeared from radar. There had been no survivors. Twenty-nine men lost their lives, leaving behind grieving widows, fathers and mothers, sons and daughters, extended families, friends, and members of a stunned shipping community struggling to understand how such a thing could have happened.

With no eyewitnesses or survivors, there could never be a final answer.

Like the *Titanic,* the *Fitzgerald* was supposedly unsinkable. At the time of its loss, the ship was less than twenty years old; it was equipped with state-of-the-art technology and boasted an experienced crew as good as any in the business. It had been in regular contact with a ship trailing it through the storm, and no one had given the slightest indication that the *Fitzgerald* was in serious trouble. When it disappeared, the reaction was almost universal: utter disbelief.

Investigations into the tragedy yielded only more questions. The *Fitzgerald*'s wreckage had been located a few days after the ship's demise, and the following spring an underwater research vehicle, equipped with television and still cameras, had been lowered to the site. The footage and images spoke of a sad, violent ending. The ship's bow section had struck the lake floor with tremendous force, plowing through mud and silt until it finally came to a halt, much of its bow buried in the muck. The stern portion, twisted by almost unimaginable torque, had torn away from the front of the ship, coming to rest in an inverted position, its propeller pointed toward the surface. The white lettering on the stern, spelling out EDMUND FITZGERALD upside down, provided stark, grim identification in the silent depths.

That same year, Canadian folksinger Gordon Lightfoot recorded "The Wreck of the *Edmund Fitzgerald,*" a ballad recalling the ship's last voyage and the perils of sailing on the Great Lakes in November, when gale-force winds and high seas could "turn minutes to hours" for anyone defying the power of nature. The song shot up the sales charts, and people who had never dipped a toe into the waters along Lake Superior's shoreline suddenly knew the name and story of the lake's latest victim.

A hotly disputed Coast Guard report, released after an extensive investigation into the accident, added to the *Fitzgerald*'s growing legend. According to the report, the freighter had gradually lost buoyancy over a substantial period of many hours, most likely as the result of taking on great volumes of water through defective or poorly fastened hatch covers. The ship probably took a nosedive after one or more large waves overwhelmed it and dropped its bow below the surface. Skeptics disputed the theory, claiming that it was more likely that the *Fitzgerald* had bottomed out in shallow water, probably somewhere around the Six Fathom Shoal, in the eastern part of the lake. The *Fitz,* they argued, had sustained damage below the waterline—fatal damage of which the captain and crew might have been unaware—that led to the loss of freeboard and the ship's subsequent plunge to the bottom of the lake. Still others believed that the *Fitzgerald* had broken apart in the violent storm, much as the ore carriers *Carl D. Bradley* and *Daniel J. Morrell* had split apart on the surface in recent Great Lakes storms.

Since there had been no survivors from the *Edmund Fitzgerald,* there were no definitive answers. The tantalizing mystery invited further debate and exploration, including a highly publicized dive to the wreckage by the crew of Jacques Cousteau's *Calypso.* Other visits to the wreckage followed. Dr. Joseph MacInnis, an underwater explorer who had visited the wreckage of the *Titanic* in the North Atlantic in 1991, studied the *Fitzgerald* in 1994 as part of a government-sponsored project examining the Great Lakes and the St. Lawrence River. "Of all the dives, the most riveting were the ones we made to the *Edmund Fitzgerald,*" MacInnis wrote in his book *Fitzgerald's Storm.* "I was overwhelmed by questions."

There were no final answers, nor would there ever be. There could only be speculation. The *Fitzgerald* had come to rest in water too deep, at about 530 feet, to permit lengthy exploratory scuba dives. Even visits in underwater vehicles were risky. After Great Lakes explorer Fred Shannon discovered a body during one of the excursions to the wreck, family members of the dead crewmen mounted a campaign to formally declare the *Fitzgerald* a gravesite closed to any future exploration. The twenty-nine men still on board the ship deserved the chance to rest in peace, without the disruption brought on by the curious. Nothing new or conclusive, the families suggested, could be learned.

*   *   *

Bruce Fuoco, however, was not descending to the wreckage for the purposes of further exploration. His objective answered a request by the *Fitzgerald* family members, many of whom were gathered on a boat anchored nearby. Fuoco's job was intended to bring a sense of closure to the *Edmund Fitzgerald* story: he would be cutting off the ship's bell and replacing it with a replica bearing the names of the men who had perished when the ship went down.

Arriving at this moment had not come easily. Only a year earlier, a court battle over the bell's removal had taken place in Lansing, Michigan—a battle that illustrated just how territorial people can be with respect to sunken ships. Fred Shannon, the plaintiff in the case, asked the court to prohibit the removal of the *Fitzgerald*'s bell. Doing so, he claimed, would destroy the historical integrity of the wreckage. Tom Farnquist and the State of Michigan, the defendants, had been approached by family members of the lost crewmen about creating a lasting memorial, and it was decided that bringing up the bell and placing it in a maritime museum would produce a fitting tribute to the *Fitzgerald*'s crew.

Both Shannon and the Great Lakes Shipwreck Historical Society had stakes in the case. Shannon had visited and videotaped the wreckage, and he hoped to write a book about the ship and his experiences with it; a television documentary was also part of the plan. Farnquist, co-founder of the Great Lakes Shipwreck Historical Society, owned and operated a maritime museum at Whitefish Point, Michigan, and he planned to house the recovered bell in the museum. Both Shannon and the Shipwreck Society had substantial monetary investments in their respective projects, Shannon in paying for his dive to the wreck, the Shipwreck Society, along with the National Geographic Society and the Canadian navy, in assembling the recovery team.

Historically speaking, such battles are not uncommon. Someone "discovers" a long-lost shipwreck, and the next thing you know, there are territorial squabbles over who owns the wreckage and who can visit it and remove artifacts—who, in general, can profit from the loss of property and, in some cases, life. Over time, numerous laws have been enacted to address these issues, but legalities don't necessarily keep professional or recreational divers from illegally removing artifacts from the sunken ships.

Shannon lost his court case when he was unable to convince the judge that removal of the *Fitzgerald*'s bell would amount to the desecration of a gravesite, or that it would diminish the marketability of his projects. The Shipwreck Society's museum would get the bell.

Bruce Fuoco went about this business like the professional he was. This was an exciting, prestigious job, and a risky one; Fuoco could count off all the dangers the dive presented. There was very little margin for error. A mistake could ignite an explosion. Or it could puncture his airline or his diving suit. At fifty stories below the lake's surface, such a mistake would be catastrophic.

Fuoco's yellow and black diving suit, called a Newt Suit by the company that designed it, had been constructed to withstand the astounding water pressure, which could collapse the lungs of a human body at this depth. Designed by a Canadian, Phil Nuytten, the Newt Suit weighed hundreds of pounds and looked like a space suit; it was capable of safely descending to 1,000 feet. It was equipped with articulated joints, electric thrusters, and a communications system that allowed the diver to talk to people on the surface. If something went wrong, a life-support system built into the suit would keep the diver alive until the diver was able to rise to the surface or a rescue team arrived.

Fuoco worked on top of the *Fitzgerald*'s pilothouse, where three steel stanchions held the ship's 200-pound bell in place. Two small Canadian navy submarines stationed nearby flooded the ship with light. Silt and other lake-bottom sediment, stirred up by a weak current generated by the subs, hung in the water. Inside one of the subs, a high-definition video camera recorded Fuoco's every move. A small fireball of light burned off the end of Fuoco's cutting torch, as if in defiance of nature itself. The phenomenon of a fire burning in more than 500 feet of water would be jaw-dropping to people seeing the video footage later.

Despite the corrosion and oxidation that had changed the bell's bronze color to a shade of light rust, Fuoco could read the engraved EDMUND FITZGERALD on its surface. A ship's bell is used to signal a change in watches or the serving of meals. It is also a timepiece, sounding on the half-hour and the hour, and is used as a signal during foggy weather. Technology has reduced the practical need for these bells, but to those calling a ship their second home, the bell symbolizes the vessel's heart. For the families of those lost on the *Edmund Fitzgerald,* the recovered bell was the memorial that they asked the Shipwreck Society to obtain, the replacement bell nothing less than a gravestone marking the names of the men entombed inside the ship. Touching the ship's original bell was as close as they would ever come to touching their loved ones.

While Fuoco worked below, family members conducted a brief ceremony on the *Northlander,* an eighty-foot yacht dispatched to the area for the occasion. Some dropped flowers and wreaths on the water; others held hands and prayed. There would be other services and memorials over the upcoming months, including a formal presentation of the bell a few days later, and a twentieth-anniversary dinner and memorial on November 10, but this modest ceremony, conducted over the site where the *Fitzgerald* had come to rest, was both solemn and exhilarating, carrying an air of finality absent to this point.

Even as this service was taking place, the bell recovery team onboard a nearby tugboat monitored Bruce Fuoco's progress. There had been no problems with the Newt Suit, and the bell's removal was moving along smoothly, if somewhat slowly. Fuoco had a tiny camera, controlled on the surface, mounted on his left shoulder, giving the recovery team a close-up look at the cutting torch burning through the bell's stanchions. They finally heard Fuoco's voice and the order they'd been waiting to hear: "Give it a tug."

The tugboat's winch strained against the weight of the bell and water resistance, but the bell broke free, narrowly missing Fuoco's faceplate, and moved toward the surface. There were a few tense moments as Fuoco and his crew waited for the bell to move beyond the *Fitzgerald*'s RDF antenna and crow's nest, but it cleared them without a problem. The *Fitzgerald*'s families would not be disappointed on this day.

The bell broke the surface of Lake Superior moments before Fuoco, towing as it swung on the cable. Relatives of the lost crewmen cried and hugged one another. The heart of the *Edmund Fitzgerald* had been recovered.

ON SATURDAY, NOVEMBER 8, 1975, A LOW-PRESSURE WEATHER SYSTEM formed in the southwestern portion of the United States; its edge ranging from southern California across northern Arizona to central Colorado. The system moved eastward at a steady pace, pulling with it cold air from the Rocky Mountains. As it moved over the Oklahoma panhandle, its air rotating counterclockwise, the system pulled in moisture from the Gulf of Mexico and warm air from Texas. Storm clouds formed and the National Weather Service predicted rain.

On that same day, a low-pressure system in Alberta, Canada, began moving eastward across southern Canada and the northern third of the United States. This system pulled frigid arctic air in its wake, setting off forecasts for snow in the north-central states of the U.S.

Such weather patterns are not uncommon during the "transition month" of November, when jet streams and upper-air patterns create strong and sometimes unpredictable weather systems. By the time the low-pressure system in the southern United States had reached central Kansas, at seven o'clock on the morning of November 9, the National Weather Service was confident in forecasting "a *typical November storm" for much of the central states and the upper Great Lakes. The storm would move north and east at a rapid pace, pass over Lake Superior, and wind up over James Bay, Ontario.*

The Canadian system continued its eastward trek, bringing down more cold air from Canada. The National Weather Service kept a close watch on this system, concerned about what might happen if it slammed into the system moving up from the southwest.

There really wasn't much room for speculation. History dictated the forecast: in the vernacular, if the two systems met, all hell was going to break loose.

CHAPTER ONE

THE TOLEDO EXPRESS

Dawn, November 9, 1975.

Moored at the Burlington-Northern Railroad dock in Superior, Wisconsin, the S.S. *Edmund Fitzgerald* was bound to catch the attention of anyone looking in its direction. At 729 feet, the *Mighty Fitz,* as the ship was often called, ranked among the largest vessels ever to sail on the Great Lakes, and even seasoned veterans were impressed by the ore carrier's size and strength. The *Fitzgerald* was a blue-collar vessel, capable of hauling mind-boggling tonnage around the lakes, but with its handsome red-and-white paint, beautiful pilothouse and twin staterooms, state-of-the-art equipment, and comfortable living quarters, it also boasted a modern beauty that other big freighters could only envy.

The *Fitzgerald,* one of the hardest-working ships in the business, had been at the Superior dock for only a few hours, and it would be gone in a few more. Over the past week, it had sailed from Toledo, Ohio, to Silver Bay, Minnesota, a port about fifty miles north of Superior, where it had picked up a full load of taconite iron ore pellets and taken off for Ashtabula, Ohio. Then it was back up the length of Lake Superior for another cargo here in Superior.

On this early Sunday morning, the *Fitzgerald* was waiting to be loaded for a routine run to Great Lakes Steel, a Zug Island processing plant near Detroit. The day looked promising. The upper Midwest could be frosty at this time of year, but today's weather was unseasonably moderate, as if fall were determined to hold off winter just a little longer. This was a relief to the small dockside crew, who had endured their fair share of raw northern Wisconsin weather. Any decent day was a bonus.

Burlington-Northern's first shift had just reported to work. Boat loader Clarence (Ed) Dennis picked up the paperwork for his day's first assignment from Donald Amys, Burlington-Northern's general foreman, and he would be supervising the loading of the *Fitzgerald*. As he walked across the deck towering over the docks, Dennis tried to place the ship at Dock Number 1. He had been a boat loader for fifteen of his thirty-four years at Burlington-Northern, but he wasn't sure he had ever loaded this ship before. Not that it mattered: the *Fitzgerald* was a traditional straight-decker, and if all went well, he'd have it ready to go within five or six hours.

The *Fitzgerald,* in fact, rarely loaded at Burlington-Northern. It usually picked up its taconite at Silver Bay and wound up in Toledo, earning another nickname, the *Toledo Express*. This was its first visit of the season to Superior.

Down below, on the spar deck of the *Edmund Fitzgerald,* First Mate Jack McCarthy supervised the removal of the ship's hatch covers. He had already delivered the loading order to Donald Amys, and he was eager to get started. His crew was on the clock, and since it was a Sunday, they'd be paid overtime—not an agreeable situation for Ernest McSorley, the *Fitzgerald*'s cost-conscious captain.

One had to be careful when removing or replacing the rectangular, 7-ton hatch covers. McCarthy had been through the process on countless occasions over his forty years of service on the Great Lakes, but he knew, all too well, that a blunder could seriously damage the hatch combings, or seals, and threaten a ship's watertight integrity. Only a year earlier, in September 1974, the crew had tried to lift a hatch cover before all the clamps had been unfastened, damaging the cover, the combing, and a few clamps. The *Fitz* had twenty-one 11' × 48' cargo openings running down its spar deck, each opening covered by, in effect, a large, flat lid. Each of the red covers was fastened down to a combing by sixty-eight clamps. The covers, constructed from thick sheets of steel, were taken off and replaced by a hatch crane that moved up and down the length of the ship on tracks.

The *Fitzgerald*'s cargo hold was divided into three sections separated by screen bulkheads; by the time this particular loading was completed, the *Fitz* would have taken on 26,116 long tons of taconite pellets. The distribution of cargo was critical, and McCarthy had carefully drawn up a loading sequence that assured the *Fitz* would stay on an even keel throughout the loading. Uneven distribution of cargo could place too much stress on a ship's hull, and, in the worst-case scenario, could crack or even sink the ship. The middle of the *Fitz* was especially vulnerable. If the ship "hogged"—bent downward at the bow and stern ends—during the loading, the hull could be seriously damaged. Poor loading had caused countless vessels to bottom out in shallow docking waters, leading to costly damage and delays. Fortunately, the *Fitz* had so far escaped such mishaps.

While McCarthy and his crew worked on the hatch covers, Ed Dennis maintained his station several stories above them, on the deck near the massive bins, or "pockets," each of which contained 100 to 300 tons of taconite pellets. The pellets traveled to the ship's hatches by chutes lowered from the pockets to the ship, and there were 187 chutes on this dock alone. Dennis directed his small Burlington-Northern dock crew on the positioning of the chutes and the flow of the cargo.

The marble-sized taconite pellets had become a vital part of Minnesota's iron production. During the first half of the twentieth century, taconite—which contains only about 30 percent magnetite and hematite, the principal ores of iron—had been discarded by the mining industry, but the increased demand for iron during World War II had depleted ore supplies to such an extent that Minnesota iron companies faced desperate times, if not extinction. The demand for steel increased throughout the 1950s, as baby boomers were born, automobile production resumed and reached all-time-high levels, and suburbs sprouted across America, creating new demands for building materials. Fortunately, Dr. E. W. Davis of the University of Minnesota, working with other researchers and scientists, developed a way of separating the iron ore from taconite. A lucrative new industry had been born.

The process, called beneficiation, was neither simple nor cheap. Taconite was tough, resilient rock, and the first step of mining it involved boring into the rock and using explosives to blast it into pieces that could be hauled, either by rail or in enormous trucks, to processing plants. At the processing plants, crushing machines and rotating mills ground the taconite into a powder, and the magnetic iron ore was separated from the rest of the rock. The iron-rich powder was then moistened, combined with clay, limestone, and bentonite, and rolled into marble-sized balls, between ⅜" and ⅝" in diameter, which were eventually fired at temperatures of 2,200 to 2,400 degrees Fahrenheit and then cooled until they became easily loaded and transported product. Huge ore carriers like the *Edmund Fitzgerald* then moved the pellets to ports near steel-producing cities, which melted the taconite down for badly needed steel.

The *Fitzgerald*'s crew finished removing the hatch covers. Jack McCarthy shouted up to Ed Dennis to indicate that he was ready to begin loading. The dock crew positioned a chute over the *Fitzgerald*'s Number 21 hatch—the last hatch at the stern of the ship—and loading commenced. Thousands of pellets spilled out of the pocket, rolled down the length of the chute, and dropped noisily into the *Edmund Fitzgerald*'s hold.

The ship's last full day had begun.

Ed Dennis would remember Jack McCarthy as "an older man, not too tall, stocky, and a very friendly guy"—not a bad description from a dock loader viewing his subject from a distance.

At sixty-two, John Henkle McCarthy was nearing the end of his long career on the lakes. Four decades had passed since he signed on as a deckhand on his first big freighter, a bulk carrier called the *Yosemite,* and since then he'd worked his way to the top and had experienced just about anything a career man on the lakes could experience. He'd learned a lot during the war years, when he worked in the Coast Guard, and he'd continued his education on any number of ships sailing for the Columbia Transportation division of Oglebay Norton.

At one point, while growing up and attending Catholic schools in Pittsburgh, young Jack McCarthy had figured he might be a writer when he grew up. He loved books and was comfortable with the English language—he won an essay contest as a boy—but the Depression ended any lingering thoughts he might have entertained about that career. His family moved to Ohio, where his father found work, and Jack took a job at a department store's soda fountain to help out with the bills. One of the store's regular customers was the marine director of the Cleveland Hills Iron Company, and McCarthy pestered him almost daily for work on one of the company's big ore boats. McCarthy's younger brother Bill worked on a freighter, and Jack reasoned it was as good a job as any.

He eventually earned his master's papers and was awarded his first command, of the *Joseph H. Frantz,* the former flagship of the Columbia fleet. By that time, McCarthy and his wife, Mary Catherine, had moved to Cleveland's suburbs, where Mary Catherine raised their four children while Jack spent nearly eight months of the year on the lakes.

A mishap in 1956 nearly ruined McCarthy's career, when the ship he was commanding, the *Ben E. Tate,* hit a rocky shoal near Kelly's Island on Lake Erie. The *Tate* was supposed to have made a turn taking it into deeper water, but for some reason continued ahead until it was too late. The grounding tore up the bottom of the ship, costing more than $200,000 in towing and repairs. Embarrassed and depressed, unable to work until an accident hearing was conducted, McCarthy spent a couple of months away from the lakes. He was allowed to return, but not as a captain. He would have to earn that privilege again.

For the better part of the next two decades, McCarthy worked on a number of ships, ultimately returning as master of the *Sylvania* and the *Tomlinson.* In 1970, while working as first mate on the *Armco,* McCarthy was reunited with Ernest McSorley, now the vessel's captain, whom McCarthy had met years earlier when both men were serving on another freighter. Their working association evolved into a close friendship, and McCarthy jumped at the chance to work as McSorley's first mate when his friend was given command of the *Edmund Fitzgerald.*

McCarthy provided a contrast to McSorley's more formal demeanor. McCarthy possessed a sharp Irish humor and an easygoing manner that endeared him to those working under him and set him apart from other first mates, who, as Ed Dennis would note, could be grumpy when doing such work as overseeing the loading of their ships. McCarthy, by Dennis's estimation, was a nice guy.

By industry standards, the *Edmund Fitzgerald* was still in its youth. Freshwater vessels were built to last a half-century or more, and the 1975 shipping season was the *Fitz*'s eighteenth year on the lakes.

The *Fitz* had stood out even before construction began. What was known as Hull 301 was going to be a behemoth of a ship, the largest ever to sail the Great Lakes. At 729 feet, it would be one foot shorter than the maximum allowed through the Sault Sainte Marie (Soo) Locks, and its 75-foot beam was exactly the maximum allowed under regulations set by the U.S. Army Corps of Engineers. The designers, however, had more than sheer size in mind. The ship would have to be able to travel at 16 miles per hour at a 25-foot draft. The combination of size and speed promised to make the *Fitz* the most impressive vessel ever to sail the Great Lakes.

But this was only the beginning of a list of firsts. The Northwestern Mutual Life Insurance Company, a heavy investor in the iron and minerals industries, had ordered the construction of the ship: the first time an American life insurance company had made such an investment. The ship's $8.4 million price tag also made it the most expensive freighter ever built. Even the construction itself was unique: whereas the traditional procedure was to form a hull by laying down the keel and building up from there, this ship's hull would be built in sections in different parts of Detroit's Great Lakes Engineering shipyard on the Rouge River. Once completed, the huge sections were floated to the main construction site, where they would be hoisted by cranes and fitted together. This method of prefabricated assembly had never been attempted before. Construction began on August 9, 1957, with the hope of having the ship ready for at least a portion of the next year's shipping season.

Almost exactly ten months later, the hull and decking had been completed, and the ship, now known as the *Edmund Fitzgerald,* was ready to launch. At more than two football fields in length and three highway lanes in width, and with a hold capable of containing more than 25,000 tons of cargo, the *Fitzgerald* delivered on its promise of being larger than life.

The ship could not have found a more deserving name. Edmund Fitzgerald, president and CEO of Northwestern Mutual, had more than a passing interest in Great Lakes shipping. His grandfather, John Fitzgerald, had been a captain on the lakes, as were John's five brothers. William Fitzgerald, John's son and Edmund's father, had been president of a shipbuilding company. Both John and William had lived to see bulk carriers named after them. Edmund continued the family tradition of involvement in maritime affairs by being actively involved in the Port of Milwaukee and by helping establish the Wisconsin Marine Historical Society.

The *Edmund Fitzgerald* was launched on June 7, 1958, with a crowd estimated at more than 10,000 gathering on that Saturday to watch from the dockside, from the roofs of nearby buildings, from piers and small vessels on the Detroit River, and from grandstands built for the occasion. The highly publicized event was attended by politicians, businessmen, and civic leaders, as well as by the men who had worked on the *Fitz,* members of the press, and thousands just interested in seeing this local celebrity lowered into the water. Edmund Fitzgerald and his wife, Elizabeth, took a place on an elevated platform near the bow of the ship, and after the typical assortment of speeches had been delivered and the vessel formally blessed, Elizabeth Fitzgerald stepped forward to christen the ship. She swung a bottle of champagne at the stem of the *Fitzgerald*'s bow, but the bottle didn't break. A second attempt yielded similar results. Finally, on the third try, the bottle shattered and the *Fitz* was officially christened.

The superstitious declared the failed attempts to break the bottle a sign of bad luck, and other ominous signs were soon to follow. The ropes securing the *Fitzgerald* to its platform were cut and the massive new vessel slid down a greased ramp, only to hit the water at an awkward angle, creating a large wave that rushed across the slip, crashed over the retaining wall, and doused the crowd watching the launch. The *Fitz* rolled precariously in the water, righted itself, and slammed into the dock on the opposite side of the slip. Spectators reacted with a mixture of shock and delight. A fifty-eight-year-old Toledo man, who had driven to Detroit to witness the launching, suffered a heart attack and died on the scene.

Despite this spotty debut, the *Fitzgerald* generated a great deal of excitement. This ship was expected to shatter cargo records for individual loads and yearly tonnage—and to travel at a pace previously impossible for large bulk freighters. In an industry dependent upon speed for healthy profit margins, this was indeed very good news. A lot of people stood to profit from the *Fitzgerald*'s efforts. Oglebay Norton, a minerals firm in Cleveland, signed a twenty-five-year lease on the ship and promptly named it the flagship of its Columbia Transportation Division fleet.

The *Fitz* spent the remainder of the summer of 1958 being fitted out with an elaborate electrical system, plumbing, communications equipment, refrigeration, firefighting and lifesaving equipment, and living quarters; the fore and aft decks were constructed, including a pilothouse with state-of-the art nautical equipment and a beautiful map room.

Not surprisingly, the *Fitzgerald*'s living quarters reflected the thoughtful planning and craftsmanship devoted to every other aspect of the ship's design. The forward deckhouse, consisting of three levels, contained living quarters, two guest staterooms, a guest lounge, and the captain's office and quarters, as well as laundry and recreation rooms. The S. L. Hudson Company, brought in to design the accommodations and furnishings, went all-out, adding touches of elegance appropriate for a ship of the *Fitz*'s status. The rooms had deep pile carpeting, tiled bathrooms, and drapes over the portholes; the captain's office housed a beautiful walnut desk. The guest lounge featured simulated-leather wall coverings, leather swivel chairs, plush furniture, and a huge rear window offering a panoramic view of the stern of the ship and the lake.

The crew's quarters, though less luxurious, were still a cut above the norm. The air-conditioned rooms, usually accommodating two crew members each, were furnished with beds, desks, closets, bookshelves, and chairs; the floors were tiled, and a porthole let in light. Each room offered hot and cold running water, and some had private showers. The nicely appointed lounge in the ship's after section had tables, chairs, both straight and upholstered, and a couch, as well as a television set, coffeemaker, and refrigerator. An enormous, fully stocked kitchen and pantry, responsible for supplying meals for two dining rooms, added to the *Fitzgerald*'s home-away-from-home atmosphere.

By late summer 1958, the finishing touches had been applied and the *Fitz* was ready to go to work. After passing a series of final inspections and making its sea trials, the ship was declared fit for its maiden voyage.

On September 22, 1958, the *Edmund Fitzgerald,* skippered by Captain Bert Lambert, left Rouge River bound for Silver Bay, Minnesota, where it was scheduled to pick up a load of taconite pellets to be delivered to Toledo. Not surprisingly, that very first load set a tonnage record when the *Fitz* passed through the Soo Locks a few days later.

The ship's life on the Great Lakes had begun.

The loading in Superior on November 9 proceeded without a hitch. While the first run of taconite pellets was delivered through each of the *Fitzgerald*'s cargo hatches, crew members, armed with walkie-talkies and positioned at either end of the ship, watched for signs of uneven distribution. Draft markings on the sides of the freighter and on the rudder indicated how deep the *Fitz* was settling in the water, and trim lights mounted on the ship's stern deckhouse revealed any listing that might be taking place during the loading. A red light meant the *Fitz* was tilting to its port side, a green light indicated a starboard list, and a white light meant the ship was level.

Each hatch accepted a full 300-ton load, and though it took only minutes to transfer pellets from each pocket, the overall process was time-consuming. At nearly 500 feet long and 30 feet wide, the *Fitzgerald*'s cargo hold wasn't quick to be filled, nor was its size indicative of the care required in loading it. Hatch combings could be damaged by careless positioning of the loading chutes, and combings were often banged around by the chutes, making a perfect seal all but impossible, so dock workers had to use caution when aligning and tipping the chutes. Ideally, a hatch cover gasket between the cover and combing sealed it and kept water from entering the cargo hold, but "weathertight" was a term left open to interpretation.

Still, a tight seal was essential. Water couldn't be pumped out of a filled cargo hold, and boarding water entering the hold during a storm presented a potentially fatal hazard. Water in the cargo hold meant loss of freeboard, which could eventually lead to the loss of buoyancy.

The taconite pellets presented other potential problems. They were heavy—127 to 140 pounds per cubic foot—and absorbent. If the cargo hold flooded, the pellets would absorb eight or nine pounds of water per cubic foot.

At some point earlier in the year, the *Fitz* had suffered minor damage to its hatch combings. At the ship's most recent inspection by the Coast Guard and the American Bureau of Shipping, on October 31, inspectors had detected minor damage to four of the hatches. None of the defects was considered serious, though, and the Coast Guard cleared the *Fitzgerald* for the remainder of the shipping season, with the understanding that repairs would be made before the freighter headed back out in 1976.

Considering all the stress and strain placed on it over the years, the *Edmund Fitzgerald* had enjoyed a relatively healthy life, with only a few mishaps marring its record. The worst of these had occurred on September 6, 1969, when the *Fitz* grounded near the Soo Locks, causing substantial structural damage. During the following winter layover, the vessel was inspected and a number of cracks were found at the keelson-to-shell connection. Repairmen welded additional steel stiffeners to the keelson, and the *Fitz* went back out on the lakes without any further problems.

The following year, the *Fitzgerald* collided with another ship, the *Hochelaga,* sustaining minor damage. Then, on three occasions—in September 1970, May 1973, and June 1974—the *Fitz* hit the walls at the Soo Locks, resulting in light damage that was repaired without loss of time. Finally, the ship lost an anchor on January 7, 1974, when an anchor link broke in the Detroit River. Compared to what some of the older freighters went through, all this was small-time stuff, certainly nothing to make anyone question the big ship's well-being.

If anything, the *Edmund Fitzgerald* was improving with age. In 1969, a diesel-powered bow thruster was installed. This mechanism—essentially, another propeller, mounted below the waterline near the bow of a ship—improved maneuverability and power when a vessel was leaving a harbor. In a ship the size of the *Fitz,* the bow thruster was a valuable addition, cutting the need for a tugboat to assist it out of the harbor.

The 1971–72 winter lay-up saw an even bigger change: the *Fitz* was converted from coal to oil. Fuel oil tanks replaced the old coal bins; the coal furnace was pulled out and a new oil-burning system was installed, upgrading the boiler system and making its operations cleaner, safer, and more efficient. The ship's chief engineer, George Holl, would complain regularly about how the new automated system caused him all kinds of grief—much more than the old coal system, which relied on manpower rather than a computer for smooth-running efficiency—but there was little doubt that the *Edmund Fitzgerald,* nearing the end of its eighteenth season, was still operating near the top of its game.

The *Fitz* settled nicely in the water as it took its second run of taconite. After finishing the first run, the ship had been moved up the dock and was now positioned beside a new set of pockets.

It was mid-morning, and if Jack McCarthy and his crew were able to maintain their current pace, the *Fitz* would be ready to go by early afternoon. This would make the boss happy. Ernest McSorley was a good company man who prided himself on delivering his cargo in good shape, on time, and as cheaply as possible. This was a matter of economics and survival. "Every captain knew it was his job to deliver cargo as cheaply and as quickly as possible," one Great Lakes captain commented long after the loss of the *Edmund Fitzgerald,* "and if you didn't measure up, the company would replace you with a captain who would measure up."

Besides, the early forecast called for some rough weather later in the day—nothing special for this time of year, but enough to make you want to move things along and miss as much of it as possible. McSorley, known as a "heavy-weather captain," was willing and able to guide his ship through stormy conditions, but, like any capable master, he had a healthy respect for the powers of nature, especially in November, when vicious storms brewed quickly.

The sooner they could get the *Fitz* out on the water, the sooner they'd be able to take advantage of some of the good weather nature had provided.

Captain Ernest McSorley was the fourth master the *Edmund Fitzgerald* had had in its short life.

Bert Lambert, the ship's first captain, had served on the Great Lakes for forty-one years when he took over the *Fitz* in 1958, and he knew from the outset that his tenure was going to be brief. His appointment, like those to follow, was largely a reward for his many years of service on other company vessels. "I remember Captain Lambert walking from fore to aft, always with his officer's uniform and hat on," recalled Eddie Chaput, who served as a coal passer and fireman on the *Fitz* during its first season. "He was an in-charge guy and no one questioned his decisions." Lambert finished out the 1958 season and retired, having set a standard for future *Fitzgerald* masters.

Captain Newman (Joe) Larsen, Lambert's successor, guided the *Fitzgerald* through an impressive run of record-breaking shipping seasons. As expected, the *Fitz* continually set new tonnage records for single loads and seasonal totals, and for number of trips taken. In 1964, in forty-five trips under Larsen's command, the *Fitzgerald* carried 1,160,952 tons of cargo through the Soo Locks, breaking the record set a year earlier by Inland Steel's *Edward L. Ryerson*. All told, the *Fitzgerald* surpassed the million-ton mark six times between 1958 and 1977.

By this time, the shipping competition was heating up. The *Fitzgerald* was still the largest ship on the lakes, but that would soon change. Other massive ore carriers were being launched, and vessels longer than the *Fitz* were being constructed. The *Fitz* even found itself in competition with its sister ship the *Arthur B. Homer,* which was owned by Bethlehem Steel. In August 1960, the

Fitz broke its old single-trip record, only to be topped by the *Homer* a few days later.

Captain Peter Pulcer assumed command of the *Fitz* when Joe Larsen retired after the 1966 shipping season. Pulcer, as colorful a character as you'd ever find on the Great Lakes, jokingly referred to himself as the Commodore, since he was master of Columbia's flagship. He loved the *Fitz,* and he ran operations with a mixture of hard-nosed business acumen and a sense of fun. Under Pulcer's command, the *Fitz* became the first Great Lakes ship to exceed the magic 30,000-ton mark for a single cargo—and it did so on four separate occasions in 1968, adding to the *Fitzgerald*'s mystique and keeping the Oglebay Norton officers happy. The next year, the *Fitz* hauled 1,349,404 tons through the Soo Locks, the highest volume in the locks' 119-year history.

Pulcer demanded the highest professional standards from his subordinates, but he also liked to keep things loose while working. He was fond of turning up the ship's loudspeaker and entertaining tourists at the Soo Locks with progress reports on the current trip as well as lessons on the life and times of the *Edmund Fitzgerald.* He also enjoyed playing classical music—or, if it was late in the season, Christmas carols—over the *Fitz*'s loudspeaker; during the summer months he was known to awaken campers along his route by blasting out marching band music in the early daylight hours. "I still get letters about that," he remarked, long after he'd retired.

Ernest McSorley, who took over in 1972, ran an entirely different ship. An old-school mariner, McSorley maintained a professional distance between himself and those working for him. To McSorley, command of the *Fitzgerald* represented the crowning achievement in a career that, in many ways, had begun when he was a boy. Born in 1913 in the upstate New York town of Ogdensburg, Ernest Michael McSorley spent his youth dreaming of working on the kind of ships he saw sailing on the nearby St. Lawrence River. As a boy, he had been quiet and intense, more a loner than a social creature. At age eighteen, he took a job as a deckhand on a saltwater vessel, but he was soon on the lakes. From that point on, he climbed the proverbial ladder, working as a wheelsman, third mate, second

mate, and, eventually, first mate on an array of ships for the Columbia Transportation Company. In 1951, at thirty-eight, McSorley was appointed captain of
the *Carrollton,* a 255-foot freighter. He was the youngest master on the lakes.

Other commands followed. McSorley established his credentials as a good businessman and very capable commander, and each new ship seemed to be a little
larger and more prestigious than the previous one, with greater attendant responsi-
bilities. In 1970, McSorley was placed in charge of the *Armco,* the flagship of the
Columbia fleet prior to the launching of the *Edmund Fitzgerald.* The *Armco*'s first
mate was McSorley's old friend Jack McCarthy, and two years later, when asked to
pilot the *Edmund Fitzgerald,* McSorley quite naturally invited McCarthy to join him
as first mate. McSorley was fifty-nine, McCarthy a few months younger. The two
had nearly seventy-four years of commercial shipping experience between them.

Asked to characterize McSorley as an individual and captain, most of the people who worked with him found him difficult to pin down. He didn't drink or
smoke, and he was quiet, not given to fraternizing with his crew.

"He kept to himself much of the time," said Thomas Garcia, who served as a
watchman under McSorley. "You may see him in port when he goes down the
ladder to make a phone call, but that's about all."

Robert Hom, who worked with McSorley on the *Armco,* saw him in two different lights. "He was a quiet guy on deck," Hom observed. "He'd just answer
your questions, but wasn't a guy who got into long conversations. In the pilothouse, with just the guys on watch, he had a great sense of humor and was very
easy to get along with."

As a rule, McSorley kept his private life to himself. He and his wife, Nellie, had
been married for a long time, but only those closest to McSorley knew that she
had suffered a stroke and was living in a Toledo nursing home, or that McSorley
was hinting about retiring and spending more time with her.

To the crewmen on the *Fitzgerald,* McSorley was simply the boss. He had to
answer to Oglebay Norton, and he based his decisions on whatever business
dictated. He was a professional, and he required from his crew the same kind of
hard work and loyalty that he himself devoted to the *Fitzgerald.*

Delmore Webster, who served as a wheelsman, deckhand, and second mate under McSorley on the *Fitzgerald,* characterized the captain as an extremely competent seaman, a "prudent mariner [who] didn't take unnecessary chances," who expected his crewmen to fulfill their duties without his having to supervise their every move. "When he came in the pilot house and asked you where you were, you had better know," Webster said.

Andrew Rajner, who also served as a wheelsman under McSorley, spoke for a number of former *Fitz* crew members in admitting that he didn't know McSorley well personally, although he could testify to his professional efficiency. McSorley, said Rajner, was "a very good man, competent, sober, about the best captain I ever knew."

Like so many captains with long careers in the shipping industry, McSorley identified with the vessel he commanded. He might have occasionally complained to his first mate or wheelsman about some of the *Fitzgerald*'s quirks, but the ship was as much his home as his house in Toledo.

"The sea was his life," his stepdaughter Dolores remembered. "He didn't even come home when he was sick. His whole life was built around the ship."

Once the *Fitzgerald* finished receiving its second load of taconite, Jack McCarthy indicated that he wanted to de-ballast, and Ed Dennis took his first extended break of the day. There was still more cargo to load, but before that occurred, the *Fitz*'s crew needed to empty the ship's ballast tanks. The process would take about an hour, giving Dennis time for coffee and maybe a sandwich.

The *Fitzgerald* contained eight ballast tanks, positioned to the sides and below the cargo hold. These long, enormous tanks were partially filled with lake water whenever the *Fitz* sailed without cargo; the weight of the water, substituting for the weight of cargo, lowered an empty ship in the water, giving it added stability in the waves. Since the ship had arrived empty in Superior, the tanks held thousands of tons of water.

De-ballasting was an important part of the loading process. Each tank had two air vent pipes rising from the tank to the deck; these vents were opened to bleed out air before the pumps were turned on. The *Fitz* was equipped with four electric ballast pumps capable of discharging 7,000 gallons of water per minute, and two auxiliary pumps capable of handling 2,000 gallons a minute. In very short order, the vents had been opened, the two auxiliary pumps were emptying the tanks into the lake, and the *Fitz* began rising slowly, almost imperceptibly, in the water.

Bob Rafferty had mixed feelings about making this trip. He enjoyed working on the *Fitz,* which, with its huge kitchen, freezers and cupboard, stainless steel tables, and twin Garland gas stoves, was a cook's delight. Rafferty, a bear of a man at six feet and two hundred pounds, was rightfully proud of his work. He'd fed a lot of men on a lot of boats over the course of his career, and he'd heard the sound of compliments often enough to know that he was very good at what he did, especially around the oven: breads, pies, and cakes had become his specialty. If he had to work on any ship this late in the season, the *Fitz* was definitely the place to be.

Still, he'd hoped to be home in Toledo by now, and he'd sent his wife, Brooksie, a postcard stating as much. At sixty-one, Rafferty was ready to pack it in and retire. He'd taken his first job on a ship when he was eighteen, and a great percentage of his life had been spent away from home. His two kids had grown up largely in his absence, and he wanted to be around to enjoy his grandchildren. His daughter, Pam, now living in Georgia, was eight months pregnant with his fourth grandchild, and Rafferty hoped to be back home in time for the child's birth. If he stayed on with the *Fitz,* he'd be cutting it close. Continuing on also meant he'd miss watching the Michigan–Ohio State football game with his son, Randy—a tradition he hated to break.

He had little choice but to stay with the *Fitz* for the duration of the shipping season. Richard Bishop, the *Fitzgerald*'s regular cook, had been out of commission for the better part of a month, recovering from a bad case of bleeding ulcers, and just when it seemed he'd be given medical clearance to rejoin the ship, the ulcers had flared up again. In all likelihood, he was finished for the season. Rafferty would be filling in for him the rest of the way.

There was something not quite right about this trip. Rafferty felt a general uneasiness about it, but he wasn't sure why. The feeling wasn't fear—over the
course of his life, he'd sailed around the world seven times; he'd served on
ships during World War II and had seen just about every kind of sailing hazard
possible—but something was bothering him. The feeling hit him on Halloween,
as he was preparing to ship out on the *Fitz* on a run from Silver Bay to Ashtabula, and it didn't go away.

His postcard home, mailed in Silver Bay before the run to Ashtabula, hinted at
his uneasiness.

"May be home by Nov 8," he wrote his wife, Brooksie, in his two-line message.
"However, nothing is certain."

Mike Armagost felt a little guilty about leaving the *Fitzgerald* and going home for
a few hours. The Burlington-Northern dock, by his estimation, wasn't the easiest
of loading docks, and he wondered whether, as the *Fitz*'s third mate, he should
have hung around and helped Jack McCarthy and his crew. Still, it wasn't often
that the *Fitz* loaded so close to his Iron River, Wisconsin home, and he relished
the thought of spending a little time with his wife, Janice, and their two kids.
He'd have to be back in Superior soon enough, and once the *Fitz* pulled away,
it would be a while before he saw his family again.

Mike's time away had always bothered Janice. She'd been raised in Monona,
Wisconsin, a small city near Madison, and she'd been a student at the University
of Wisconsin when they met one summer while her family was vacationing in
Iron River. The long-distance courtship had been difficult enough, but even
tougher were Mike's extended absences when he was out on the lakes. It took a
while, but Janice had learned to live with it, especially after she and Mike married and moved to Iron River, and their two children, Michele and Christopher,
were born.

Mike had been working on ships, including a brief tour on a saltwater vessel,
since 1957, and for a while he dreamed of eventually using his savings to buy
and run a lodge or tavern. The realities of raising a family changed that. Working

on the freighters meant making better money, so he stayed in the shipping industry. With any luck, he'd have his master's papers someday.

On this particular Sunday, Mike spent his time with Janice and the kids; then, before he headed back to the docks in Superior, they all stopped in for a brief visit with his mother, and, after that, with one of his closest friends. Then it was back to the dock.

Mike kissed his wife and kids goodbye at the Burlington-Northern gatehouse and returned to the ship. It was a little after noon, and the *Fitz* was almost loaded. They'd be pulling out soon enough, but he wouldn't be on duty until later, so he went to his room to relax.

Ransom Cundy and Frederick Beetcher reported to duty as they always did: together. To the outsider, the tall, slender Cundy and the short, husky Beetcher might have looked like a peculiar pair, but the two were the closest of friends, joined not only by their jobs on the *Fitzgerald* but by recent events that both were trying to escape.

Cundy, known as Ray by his family and friends, worked as a watchman on the *Fitz,* and with the exception of five years in the 1960s, when he'd taken a job onshore, he'd known nothing but life on the ships. He had served in the Marine Corps during World War II and fought in the battle of Iwo Jima before returning home, getting married, and taking jobs as a watchman with the National Steel Company, the Hanne Company, and, eventually, Oglebay Norton.

A supreme practical joker, Cundy was one of the most popular crewmen on every ship on which he served. He was the kind of guy you'd turn to if you wanted to air out a problem or gripe, or just needed some cheering up, and there was plenty of time for that on the long trips down the lakes, when you had nothing but time on your hands.

Cundy's lighthearted style changed dramatically on March 30, 1974, when his twenty-six-year-old daughter Janice was shot to death by her husband in a gruesome murder-suicide, leaving behind three very young children. Cundy, who had divorced his first wife and remarried, dropped into a deep yearlong depression that left him, in the words of his older daughter, Cheryl, "a sad and beaten man."

Fortunately, he had Fred Beetcher to help him along during this dark period. Beetcher knew something about grief and its effects, and he could use his own story as an example of what could happen if you let your anguish rule your life. Like Cundy, Beetcher had lost a loved one. His wife had passed away not long after giving birth, leaving Fred with their infant son, Eugene. With no one to look after his son during his long stays away from home, Beetcher watched as Eugene was moved from foster home to foster home. Beetcher's life spiraled downward into gloomy alcoholism and, for a while, it seemed as if he was determined to drink himself to death.

Then he met Ray Cundy. Both men lived in Superior, Wisconsin, and both shared a kind of grief that the others on the ore boats could only imagine. The two started hanging out together, both at work and at home, and they began to see the future as something other than time.

On this late-season trip, Beetcher, a porter on the *Fitz,* would be working with porter Nolan Church, a fifty-five-year-old newcomer to the ship, and the two would be answering to second cook Al Kalmon, a former restaurant cook just completing his first year on the lakes, and Bob Rafferty, who was filling in for the *Fitzgerald*'s regular first cook. The group would be responsible for seeing that no one went hungry for the next few days, which was about as likely as the *Fitzgerald*'s huge pantries running out of food. Rafferty was an exceptional baker, but even he was topped by Kalmon, who could make sinfully good breads and pastries. If anything, the crewmen on the *Fitz* would have to loosen their belts a notch by the time they'd reached Detroit.

Loading the *Fitz* ate up just under six hours. The last pocket was emptied into the hold, the ship's fuel tanks were topped off with 50,013 gallons of Number 6 fuel oil, and the dock crew started fastening down the hatch clamps. Crewmen hosed down the deck, clearing it of loose taconite pellets and a film of pellet dust. Jack McCarthy measured the ship's draft—27 feet, 6 inches at the stern, and 27 feet, 2 inches at the bow—and reported the numbers to Ed Dennis.

In the chart room behind the wheelhouse, Captain McSorley looked over the Lake Survey Chart Number 9 map of Lake Superior and ran over his mental checklist of the early portion of the *Fitzgerald*'s journey across the northern part of the lake. The *Fitz* would spend the rest of the day heading in a northeasterly direction before turning and heading southeast to the Sault Ste. Marie Locks. The entire trip, from Superior to Detroit, measured around 700 miles and would take just over two days. If the weather held, the *Fitz* would be docking at the Zug Island harbor sometime around five o'clock on Tuesday afternoon.

The deck crew was still dogging down the *Fitzgerald*'s hatch covers when the ship pulled away from the dock. Jack McCarthy waved at Ed Dennis and his assistant, Elmer Koski, as the *Fitz* set out.

"So long, boys," McCarthy called to the men. "Good luck."

It was just before two in the afternoon when the *Fitz* made its way through the breakwater and onto Lake Superior, its engine set at full ahead, the Wisconsin shoreline receding by the minute. The ship was in its element.

Janice Armagost parked the car and walked her two kids to a spot near the Lake Superior breakwater. The *Fitz* was pulling away from the dock, and she was hoping to wave goodbye to Mike as the ship went by. Mike would be back in a couple of weeks, in plenty of time for Christopher's third birthday on November 27, but she'd started missing him almost as soon as she watched him walking away at the Burlington-Northern gate.

After dropping Mike at the gate, Janice had taken the kids out for burgers. The next six weeks would be busy, exciting times. Besides Christopher's birthday, Thanksgiving, and the beginning of the holiday season, there was the excitement of having Mike back home for the winter. On top of all that, Michele would be turning six on December 21.

The *Fitz* passed very near to where Janice and her children waited. Several hands were out on the deck, dogging down hatch covers. Janice had been on the *Fitz* before, and had met some of Mike's fellow crew members, but to her, the *Fitz* was simply a big boat, a place where her husband worked.

She looked for Mike as the *Fitz* went by, but he was nowhere on deck.

"Where's Mike?" she called out to one of the deckhands.

"He's down below somewhere," the crewman called back.

Janice continued to watch as the massive ship made its way out onto the lake. She had no way of knowing that, at that moment, she and her children had become the last people to see anyone alive on board the *Edmund Fitzgerald*.

CHAPTER TWO

THE FINAL VOYAGE

TWO AND A HALF HOURS AFTER THE *EDMUND FITZGERALD* SET OUT, AN-
other huge ore carrier, the S.S. *Arthur M. Anderson,* left port at Two Harbors,
Minnesota. The weather was still warm and the seas quiet, with waves coming in
little more than ripples. The *Anderson,* carrying a full load of taconite pellets,
was bound for Gary, Indiana.

Named after the director of U.S. Steel Corporation and vice president of the
J. P. Morgan Company, the *Anderson,* at 767 feet, was actually longer than the
Fitzgerald. When launched on February 16, 1952, the ship had measured 647
feet, but an additional 120 feet had been added over the winter of 1974–75, in-
creasing the *Anderson*'s cargo capacity from 20,150 tons to 26,525 tons. Like the
Fitzgerald, the *Anderson* had earned its reputation as a hardworking ship.

Captain Jesse (Bernie) Cooper, a veteran of thirty-eight years on the water,
mastered the *Anderson.* Cooper's career had followed the usual pattern for lifers
on the lakes. He'd started as a deckhand and worked his way up to third mate before World War II broke out and he interrupted his career with a stint in the Navy.
After the war, he returned to the Great Lakes and resumed his rise in the ranks,

finally earning his master's papers. The 1975 shipping season was his third full year as master of the *Anderson*.

As Captain Cooper directed his ship out of the breakwater and onto open water, he could make out another ship on the lake behind him.

"It was a beautiful, clear November day," Cooper recalled. "As we backed out of Two Harbors, we could see on the horizon the *Fitzgerald*. We knew it was the *Fitzgerald* because we heard her security report coming out of Superior."

It would only be a matter of time before the *Fitzgerald,* the faster of the two ships, overtook him, but it would be good to have another ship around if the weather took a turn for the worse.

The forecast, as Cooper knew, was unpromising. Initially, the National Weather Service had predicted the storm would pass to the south of Lake Superior by 7:00 P.M. on Monday, November 10, but an amended forecast now predicted the storm would cut into the southeastern portion of the lake before heading up to Canada. And the storm was proving to be deceptively strong. It had gained power throughout the day as it roared through Kansas and into Iowa, generating stronger than anticipated winds as it moved in its northeastern direction. Bernie Cooper had no sooner guided the *Anderson* out of Two Harbors than the National Weather Service posted a new bulletin, this one calling for gale-force winds for all of Lake Superior.

Cooper wasn't at all worried. The *Anderson* was a big, powerful ship, and it had faced this kind of weather before.

"At the time, the gale warnings were fringe," Cooper would remember. "When I say fringe, I mean 34–38 knots, which is not unusual at this time of year."

Still, it wouldn't hurt to stay vigilant. Cooper had made a point of learning all he could about weather systems and how they affected ships out on the lakes, and as soon as he heard the updated forecast, he began plotting his own weather chart of the system. Then he called the ship sailing behind him.

Cooper didn't know Ernest McSorley, but he knew the *Fitzgerald* by reputation. Both the *Anderson* and the *Fitzgerald* were weather-reporting ships, outfitted with a variety of measurement devices. Four times a day, the crews would measure temperature, wind velocity, and wave height and send their findings to the National Weather Service, which, in turn, would transmit the readings to other ships and Coast Guard stations in the Great Lakes region, all in an effort to keep forecasts and readings as up-to-the-minute as possible. The *Anderson* and the *Fitz,* Cooper reasoned, not only had a mutual interest in keeping an eye on the developing storm and altering their courses if nature so dictated, they also had the equipment to regularly monitor the storm's intensity.

The two captains discussed the forecasts and how they should direct their ships in the deteriorating weather. McSorely had also heard the gale warnings, but, like Cooper, he wasn't inclined to alter his course—not just yet. Both vessels were making good time, and if they continued to travel at their present pace, they would be passing south of Isle Royale right about the time the really nasty weather was expected to kick in. The large island on western Lake Superior would provide shelter from the storm.

But neither captain took lightly the forecast of gale-force winds, because wind determines the size of the waves. Three factors—wind speed, duration, and fetch—play into an equation known all too well by both Ernest McSorley and Bernie Cooper: the stronger the constant wind speed, the bigger the wave; the longer the wind blows, the bigger the wave; and the greater the fetch—the distance of open water over which the wind travels—the bigger the wave. The National Weather Service's forecast of a gale warning meant winds of roughly 39 to 46 miles per hour. The forecast also indicated that the storm would last well into the next day, meaning there would be plenty of time for the seas to build.

Captains McSorley and Cooper also understood that if the low-pressure system passed directly over Lake Superior, they would be facing the weather phenomenon known as a nor'easter. The low-pressure system's counterclockwise movement would bring in strong, harsh winds from the northeast, whipping up mountainous waves that could batter even the sturdiest modern vessel. Nor'easters generally visit the Great Lakes in November, when cold air moves over water still warm from the summer, and they have a well-earned reputation for brutality. Native Americans spoke of angry spirits generating these storms, and mariners referred to nor'easters as the witch of November. You had to respect these storms. Countless ships had encountered them, and of all the ships that had sunk on the Great Lakes, the vast majority had gone down in the jaws of nor'easters.

To Native Americans looking out over the vast expanse of icy cold water hundreds and thousands of years ago, Lake Superior must have seemed as boundless as the forests around them. There was no distant shore in sight, and to travel by canoe or other small craft over the lake's 350-mile length, across unpredictably treacherous waters, was out of the question.

The lake that the Ojibwa called Gitche Gumme originated more than a billion years ago, when the Mid-Continent Rift began to split North America apart. For 22 million years, molten basalt pushed up from the center of the earth, reshaping the surface of the area extending from what is now Michigan to Minnesota, creating a basin that deepened over time and extended as far south as Kansas. Erosion and the formation of shallow bodies of water left mud, rock, and sand that further changed the sculpted topography of the area. Then, around two million years ago, glaciers finished the work, carving up anything in their paths and settling into the area that became Lake Superior. When the glaciers retreated, the ice in the basin melted and the largest of the Great Lakes was born.

But Lake Superior is more than just the largest and deepest of the lakes in North America. It boasts the greatest surface area of any body of fresh water in the world—roughly 10 percent of the planet's fresh water—and only two freshwater lakes, Lake Baikal in Siberia and Lake Tanganyika in Africa, hold more water. The water from all four of the other Great Lakes could fit into Lake Superior, with room to spare, and its shoreline is 1,826 miles long, roughly the distance between Duluth and Miami. At its deepest point, Lake Superior would cover the Empire State Building in New York or the Sears Tower in Chicago. Three states (Minnesota, Wisconsin, and Michigan) have shorelines along Lake Superior, as does Canada.

French explorers reached Lake Superior in the early 1600s, a few years before the *Mayflower* anchored at Plymouth Rock. They navigated the lake's shores in birch bark canoes and wooden bateaux, trading for furs while their missionaries tried to bring Catholicism to the native tribes. Although trading continued for two centuries, and settlements and trading posts sprang up near the shores of what became Minnesota, Wisconsin, and Michigan's Upper Peninsula, Lake Superior was largely ignored by the expanding new nation's big commercial interests. This changed dramatically in the late 1800s, when construction began on the Lake Superior & Mississippi Railroad. Huge numbers of Scandinavian immigrants moved into the area, and the population exploded. At the beginning of 1869, fourteen families lived in the port city of Duluth; seven months later, the population was 3,500. The grain, commercial fishing, and lumber industries thrived, and with the booming economy came more travel on the lake.

The mining of Minnesota's rich supply of iron ore began at about the same time. Scientific surveys around Lake Vermilion revealed an incredibly rich supply of iron ore in the area, and with the establishment of mines on the Vermilion Range—and, a short time later, the Mesabi Range—came the need for transport on Lake Superior. Two Harbors became Minnesota's first iron ore port, with others established soon afterward. Bearing in mind that the *Edmund Fitzgerald* had carried 30,000 tons in its hold on a number of occasions, early shipping totals were downright minuscule. The first recorded shipment of iron ore, on June 18, 1856, consisted of 269 tons transported from Marquette to Cleveland on the steamer *Ontonagon,* for the Cleveland Mining Company. The company's total shipping for that entire year amounted to 6,343 tons—less than modern freighters carried in water ballast when sailing without cargo.

The industry grew rapidly, however, becoming the hub of Minnesota's economy. The Vermilion Range alone produced at least a million tons of iron ore between 1892 and 1952. John D. Rockefeller earned a fortune by investing in a Mesabi Range enterprise and expanding into shipping. By the turn of the twentieth century, mines around Lake Superior produced three quarters of the nation's iron ore.

Methods of transporting the iron ore evolved with the burgeoning industry. In the early years, barges were pulled by wooden schooners; later, steel "whaleback" steamers provided the muscle, but the process was expensive. The development of the "long ships"—freighters exceeding 500 feet in length and capable of hauling enormous cargoes—drastically changed the industry, not only in terms of the tonnage moved around on the lakes, but in the way the shipping business was conducted. These huge ore carriers could do double duty, delivering iron ore to ports in Ohio and returning with their cargo holds filled with coal, making the costs of both fuel and shipping more competitive.

Lake Superior claimed its share of victims as the traffic increased on its waters. This was inevitable. But it was more than just a matter of simple math: the demand for iron ore was high; to meet the demand, bigger ships were designed and built, and more trips across the lake were scheduled. The shipping business had always been dangerous, but tougher ships and improved safety measures cut down the number of sailors lost on the lakes; they also created a false sense of security that could be lethal when the skies darkened, the winds howled in from the northeast, and the waves began to build. The captains of the smaller boats usually had the good sense to anchor and wait out a storm; the masters commanding the bigger ships, as history would show, were sometimes guilty of placing the demands of commerce and their faith in their vessels above the potential for disaster.

By early evening on November 9, the *Edmund Fitzgerald* was encountering the anticipated deteriorating weather conditions. The wind was blowing harder and the seas were choppy, but from the perspective of those occupying the *Fitzgerald*'s pilothouse, it was business as usual. The *Fitz* just moved along steadily, at about 15 miles per hour. It had yet to catch up to the *Anderson,* but that would happen sometime during the night. If all went well, the *Fitzgerald* would be passing just south of Isle Royale around midnight. By that time, most of the crew would have quit playing cards or watching television, and settled into their rooms.

One could not have asked for a more experienced crew. With more than seven decades' experience between them, much of the time spent as masters of big freighters, Ernest McSorley and Jack McCarthy were a formidable one-two combination. McSorley and all three of his mates had pilots' licenses for the Great Lakes, but they were only the beginning. Five of the twenty-nine men on board were in their sixties, twelve more in their fifties. George Holl, the chief engineer, was only the second person to hold that position in the *Fitzgerald*'s existence. With only a few exceptions, the crew hailed from the area around the Great Lakes, from blue-collar shipping and steel-producing communities in Ohio, Minnesota, and Wisconsin. The crewmen might migrate from ship to ship, from season to season, but their combined experience was as impressive as you would find on any freighter on the lakes.

You didn't get rich working on an ore carrier, but the pay wasn't bad, either. Base pay for a crewman was $5.63 per hour, a decent enough wage in 1975, but with overtime, bonuses, and cost-of-living allowances sweetening the pay-checks, the annual earnings were substantially more than the base rate allowed. The master, mates, and engineers did even better. A master, with end-of-the-season bonuses for trips and tonnage, earned enough to live quite comfortably.

For most, however, money wasn't the main incentive for working on the lakes. You could earn more at the automotive plants in Michigan, Wisconsin, or Ohio, without facing anything like the hazards of sailing. Granted, shipping wasn't what it had been a century earlier, when sailors treated their careers like a sacred vo-cation. Modern sailors were just as apt to spend their early years on the lakes and then move on to work that kept them closer to their families and homes.

Over the centuries, one constant remained: the almost mystical draw to the water, and the sense of independence you felt when you were on it. On this trip, the men would go two and a half days without setting foot on land, and more than half of that time would pass without their seeing it. Tourists spent large sums of money to experience the feeling these men took for granted. The world was becoming an increasingly enclosed, claustrophobic place; to stand on the deck of the *Edmund Fitzgerald* and look out over the endless expanse of water was to understand a type of freedom that land could never provide.

By the early morning hours of November 10, Captain Ernest McSorley knew that he and his crew were facing a storm of considerable strength. At 1:00 A.M., when the *Fitzgerald* filed its regular report with the National Weather Service, rain was beating down heavily on the lake, and northeasterly winds were measured at 52 knots (nearly 60 miles per hour). Ten-foot waves chopped away at the side of the ship, and the temperature had dropped to 37 degrees. Visibility was down to 2 to 4 miles. The *Fitz* was about 20 miles south of Isle Royale.

The storm, now located over central Wisconsin, moved toward Lake Superior at 33 miles per hour. The barometric pressure continued to fall, which worried the meteorologists tracking the storm at the National Weather Service in Chicago: at the rate and direction the storm was heading, it was likely to cause all kinds of problems for any vessel unlucky enough to be out on Lake Superior when the low-pressure system passed over. Within an hour of hearing from the *Fitzgerald,* the National Weather Service issued a new bulletin, this one a storm warning calling for "northeast winds 35 to 50 knots, becoming northwesterly 28 to 38, [with] waves 8 to 15 feet."

This proved a conservative estimate. The *Fitzgerald* and *Anderson* had already confronted as much—and worse—as they moved along on open water. They were taking the brunt of the storm, yet both ships, stabilized by their loads of taconite, rode well in the water. Spray from the waves hit their spar decks, and heavy seas made the ships work a little harder than usual, but neither McSorley or Cooper worried for the safety of his vessel. To Bernie Cooper, the storm was nothing he hadn't faced before. "We were having a fringe gale," he would remember, "30 to 35 knots, taking spray and no green water on deck."

Green water—solid water, rather than spray—washing over decks was legitimate cause for concern. To wash over the decks, waves had to be 25- to 30-foot monsters, and their sheer weight and force presented serious hazards to the ships they were boarding. Green water could destroy a ship's superstructure, cave in hatch covers, or reduce a pilothouse to rubble. Waves washing over the stern and rolling up the length of the ship could push a ship's bow deep into the water and threaten its buoyancy. In extreme cases, they could roll or capsize a ship.

The most recent ore carrier to sink on Lake Superior was a case in point. The *Henry Steinbrenner,* a 427-foot straight-decker carrying 8,800 tons of iron ore, had sunk on May 11, 1953, after taking on high seas that collapsed hatch covers and flooded its cargo hold. The fifty-two-year-old ship had left Allouez, Wisconsin, early in the morning of Saturday, May 10, downbound for a steel mill on

Lake Erie. The weather, like the pleasant conditions the *Fitzgerald* and *Anderson* had enjoyed when they left their respective ports twenty-two years later, was clear and the seas calm, with temperatures in the mid-sixties when the *Steinbrenner* pulled away from the dock. Forecasts, however, called for stormy conditions ahead, with 30- to 35-mile-per-hour winds and thunder squalls on the western half of Lake Superior.

Weather conditions deteriorated significantly, with torrential rains hitting the lake and temperatures plummeting until the rain changed to snow. By late that evening, winds gusting up to 80 miles per hour had whipped the lake into a churning tempest. Thirty-foot waves battered the *Steinbrenner* and green water swept over the deck, loosening a hatch cover. Three crewmen, tethered to a lifeline cable, braved the wind and seas to secure the hatch. A wave swept one of them into the cargo hold, but, miraculously, he came away only slightly injured.

The hatch cover held until around 3:30 in the morning, when boarding seas worked it loose again. By this point, conditions on the deck were so hazardous that it was impossible to attempt to re-secure the cover. The *Steinbrenner*'s pumps worked nonstop to offset the water gushing into the ship's hold, with little success.

The Coast Guard narrative of the *Steinbrenner*'s fateful journey, published in its accident report, recounted the ferocity of the storm in frightening detail: "Actual weather conditions continued much heavier than predictions—seas were pounding the ship and covering the hatches. With the ship heading into the wind, sea was pouring on board from both sides, rushing down the spar deck around the after deck house to the fantail area."

The freighter was all but dead in the water, defenseless against nature. Water rushed into the open cargo hatch, and by morning more hatch covers were working loose and the ship had lost almost all of its freeboard. Throughout the night, the ship slogged along, averaging about 4–5 miles per hour and just before dawn, when it was about 15 miles south of Isle Royale, the *Steinbrenner* became "sluggish," with no hope of staying afloat or reaching safe harbor. The captain radioed for help and instructed his crew to don life jackets. A half hour later, three more hatch covers gave way and the captain ordered the engines to be shut down. The "abandon ship" whistle sounded.

The *Steinbrenner* sank quickly. Some of the crew were able to escape on a life raft and lifeboats, while others went down with the ship. One unfortunate group had been unable to reach life jackets in time. In the chaotic moments before the freighter sank, crew members desperately struggled to launch the lifeboats. The Coast Guard offered a grim report on the futile efforts to abandon ship by the men lost in the disaster: "Seventeen crew members were lost, evidently due to difficulty in launching lifesaving equipment and an apparent lack of confidence in the lifesaving equipment by some of the crew members who made no effort to abandon the vessel."

Fourteen of the thirty-one men on board, including the ship's captain, survived the sinking, and were rescued after spending between four and four and a half hours on the lake. After investigating the events leading to the demise of the *Steinbrenner,* the Coast Guard concluded that "the cause of the *Steinbrenner*'s foundering was heavy seas dislodging the after three (3) hatch covers . . . permitting flooding of the cargo holds." The ship, the report noted, had been seaworthy, and had "received timely weather reports of the impending strong weather conditions from the time of her departure to her foundering."

The *Steinbrenner* had had a tumultuous history—it had sunk after colliding with another ship in 1909 and had collided with still another in 1923. In the wake of the 1953 sinking, new practices were set for the availability of lifesaving equipment. Ultimately, however, the ship had been brought down after a journey eerily similar to the one now being made by the *Edmund Fitzgerald* and the *Arthur M. Anderson*—a routine run that had turned difficult along the way. A ship could take only so much pounding from the waves.

When the National Weather Service issued its storm warning in the wee hours of November 10, Bernie Cooper radioed Ernest McSorley and the two captains considered a change in direction. A more northeasterly course, they agreed, might be best. The wind was still howling in from the northeast, and if the two ships moved a little closer to the Canadian shore, they would be getting at least minimal protection from Ontario's lee shore. As it was, they'd been heading almost directly into the storm for hours. The two vessels had so far managed with very little difficulty, but the recently posted storm warning meant even heavier seas ahead. By moving toward the Canadian shore, they would cut the wind's fetch and avoid the worst of the building seas.

McSorley had taken this route on any number of occasions, and he knew it well. That it lay farther north and east than the usual shipping route translated into more time on the lake, but at this point, with the shipping season almost completed and some downtime ahead, a few extra hours wasn't that big a deal. There would be plenty of time to relax when he returned to Ohio in a couple of weeks.

The *Fitz* moved full speed ahead. Rain pelted its decks and the wind rattled its wires. Around three in the morning, it passed the *Anderson,* and as the night wore on and dawn approached, the distance increased between the two ships.

The sky was just beginning to grow light when the storm reached Michigan's Upper Peninsula and the southern shores of Lake Superior. The cold front from Canada, sweeping down in the wake of the high-pressure system that had passed to the north during the previous day, was dropping the temperatures that had been so uncommonly warm only twenty-four hours earlier. The rain would soon be changing to snow.

McSorley and Cooper both knew that they had a day of hard sailing ahead of them. They'd be turning their ships and heading south in a matter of a few hours, and then they would be sailing into the eye of the storm. Once the storm had passed north of them, the winds would shift from the northeast to the northwest, and the freighters would be dealing with following seas—waves that built up from the west and crashed into them from behind. At that point, things could get nasty.

At seven A.M., McSorley picked up his radiotelephone and called the Oglebay Norton offices in Cleveland.

"Our ETA at the Soo," he told them, "is indefinite because of the storm."

"If you don't like the weather, just wait an hour. It'll change."

The old saying rang true on all five Great Lakes. Weather conditions could change maddeningly fast, with blue, bright skies turning dark and stormy without warning. Foggy mornings gave way to clear, sunny afternoons, and balmy days could grow chilly within a matter of hours. Anyone living near the shore of a Great Lake was familiar with "lake effect" snow: an area approximate to a lake might be buried in snow when only a few miles away, there might be only a dusting of snowflakes on the ground. The lakes cooled temperatures in the summer and moderated them in the winter.

Familiarity with such weather conditions and respect for their fickleness were prerequisites for anyone piloting the big boats on the lakes, particularly in November, when sudden and unpredictably intense storms could turn a calm sea into a maelstrom. Great Lakes shipping veterans, well versed in the history of the lakes' epic storms, could lean back in the mess halls and rec rooms of their ships and repeat, in excited tones, the finest details of the monster storms that stood apart from all the rest—storms that had confounded meteorologists, tossed huge vessels onto the rocks, capsized ships caught in the middle of boiling seas, and created widows and fatherless children all across the upper Midwest. Some storms, like the shipwrecks they made, became legendary.

Each of the Great Lakes could boast its own history of killer storms. As a rule, these storms were far more violent than weather forecasters had anticipated, with hurricane-force winds and waves as high as two- or three-story buildings. Such storms exacted mind-numbing tolls in vessels and lives. People working on the lakes had a long tradition of debating the intensity of storms—especially the ones they had just sailed through—but in some cases, there was simply no room for dispute.

One such storm racked Lake Superior from November 27 to 29 in 1905. For three days, the lake was nailed with a murderous combination of constant 70- to 80-mile-per-hour winds, subzero temperatures, blinding snow squalls, and massive waves. All told, thirty ships were destroyed and many others grounded or severely damaged.

The wind tossed ships around like paper cups. Lost in the blizzard or crushed to tinder by waves, they wound up on beaches or rocky shoals, their unfortunate crews still luckier than the nineteen men of the *Ira H. Owen,* who went down at the height of the storm. One vessel, the *Western Star,* was tossed so far ashore that people were actually able to walk around the wreckage. The Pittsburgh Steamship line, owned by U.S. Steel, saw seven of its freighters, including the company's flagship, and three barges badly damaged or totally destroyed.

Perhaps the most dramatic—and heartbreaking—of the disasters occurred in Duluth on November 27, when the *Mataafa,* a 430-foot freighter loaded with iron ore and towing the *James Nasmyth,* a 366-foot barge, ran aground just outside the Duluth harbor, within view of thousands on land. The *Mataafa* had sailed in relatively calm seas, only to head straight into the teeth of a vicious nor'easter and blinding snow. When heavy seas boarded the decks and threatened to capsize the ship and its consort, R. F. Humble, the *Mataafa*'s master, decided to return to Duluth. The two vessels fought the storm for hours, barely making way through the gigantic waves and blizzard, but they finally arrived at the entry of the Duluth harbor. Seeing that the *Nasmyth* could never maneuver back through the piers, Captain Humble ordered it cut loose, leaving its crew at the mercy of a pitiless storm. The barge dropped its anchors; just when it seemed it would be tossed onto the rocks, the anchors took hold and the *Nasmyth* was able to ride out the storm.

Those aboard the *Mataafa* were not as fortunate. For a brief period, it looked as if the ship would make it to safety, but as it was inching between the piers, the wind and waves combined to smash it against a concrete pier head, spin it around, and sweep it back out toward the open sea. The *Mataafa*'s rudder was torn off; unable to steer, the ship had no chance. The wind dashed it against the rocks about a hundred feet from the beach. The *Mataafa* broke and settled low in the water.

Rescue was impossible in the winds and high seas, and with temperatures plunging to 20 below and a blizzard burying Duluth in drifting snow, there was little doubt about the fate of the *Mataafa*'s crew. The boilers had been disabled by water entering the stern section of the ship, and without heat the men were doomed to slowly freeze to death. A crowd estimated at more than 10,000 gathered near the dock and along the shore, building fires and holding prayer vigils.

By morning, the storm had dissipated enough that the Coast Guard was able to dispatch a lifeboat to the wreckage. As expected, the nine men in the stern section had perished. Five were missing and presumed washed overboard, and four were found dead of exposure, their frozen bodies encased in ice. Axes had to be used to chop the bodies out of the wreckage. The men in the bow section had survived by chopping up the captain's bathroom, burning the wood in his bathtub, and huddling together for warmth.

As deadly as the storm of 1905 had been, it paled when compared to the November 9–12 storm eight years later—a four-day blow that hit all five of the Great Lakes, sinking ten ships, seriously damaging or destroying thirty others, and claiming the lives of 235 men. On Lake Huron alone, eight ships were lost with all hands, a toll of 178 lives. To Great Lakes historians then and now, this was truly the storm of the century, if not the worst ever on the lakes.

The entire upper Midwest fell victim. Twenty-two inches of snow piled up in Cleveland, bringing the city to a halt. In Chicago, wind blew down the buildings in a park and scattered all their equipment. In Milwaukee, Lake Michigan waves pounded a newly built breakwater to scrap. Three coal bridges were knocked down in Duluth. Telephone and electrical lines snapped and highways were shut down by blowing and drifting snow. Areas around Lake Huron reported four-foot drifts. Most storms move rapidly through a region, but this one took its time, gaining incredible power as it moved down Lake Superior and over Lake Huron. By the time the storm had moved out of the region on Tuesday, November 11, bodies from eight Lake Huron shipwrecks were washing ashore, many still in life preservers, most encrusted in ice.

Mariners were given plenty of advance warning that the storm, approaching from the northwest, was not an ordinary autumn blow. The Coast Guard posted storm warnings along Lake Superior at noon on November 7; only a few hours later, the storm warnings were replaced by a rare hurricane warning. Winds were already exceeding 50 miles per hour.

The forecasts failed to discourage some of the captains scheduled to sail. Business was business, and a canceled trip this late in the season meant lost revenue that, in all likelihood, couldn't be made up later. Heavy-weather captains, so called for their willingness to sail in conditions that drove others to shelter, weren't easily intimidated. They commanded strong ships and they had faced nasty storms in the past.

The *Huronic,* a luxurious 321-foot passenger liner, became one of the storm's earliest victims. Downbound on Lake Superior, the liner wrote a wild ending to its last scheduled cruise of the season when, suddenly and without warning, wind gusts blew in the ship's pilothouse windows and began shaking the pilothouse apart. With massive waves boarding his decks and wind dismantling his ship's superstructure, the *Huronic*'s captain ordered his crew to chop away the splintered pilothouse while the ship made a desperate run for Whitefish Point. The captain managed to ground his badly mangled vessel near the point, averting a sinking and saving the lives of its passengers.

Other ships suffered similar fates. Experienced sailors, accustomed to the Witch of November, were nevertheless lost in blizzards, their vessels blown wildly off course and onto rocky shoals or beaches. If they were lucky, the crewmen were rescued before wind and waves tore their ships apart. If not, they found themselves in a very different battle: survival without food or water, in wet (and eventually frozen) clothing, with minimal shelter.

The eighteen-member crew of the *Turret Chief* encountered such difficulties when, at about 4:00 on the morning of November 8, the 253-foot Canadian freighter was thrown onto a rocky reef near the shore of the Keweenaw Peninsula, about five miles from Copper Harbor, Michigan. Hopelessly lost and with nothing to eat and no way to build a fire, the crew huddled together in a makeshift shelter and prepared for the worst. Two days passed. Then, on the morning of Monday, November 10, they watched in disbelief as a group of Native American trappers appeared out of nowhere. The trappers ushered them to safety.

The crew of the *L. C. Waldo,* a 472-foot ore carrier loaded with iron and bound for Cleveland, endured a similar ordeal. Boarding waves had torn the pilothouse apart and encased the ship in sheets of ice. The *Waldo*'s captain, using only a lifeboat compass and auxiliary wheel in the after deck house, struggled to find any kind of shelter for his ship, but the vessel was ultimately swept onto Gulf Rock near Manitou Island. The twenty-four-member crew sat helplessly as the waves made fast work of the *Waldo,* ripping away its forward deckhouse and ultimately breaking the ship in two. The crew fled to the small windlass room at the front of the ship and, for two days, stayed alive by chopping the remains of the *Waldo* to pieces and burning the wood in a bathtub. A passing ship spied the wreckage and the distress flag, and alerted the Coast Guard. Two harbor tugs were sent to the scene to rescue the hungry, exhausted, and nearly frozen crew.

Two ships simply disappeared. The *Henry B. Smith,* a 525-footer loaded with 10,000 tons of iron ore, and the *Leafield,* a 250-foot Canadian freighter carrying grain, left their ports, disappeared in the storm, and were never heard from again. Wreckage and bodies of the *Smith* victims were eventually discovered, but the *Leafield* left no trace that it ever existed. Neither a scrap of wreckage nor any of the seventeen victims was recovered. The *Smith* story offered a shocking illustration of the chances taken in the name of commerce: Captain Jimmy Owen was reportedly reluctant to sail in such conditions, but the ship's owners warned him that he would be fired if he didn't honor his schedule.

The destruction on Lake Huron was exponentially greater than on Lake Superior—the 1913 storm would eventually be called the Lake Huron Storm— and would spawn scores of books and articles about the "white hurricane"'s devastating force. October 20, 1916, when a freshwater hurricane brought down four ships on Lake Erie, became known as Black Friday. The November 18, 1958, gale that broke the *Carl D. Bradley* in two was labeled the *Bradley* Storm. Such historical shorthand conjured up long, colorful stories told in the bellies of modern freighters, where crewmen gathered in mess halls and rode out what they were convinced would be the next big storm.

The November 9–10, 1975, tempest on Lake Superior eventually earned its own title: the *Edmund Fitzgerald* Storm.

The *Fitzgerald* twisted and rolled as it made its way down the lake, its hull groaning in protest to the way it was being lifted and dropped in the turbulent waves. Like all modern Great Lakes vessels, the *Fitz* had been built to absorb punishment. Its hull had been constructed out of steel flexible enough to handle the action of the waves, but now, with the eye of the storm north of it and the seas building at an alarming pace, the *Fitz* was being pressed to its limit. A ship's working in these conditions could unnerve even hardcore veterans, who were known to crawl down access tunnels to get from one end of a ship to the other. Some never quite got used to the fact that the ship could be working so hard that the after section would rise to such an extent that they couldn't see the end of the tunnel, or that it could bend to such an extent that they were literally walking on the walls to maintain their balance.

In the aftermath of the loss, former *Fitz* crewmen disagreed about the way the ship worked in heavy seas; there was even talk that Ernest McSorley himself worried about the action in his vessel.

Delmore Webster, who served on the *Fitz* as a wheelsman, took a certain amount of rolling for granted.

"When you are in a heavy sea, in heavy weather, it rolled," he said of the *Fitz*. "It wasn't in excess of other boats I have been on. I mean, it is not like she had an unusual characteristic for rolling."

Richard Orgel, who was briefly a third mate on the *Fitz,* took issue with this assessment. The ship, he insisted, would bend and spring "considerably" in heavy weather, more than other ships he'd served on.

"When you are standing forward and looking aft," he said, "it would remind you of a diving board just after somebody jumped off—the board, the diving board of a swimming pool. She did this whippingly."

This action, Orgel pointed out, began somewhere near the middle of the ship and ended at the stern. For a very brief period—no more than two or three seconds, by Orgel's estimation—the *Fitz* would shudder and stop, only to repeat the process a few seconds later. The springing struck Orgel as being highly irregular.

"It seems that when the sea piles up under her stern and then falls away, she just doesn't drop down into the trough," he stated. "The stern doesn't drop into the trough like you would expect it. It whips, is the best word—or springs, is the best way I could describe it."

"It is a funny feeling to walk down the ship and have that ship springing," noted Andrew Rajner, who had relieved Jack McCarthy as first mate on the *Fitz* from September 12 to October 3, 1975. "Even if you go down the tunnel, it is a long way down to the other end. You have something moving underneath you, and you really are not sure of what you are standing on, but after a while, you get used to it. You just forget about it."

Orgel recalled a time when the *Fitzgerald* encountered heavy weather after leaving Whitefish Point, upbound for Silver Bay. Ernest McSorley had chosen to take the safer, northern course, but the *Fitz,* sailing almost head-on into the storm, was working noticeably.

"I asked him if it was possible that this action could actually cause the hatch clamps to come off," Orgel remembered. "He said no, he had never seen that happen, and I remarked to him that there was sometimes a lot of action back there."

At the time, McSorley was preparing to leave the pilothouse and head to his quarters for a short nap, and Orgel was relieving him. While they talked about the *Fitzgerald,* McSorley confessed his own misgivings about the way the ship worked in heavy seas.

"Oh, this thing," he told Orgel, "this sometimes scares me."

Before retiring to his room, McSorley left special instructions with his third mate.

"He told me if she started working too much, I should alter course and call him," Orgel said. "He said he was going to be laying on top of his bed. He wasn't going to undress or anything, and if I had any problems or thought it was working too much, I should call him."

Peter Pulcer, master of the *Fitzgerald* just prior to McSorley's arrival, admitted that he'd encountered plenty of pitching and rolling in heavy seas during his six years with the ship—"I have walked the walls already, I can tell you that"—and he'd seen water rolling over the decks of the ship. But the *Fitz* had been strong throughout the worst of it.

"I have seen her roll too much," he admitted. "She would roll to a certain extent, but the seas on the quarter, they would come aboard and roll along the deck. I had never seen any damage done."

The pitching and rolling, and bending and springing, in Pulcer's view, were nothing special. He'd never had any serious problems with the *Fitz*.

"She handled like a good little girl," he insisted. "That's all I know."

Buck Champeau couldn't wait for the shipping season to end. The *Fitzgerald*'s third engineer was building a cottage on Lake Clark in Wisconsin, not far from Sturgeon Bay. The place was getting close to completion, and Champeau wanted to be around when the carpeting and drapery arrived. Since his divorce, he'd lived on and off with his mother, and he'd kept an apartment in Milwaukee, but he longed for a place in beautiful country, where he could sit back and relax, host his daughter, Debbie, when she visited, and enjoy the hunting and fishing. He went back and forth on the idea of staying on the *Fitz*. It was a big, safe boat, but he'd had an uneasy sense about it ever since the night he'd knocked back a few drinks and agreed to let someone in the bar read his palm. Something terrible had been revealed—something he refused to discuss even with his family—but he went home and rewrote his will and put his affairs in order.

Champeau wasn't an easy man to frighten. Stocky and well muscled, with thick jet-black hair and a handlebar mustache, Oliver Joseph Champeau was the oldest of his parents' five children. When his father died, Buck, then thirteen, assumed the traditional role of head of the household, helping raise his two brothers and two sisters, and working as a paperboy and babysitter to augment what his mother earned washing clothes and cleaning houses. Family meant everything to him. He taught his younger brothers how to defend themselves in schoolyard fights, and he enjoyed spending lazy hours on the weekends in a nearby orchard, picking cherries with his sister Mary. He carried these tough and sensitive characteristics with him throughout his life, manifest in everything from the Marine Corps tattoo on his left forearm to the way he befriended down-and-outers at the local mission and brought them home for meals. One of them was a particularly gnarled character with the unlikely name of Kaput, and Buck made his family promise to look after Kaput after he'd returned to work.

Maybe he got some of that empathy from his own hardscrabble days; maybe it was just his nature. He'd quit school and taken on different jobs, including one driving a coal truck, before signing on for a stint in the Marine Corps during the Korean War. He served on the U.S.S. *Oriskinay,* and when he returned home, he decided to look into finding work in the shipping industry. Most evenings, he'd study in the basement, away from the noise upstairs, trading books with his brother-in-law, who also worked on the lakes. In time, Champeau earned certification as a second engineer, a position he might have held on the *Fitzgerald* if the two second engineer positions hadn't already been taken.

He'd been with the *Fitz* for three years, but he wasn't terribly fond of it. Probably he just needed something new. He'd been sailing since 1961, when he took his first job on a car ferry, and, like a lot of men in the business, he'd bounced from ship to ship. Maybe next year he'd find another . . .

In the meantime, he had a job to do on the *Fitz.* The storm was raising a tremendous racket, and the *Fitz* was moaning like the loser in a schoolyard fight. But the *Fitz* still had plenty of fight. There had been no problem in the engine room, and the freighter just kept on plowing ahead, cutting through the building seas at full speed.

Thanksgiving was only a few weeks away. If all went well, Champeau would be overseeing the carpet layers and doing some more finishing work. He'd even put together a room for his daughter, had it painted yellow, just like she wanted.

From a distance, the big Great Lakes straight-deckers looked as if their bows and sterns had been stretched like taffy until the fore and aft sections were separated by an abnormally elongated midships section, the pilothouse in front, the boilers, engines, and afterdeck in back, the cargo holds between. Great Lakes storms put tremendous stress on these long, gangly vessels, when waves would lift and violently slam down the bows and sterns of the ships. A propeller could be lifted out of the water. Hulls could be twisted until rivets popped and were sent flying like bullets. The midsection of a ship could buckle, or "hog," until it fractured and water gushed into the cargo holds. In the worst-case scenario, hogging could tear a ship in two.

In two of the Great Lakes' most storied modern disasters, the *Carl D. Bradley* and the *Daniel J. Morrell* had broken apart in just such a fashion, victims of the gales of November.

Launched in 1927, the 648-foot *Bradley*, a bulk carrier, was the longest Great Lakes vessel of its time. The *Bradley* set a number of gross tonnage records on the lakes, including, in 1929, the mark for the largest single cargo ever hauled: an 18,114-ton load of limestone.

Time, however, had noticeably aged the *Bradley*, so much so that in the fall of 1958, its master, Roland Bryan, expressed reservations about its seaworthiness. "This boat is getting pretty ripe for too much weather," he wrote a friend. "I'll be glad when they get her fixed up."

Captain Bryan's concerns were justified. Over the previous two shipping seasons, the *Bradley* had been involved in three incidents that might have weakened its hull. The first, a collision with another ship on April 3, 1956, damaged the *Bradley* seriously enough that it had to be drydocked for repairs. A year later, in the spring of 1957, the ship had bottomed out while leaving the harbor in Cedarville, Michigan, sustaining minor damage. Finally, in November 1958, shortly before its final journey, the *Bradley* grounded in Cedarville again, sustaining a fourteen-inch fracture that was repaired by welding while the ship was still afloat.

The *Bradley* had passed its annual inspection in April 1958, and a safety inspection had occurred during a fire and lifesaving drill on October 30, less than three weeks before the freighter pulled away from a dock for the final time. Nevertheless, the *Bradley*'s owner, the Michigan Limestone Division of U.S. Steel Corporation, recognized the urgent need for heavy-duty work on the ship; it planned to install an $800,000 cargo hold and make other repairs at the end of the 1958 shipping season.

When the big freighter pulled out of the Huffington, Indiana, harbor on the evening of Monday, November 17, 1958, in what was scheduled to be the ship's last trip of the season, Captain Bryan and his crew of thirty-four knew they were in for a long night. The weather forecast called for 25- to 35-mile-per-hour winds from the south to increase to a gale-force 50 to 65 miles per hour from the southwest, stirring up predictably high seas. With no cargo in its hold, the *Bradley* used 9,000 tons of water ballast to stabilize it during its run to Calcite, Michigan.

Throughout the next day, the *Bradley* held its own against the deteriorating weather, making its way up the Wisconsin coast at about 15 miles per hour, holding a course that kept it between 5 and 16 miles from shore. With the winds behind them and at least minimal protection from the storm, the crew of the *Bradley* expected to be in safe harbor by the early morning hours of Wednesday, November 17.

Other vessels, traveling north of the *Bradley* on Lake Michigan, reported fighting heavy seas, but these ships were few and far between. Most had taken shelter in such ports as Green Bay, Garden Island, or the Straits of Mackinac, prepared to wait until the storm abated.

The *Bradley* moved along with no difficulty at all, despite 20-foot waves hitting the ship at 50- to 75-foot intervals. No green water washed over the decks, and the *Bradley* was riding so smoothly that sideboards weren't even used on the mess table. Watchman Frank Mays, one of the disaster's two survivors, walked the length of the vessel in one of its access tunnels, and, as he would later testify, he observed nothing unusual.

In the pilothouse, Captain Bryan and First Mate Elmer Fleming talked about how they intended to guide the *Bradley* through the Beaver Island archipelago. Suddenly, at 5:31 P.M., a loud thud, followed by a shuddering of the ship, interrupted their conversation. Bryan and Fleming instinctively looked back toward the ship's stern, and were horrified to see it sagging in the water. The *Bradley* was breaking apart.

Bryan sounded the general alarm and blew the abandon ship whistle while Fleming transmitted a mayday on the ship's radio. The *Bradley,* Fleming told the person answering his call, was mortally wounded, about 12 miles southeast of Gull Island. Fleming had just sent out a second mayday transmission when the *Bradley*'s lights flickered and the power went out. The vessel hogged again, its midsection heaving upward until the *Bradley* split into two almost equal pieces. Both sections sank quickly, within minutes of the initial hogging, the stern portion sending up an explosion of steam, bright yellow flames, and smoke when the cold Lake Michigan water flooded the boiler room.

Meanwhile crew members scrambled for life jackets and headed for lifeboats and rafts. Some jumped overboard when the ship sank, but many were thrown into the freezing water when the two sections rolled and plunged to the bottom of the lake. Shouts and cries for help were absorbed in the shrieking wind and mountainous waves.

For Frank Mays and Elmer Fleming, the ordeal was just beginning. Both had been dragged underwater when the *Bradley* sank; they survived the plunge and, upon surfacing, found a life raft. Two others joined them on it. The waves pushed them away from the scene of the sinking, tossing the raft and sending the four overboard on numerous occasions. The men huddled together for warmth, praying and hoping that a rescue ship would arrive before hypothermia finished them off.

Rescue ships had heard Fleming's mayday and headed for the area where the *Bradley* had gone down, but their search was futile. The ship had sunk shortly before six in the evening, when it was dark on the lake, and it was impossible to see survivors amid waves that crested as high as thirty feet. A Coast Guard aircraft joined the search, dropping flares that pierced the night, but found no one.

The four men on the raft hung on. The hours passed; one by one, two of the men disappeared when the lake tossed the raft and they were flung off. Daylight broke, with Mays and Fleming still clinging to the raft, now nearly twenty miles from where the *Bradley* had sunk. Ice had formed on their clothing, and rescue seemed like little more than a cruel fantasy. Finally, at 8:25 on Wednesday morning, more than fourteen hours after the *Bradley* had foundered, the *Sundew,* a Coast Guard cutter searching in the area, spotted the raft and pulled the two men aboard.

Eighteen bodies (of thirty-three victims) were recovered from Lake Michigan. In its report on the loss of the *Carl D. Bradley,* the Coast Guard blamed "excessive hogging" for breaking the ship apart. "This casualty," the Coast Guard concluded, "has emphasized the need for the programs of technical evaluation to determine if there is any evidence of structural defects in other vessels of the Great Lakes fleet."

Concerns over the structural integrity of older ships sailing the Great Lakes during the stormy shipping season weren't new, nor would they be resolved despite the good intentions stated in the Coast Guard's report on the *Bradley*. Less than a decade later, following the loss of the *Daniel J. Morrell*, Joseph J. O'Connell, Jr., chairman of the National Transportation Safety Board, dispatched a letter to Admiral Willard J. Smith, commandant of the Coast Guard, expressing identical concerns.

"The National Transportation Safety Board is concerned that a similar tragedy may occur to other bulk carriers under similar circumstances," O'Connell wrote. "The fracture sustained by the [*Morrell*'s] sister ship S.S. EDWARD Y. TOWNSEND in the same vicinity and under like conditions substantiate[s] this concern. Another example is the breaking and sinking of the S.S. CARL BRADLEY in Lake Michigan on November 18, 1958, which was attributed to an undetected structural weakness or defect."

At the white-hot center of these concerns stood two conflicts as old as the history of shipping on the Great Lakes—man versus nature, commerce versus safety—and while no one wanted to think it, let alone say it out loud, human arrogance often cast the deciding vote. While the shipping industry and those sailing on the lakes always maintained a healthy respect for the devastating powers of nature, it still seemed inconceivable that massive ships, designed and operated by the most capable minds in the business, could be bested by forces they were supposedly equipped to handle.

If anything, the shipping industry was becoming bolder. By the early-1970s, thousand-foot vessels were being designed, weather was being more accurately and quickly predicted, and state-of-the-art radar, communications technology, and safety equipment, largely developed in the wake of past failures, pushed the envelope to new limits. Minimum draft requirements had been altered, allowing

the big ore carriers to carry much larger loads in the fall and winter seasons, and
ships were now working year-round.

Ships like the *Daniel J. Morrell* and its sister ship, the *Edward Y. Townsend,*
were becoming the dinosaurs of the Great Lakes. They had been built well before 1948, when more flexible materials began to be used in the construction of
ships to combat the bitter cold and pounding waves in Great Lakes storms; the
Morrell and *Townsend* were still good, serviceable vessels, but it was becoming
evident that their time had come, that they were being replaced by more highly
evolved specimens.

When the *Daniel J. Morrell* left the harbor of Lackawanna, New York, near
Buffalo, on the evening of November 26, 1966, it should have been finished for
the season, but after conferring with the ship's owners, Captain Arthur Crawley
learned that one additional run was required to fulfill its tonnage commitments.
The *Morrell* would have to return to Taconite Harbor, Minnesota, for one last
load of iron ore. The 603-foot bulk freighter had been working on the lakes
since 1906, and had completed thirty-three trips during the 1966 shipping season, so one more voyage, although disappointing to crew members eager to return to their families for the winter, was not a major inconvenience.

The *Townsend* was scheduled for a similar trip to Taconite Harbor, and it left
Lackawanna a few hours after the *Morrell.* Neither ship was hauling cargo, and
both had water in their ballast tanks for what looked to be a rough ride on Lake
Huron. The forecast out of the National Weather Service offices in Chicago
called for high winds for the southern two thirds of the lake, and gale warnings
for the northern third, with rain or a mixture of rain and snow for the entire
lake.

The forecasts were accurate. After an uneventful start, the two ships faced
gradually worsening conditions on the lake. The *Townsend,* in particular, took a
pounding from the waves, and the captains kept regular radio contact with each
other, discussing their concerns about the weather and how they would direct
their vessels through it. Both ships were rolling considerably, and Captain Thomas
J. Connelly of the *Townsend* worried about his ship's hitting troughs in the high
seas. Both officers considered turning back to Port Huron, or making a run to the

shelter of Thunder Bay, but they decided that the maneuvers required in doing either might be more dangerous than just proceeding on the open water.

Both ships struggled on, the wind blowing them off course and producing waves that Connelly would later characterize as "tremendous." The *Townsend* seemed especially vulnerable, taking green water on its decks and pitching and rolling in the seas, its sixty-year-old hull twisting and groaning as 25-foot waves lifted it from the water and dropped it down again. Connelly would later testify that he had never encountered such conditions in all his years on the Great Lakes, adding that he would have been unable to launch his lifeboats in the storm, had it become necessary. When the *Townsend* limped into Lime Island for refueling on November 30, the storm's toll on the ship was shockingly evident: rivets in the deck plating had come loose, and a crack was found near one of the hatches.

During his conversations with the *Townsend,* Captain Crawley expressed no grave concerns over his ship's safety. He conceded that the *Morrell* was taking a battering in the storm, pitching and rolling as the *Townsend* was, but there was no panic in his voice when he spoke to Connelly. It was the *Townsend* that was struggling. During one of their last conversations, at about 11:00 on November 28, Connelly had cut the call short when the *Townsend* began to broach in the high seas. "I'll call you back," he told Crawley, hanging up the phone.

The *Morrell* might have had more problems than Crawley realized. Only three hours after the abbreviated talk with Connelly, at 2:00 A.M., *Morrell* crew members were awakened by a loud, explosive banging that sent a shiver throughout the ship. A second, louder banging followed and the men scrambled to the sound of the general alarm.

The *Daniel J. Morrell,* hogging in the storm, was breaking apart, its middle section buckling between the eleventh and twelfth hatches. Severed electrical lines sent sparks flying in the night. The lights at the front of the ship were out. Friction from the two sections slamming against each other and tearing further apart sent out a horrific grating sound. No one doubted what was happening. Half-dressed men hurried to the life raft positioned on the stern, but the lifeboats on the stern were inaccessible. The crewmen piled on the life raft and

waited. Launching the raft into the tortured seas below was risky, with no guarantee that the men would be able to jump overboard and reach it, so after some
discussion, they decided to wait on the raft until the bow of the *Morrell* sank
and they floated free of the wreckage.

Within minutes, the ship broke in two. The stern section, still under power
with its boilers running and propeller churning, slipped away from the bow section and rammed it repeatedly until it had broken completely free. The men in
the raft watched in disbelief as the stern proceeded on, its running lights still
working, into the night. The bow started to settle in the water, just as a huge
wave washed its deck, throwing the men and raft overboard.

Freezing water presented a stunning, almost unimaginable shock to the system,
as watchman Dennis Hale, clad in only his undershorts, a peacoat, and a lifejacket, quickly learned. He plunged beneath the lake's surface, struggled to swim
upward, and, gasping from the shock, looked frantically for signs of the raft and
his fellow crew members. The raft, bobbing on the water, was about ten feet
away, and Hale swam to it. He was quickly joined by three other crew members—
deckhands Arthur Stojek and John Cleary, and wheelsman Charles Fosbender.
They neither saw nor heard any of the other men who, only moments earlier,
had been seated with them on the raft.

The *Morrell's* sinking had been very sudden—only an estimated eight minutes
passed between the initial emergency alarm and the moment when the ship split
in two—and since the ship had lost its power when the electrical lines were severed, no mayday signal had been transmitted. The men were on the lake alone;
no one knew the *Morrell* had disappeared in the storm. Still, the four on the raft
hoped to be rescued by one of the vessels known to be in the area. Hale fired
off several distress flares and the men huddled together on one side of the raft.

No immediate help arrived. Hale had plenty of time to contemplate the irony
of his situation. By all rights, he should have been somewhere else. Only a couple of days earlier, he had missed the *Morrell's* departure from Lackawanna. He
and another crew member talked a friend into driving them to Detroit and they
boarded the *Morrell* in Windsor, Ontario, when the ship had anchored there for
refueling. Even the ship's sinking had a surreal quality. When awakened by the

first banging sound, Hale had paid little attention to it. Ships made all kinds of strange noises while fighting storms. The second banging had sent books flying off his bookshelf, prompting him to leave his room to investigate what was going on. Hearing that the ship was breaking apart, he had raced back to his room for clothes. The power was out, and he groped around in the darkness, eventually grabbing his peacoat and heading to the deck and life raft.

"The main deck was starting to tear," he remembered, years later. "There were sparks, little puffs of smoke. I watched it separate. I was looking over my shoulder, thinking, 'God, I hate to get wet.' I wasn't in a panic. I always thought that was quite strange."

Now here he was, sharing a raft with three others, trying to find a way to retain his body heat in savage winds and rolling waves. Cleary and Stojek died of exposure just before dawn on November 29; Fosbender passed away later that afternoon. Hale managed to hang on for another day. He burrowed beneath his dead crewmates for shelter and drifted in and out of consciousness, suffering nightmares when he was unconscious and hallucinations when he was awake. At one point, when he tried to eat the ice off his peacoat to quench his thirst, Hale saw a ghostly presence who warned him that he would get pneumonia if he ate the ice. Hale prayed and, despairing as the hours passed and he felt he was being punished for surviving the shipwreck, he talked to his dead shipmates. The raft eventually ran aground near the shore, but Hale was too weak to lift himself off the raft.

Finally, around four o'clock in the afternoon of November 30—thirty-eight hours after the *Morrell* had sunk—a Coast Guard helicopter spotted the raft near Harbor Beach and rescued Hale. Apart from severe frostbite to his toes and right hand, and a minor case of shock, he was in surprisingly good condition.

That he had been found was close to a miracle. Since no SOS had been issued by the *Morrell*, no one knew the ship was missing until shortly after noon on November 30, when the Coast Guard Rescue Coordination Center in Cleveland, concerned that the *Morrell* had yet to report at the Soo Locks, began a search. A short time later, a body was found floating not far from the Harbor Beach Breakwater Lighthouse. Additional bodies were discovered by other ships in the area.

When a Coast Guard helicopter spotted the raft, the pilot was convinced that he would be picking up four more bodies, and his crew discovered that Dennis Hale was alive only when a guardsman boarded the raft.

In the aftermath of the *Daniel J. Morrell's* sinking, a lot of questions were asked about the construction of the older ships on the Great Lakes and about the seaworthiness of all ships traveling in rough weather. The *Morrell,* it turned out, had probably been suffering from structural weakness or failure hours before it broke up. When Dennis Hale was on his normal 4 P.M.–8 P.M. watch on the evening of November 28, he was directed to examine the cargo holds and mark any leaks or damages. He found a leak near the ship's Number 6 hatch, and two leaks near the Number 8 hatch. All, in his words, were "spurting water." Even more disturbing, he found surface water in two of the cargo holds. He reported the damage and leaks to Captain Crawley.

In its accident report, the Coast Guard stopped short of blaming any single point for the *Morrell's* structural failure. Instead, it pointed to a combination of four factors: "high load due to extremely heavy weather conditions"; "notch sensitive steel"; "a notch"; and a "temperature of 33 degrees F, which was below the nil ductility temperature of the steel." The problems found during Dennis Hale's inspection were also cited as possible contributing factors: "The free surface water in cargo holds 2 and 3 might have caused an unusual strain to an already weakened area as a result of the dynamic forces of shifting weight due to pitching, rolling, pounding, and possible twisting of the vehicle as its bow was blown around."

The Coast Guard pondered the rapidity of the sinking and wondered what might have happened if the ship had been equipped with watertight bulkheads: "Had the two screen bulkheads located in the cargo holds been of watertight construction, it is possible that one or both sections of the vessel would have remained afloat."

Dennis Hale never worked on the lakes again. By his own admission, he suffered from a form of post-traumatic stress syndrome, haunted by the fact that he had been the tragedy's only survivor. He eventually wrote a book, *Sole Survivor,* about his ordeal.

The *Edward Y. Townsend,* which had sustained a fracture in its deck plates almost exactly where the *Morrell* split apart, never hauled another load on the Great Lakes. It was eventually sold to a scrap company in Spain, but it broke up and sank in the Atlantic as it was being towed across the ocean.

Sometime around one o'clock in the afternoon, the weather broke and the *Fitz* sailed in moderate seas, under sunny skies. This was the eye of the storm. The crew welcomed the break. The ship had turned south an hour earlier, and while the early portion of the trip down the lake hadn't been as brutal as the hours when it was running headfirst into the storm, the *Fitz* still faced heavy seas.

The storm, as forecast, had passed just west of Michipicoten Island and was heading northeast to Canada. The *Fitz* had moved into Canadian waters a couple of hours earlier, and it would remain there until the very end of its trip, when it would angle slightly west, toward Whitefish Bay.

No one aboard had any illusions about the benign weather they were now facing. As soon as the storm moved away from them, they'd be facing the roughest sailing of the trip. The wind would change direction at about the same time that the *Fitzgerald* was making its passage between Michipicoten and Caribou Islands, the only two islands of note on eastern Lake Superior.

Ernest McSorley had kept in touch with the *Anderson* about its plans for this leg of the journey. Caribou Island, a heavily wooded seventeen-mile strip of land rising out of the lake, presented a possible hazard to any ship straying too close, as did the stretch of water between it and Michipicoten Island, which lay just to the north. In between the two islands, the lake's depth varied greatly, from 600 feet at its deepest point to 36 feet at its shallowest. In a storm, the shallower areas could be rough, and Bernie Cooper told McSorley that he intended to alter his course.

"I'm going to haul to the west for a while," he informed the *Fitzgerald*'s captain. Cooper anticipated some extremely strong winds once the storm had moved further north, and he favored putting extra distance between the *Anderson* and Michipicoten Island in the event that he started taking heavy seas off his stern. Even the big ships could be knocked off course by a storm, and Cooper wanted to play it safe.

McSorley preferred to remain on his present course although, as he told Cooper, the *Fitzgerald* was "rolling some." The seas had picked up since the *Fitz* moved out of the eye of the storm, but the ship was still moving at full speed and experiencing no serious problems. McSorley figured he'd angle the *Fitz* between the islands; this would give him a straight shot into Whitefish Bay. The *Fitz* had already lost some time by taking the northern route after the storm warnings were posted; as long as it continued to handle the storm, there was no need to spend any more time on the lake than necessary.

One could only imagine what lay ahead. The sky had grown dark again, and it was starting to snow. Twelve-foot waves hit the side of the ship, sending spray over the spar deck. The wind rattled the fence wires running down the length of the deck, adding to the constant din that put everyone on edge.

The older members of the *Fitzgerald*'s crew had lived through any number of storms during their time on the lakes. They took for granted that the month of November could serve up some bad weather, from bone-numbing cold to seas rough enough to send your possessions flying across the room. Lake Superior wasn't called Old Treacherous for nothing.

These men had learned how to ride out the worst of it. You were essentially confined to your quarters, or at least to your end of the ship, since nobody was going to walk anywhere outside when even moving down the access tunnels could be a challenge. You were better off staying in your room and catching up on some reading, or watching television. Or you might sit around and chew the fat with some of the others in the rec room or dining room. Or, if you were coming off your watch, you might try to catch a little sleep, which wasn't the easiest task when the ship was rolling and groaning, and the wind and waves contributed all kinds of noise to disrupt you. You might have been through a couple of big blows, but each storm was different, playing games with your nerves and putting you on constant alert. But why worry? You were in a good, strong ship; all you had to do was get through a few more hours and you'd have reached safe harbor or moved out of the storm's reach.

For five of the crewmen, all in their early twenties, this was largely new, uncharted territory. All had spent some time on the lakes, but none had witnessed anything of this magnitude. Twenty-three-year-old oiler Tom Bentsen was the most experienced of the group. Bentsen had attended the Great Lakes Maritime Academy in Michigan, and when the 1975 shipping season ended, he would have earned enough credits for his third assistant engineer's license. The *Fitzgerald*'s massive engine room was possibly the safest, most stable place on the ship, and working with an experienced seaman like George Holl and his second assistants undoubtedly provided Bentsen with an additional sense of security when the *Fitz* rolled in heavy seas.

Deckhands Bruce Hudson and Paul Riipa had worked together in the past, on the *Ashland,* and they'd arrived on the *Fitzgerald* for very different reasons, Riipa because he was unhappy on the *Ashland,* Hudson as a kind of promotion for the work he'd done as an oiler on the *Ashland.* Hudson, a former Eagle Scout and a devout Methodist, had befriended another young crew member, David Weiss, and the two planned to take a road trip to California as soon as the shipping season ended. Mark Thomas, a twenty-four-year-old from Richmond Heights, Ohio, rounded out the group of *Fitzgerald* deckhands.

They made an interesting fraternity. Weiss, who had only recently found a direction in his life after an aimless, rather troubled youth, couldn't have been more different from Riipa, an intensely religious man given to reading the Bible during his off hours. All had seen their duties changed by the storm: rather than work out on the deck, where they might be found painting a hatch cover or greasing a vent cap, they were limited to maintenance jobs below the decks or in the after deck.

As the storm intensified and did its work on the *Fitzerald,* they all heard the stories from their elders—those who'd insist that they had been through worse, and those who brought up the stories of the *Bradley* and *Morrell* and hoped the *Edmund Fitzgerald* was stronger than those two ill-fated ore boats.

Captain McSorley pushed his ship through the storm. He had been in some horrible weather in his forty-four years on the lakes but had never encountered anything like this. The eye of the storm was now behind him, and the winds, stronger than ever, had changed direction. They were blowing in from the northwest, so the *Fitz* no longer enjoyed even marginal protection from the Canadian shore. Instead, the winds ripped across the water for most of the length of Lake Superior, building enormous waves that rammed relentlessly into anything in their path, wave quickly following wave, with a devastating cumulative effect. This kind of weather could inspire seasoned veterans to pray.

The *Fitz* managed well. By mid-afternoon, it had passed Michipicoten Island and was heading south toward much tinier Caribou Island. In calm seas, passage through this area demanded vigilance but was relatively safe. Here lay some of eastern Lake Superior's most treacherous shoals, and a seasoned captain like Ernest McSorley knew the danger they posed to a fully loaded ship bouncing in stormy waters.

Shoals could destroy a ship in no time, especially if it grounded during a storm, when it could be dismantled by winds and waves before it was discovered and its crew removed by a rescue ship. Lake Superior's underwater terrain, particularly around the islands, could be extremely rugged, with the lake's floor rising from hundreds of feet in depth to less than fifty feet in very little distance. The waters around Isle Royale were littered with the remains of ships that had grounded on reefs. The worst loss of the nineteenth century occurred on November 7, 1885, when the 262-foot Canadian passenger ship *Almoga* hit the rocks near Isle Royale in a storm, breaking apart at the cost of forty-eight lives. On November 6, 1918, the *Chester A. Congdon* earned the distinction of becoming Lake Superior's first million-dollar loss, when the 532-foot freighter hit bottom on Isle Royale's Canoe Rocks. The *Kamloops*, a 250-foot Canadian package freighter, disappeared in a storm on December 7, 1927, with a loss of twenty men, and wasn't found until 1976, when sport divers located its remains near Isle Royale. Exactly six months after the loss of the *Kamloops*, on June 7, 1928, the *America*, a 164-foot steamer, grounded on a reef in Isle Royale's Washington Harbor, the wreckage sloping downward from four feet of water to eighty-five. Another Canadian freighter, the 525-foot *Emperor*, struck the Canoe Rocks not far from the *Congdon* on June 4, 1947.

The twenty-two-mile channel between Michipicoten and Caribou Islands, though historically less lethal to ships than the areas around the Apostle Islands or Isle Royale, offered its own hazards to vessels passing through. More than half a century had passed since the Canadian Hydrographic Service had charted the area in 1916 and 1919, and the charts produced during those surveys were still in use when Ernest McSorley and the *Edmund Fitzgerald* sailed into the area on the afternoon of November 10. One reef, known as Chummy Bank, was located south of Michipicoten Island, and a much larger, deadlier reef, known as the Six Fathom Shoal (or North Bank Shoal) awaited north of Caribou. This treacherous area found the lake bottom rising from a depth of about 600 feet to 36 feet—a shallows that spelled potential disaster if a huge ore carrier, loaded with cargo and being rocked in violent seas, slammed into the lake bottom.

Worse yet, an even shallower area, uncharted by the Canadian Hydrographic Service, lay directly in the *Fitzgerald*'s path. After the wreck of the *Fitz,* the Canadian Hydrographic Service, at the request of the U.S. Coast Guard, would survey the area and discover that the Six Fathom Shoal actually extended a mile farther north than previously charted. In this area, the depth was as little as 31 feet.

Although it will never be known for certain whether the *Fitz* touched bottom on this shoal, it is certain that something very serious, quite possibly catastrophic, happened to the *Edmund Fitzgerald* while it was making its way through these waters. The ship, pounding up and down in increasingly heavy seas, its hull bending to accommodate the action of the waves, strained to handle nature's abuse. Controlling the ship's movement in these seas became a major challenge, and those in the pilothouse labored to keep the *Fitz* away from troughs, which could break or capsize a vessel without warning. Blinding snow eddied outside the pilothouse windows, obscuring what little visibility the *Fitzgerald* had under the darkening skies. Waves washed over the rails and onto the spar deck. The ship and its crew had never been more vulnerable.

About fifteen miles behind the *Fitz,* Bernie Cooper watched the *Anderson*'s radar with growing concern. In directing his crew to take a course that would pass farther west of Michipicoten Island than the *Fitzgerald*—a course that had widened the distance between the two ships—Cooper had also chosen a course that would keep the *Anderson* a safer distance from the Six Fathom Shoal. Captain McSorley might have been shortening his trip by taking the course he had chosen, but he was also maneuvering his ship through very dangerous waters.

"Look at this, Morgan," Cooper said to his first mate, pointing to the radar screen. "That's the *Fitzgerald*. He's in close to that six-fathom spot."

Morgan Clark looked at the screen and agreed. "He sure looks like he's in the shoal area," he said.

"He sure does." Cooper said. "He's in too close. He's closer than I'd want this ship to be."

Cooper's worries were well founded. At 3:35 P.M., only minutes after observing the *Fitzgerald*'s position on his radar, he was on the radiotelephone with Ernest McSorley, who had called the *Anderson* to report a problem: the *Fitzgerald* had sustained some damage.

"I've got problems," McSorley said. "I've got a fence rail down, some vents torn off, and I got a bad list."

"Do you have your pumps going?" Cooper asked.

"Yes," McSorley replied. "Both of them."

Cooper thought he detected concern, but not worry, in the captain's voice. Cooper wondered again about just how close the *Fitz* had come to the shoal.

"Will you shadow me down the lake?" McSorley continued. "I'll reduce my speed so that you can overtake me."

"Okay," Cooper said. "We will do our best."

After signing off, Cooper considered what might have happened to the *Fitzgerald*. The damage itself wasn't serious enough to sink the ship, but it seemed to indicate that the *Fitz* had hit a shoal. A fence rail just didn't come down in a storm; it had to experience an extreme change in tension—the kind of change that might occur if the ship hogged, either from actually striking a shoal or from tremendous bending in the turbulent waters around the shoal. Cooper had never heard of an instance where a wave had taken down a rail. The more he thought about it, the more convinced he became that the *Fitzgerald* had touched bottom somewhere near the Six Fathom Shoal.

But, for the time being, he had worries of his own. The *Anderson* was approaching Caribou Island, and Cooper had to see his ship through the area.

While attempting to obliterate any vessel still out on the lake, the storm also worked furiously on all things anchored to land. Fierce winds snapped power lines everywhere; trees were torn from the ground by their roots. Michigan's Upper Peninsula, accustomed to foul wintry weather that tested all but the heartiest souls, was relentlessly battered.

The Great Lakes historian Fred Stonehouse, in his book *The Wreck of the Edmund Fitzgerald,* recalled being in Marquette, Michigan, on the evening of November 10, and he was awed by the ferocity of the storm.

"I went down to Presque Isle Park and watched the waves sweep over the island," he wrote. "From what I could see, it was one of the worst storms in years. I shot some 16-millimeter film of some of the waves sweeping over the breakwall and coming up the cove. I had never seen waves that large before."

Winds swayed the Mackinac Bridge, the five-mile suspension bridge connecting Lakes Michigan and Huron and the Upper and Lower Peninsulas of Michigan. The bridge had been busy since opening to traffic on November 1, 1957, but on this afternoon, it was no match for the elements. Authorities ordered it closed when a truck was blown over onto a car in the adjacent lane.

The Soo Locks, facing winds of up to 90 miles per hour, had been turned into slips of churning water, with waves surging over the lock gates. Authorities shut down the locks, closing the shipping traffic for the day. A Coast Guard broadcast alerted ships of this development, and advised all vessels on Lake Superior to immediately seek safe shelter. Nothing, small or large, was safe on the water.

Red O'Brien had as much as he could handle in steering the crippled *Fitzgerald* through seas that constantly threatened to knock the ship off course. The *Fitzgerald*'s wheelsman had been through any number of Great Lakes storms in his three decades of sailing, and he'd never feared for his safety or doubted his abilities, but this storm was special. O'Brien had begun his four-hour shift at four o'clock, not long after Captain McSorley had reported the ship's damage to the *Anderson,* and barring any unforeseen problems over the next couple of hours, he would be in the pilothouse when the *Fitz* finally reached Whitefish Bay.

O'Brien was the right man to have on the bridge under these circumstances. He was perfectly at ease with his two fellow Irishmen in the pilothouse—Captain McSorley and Jack McCarthy, whom he numbered among his friends—and his skills at the wheel and easygoing temperament were badly needed in times like this. O'Brien loved to play cards—he was jokingly referred to as the Great Lakes Gambler—and he was good enough at it to know that success usually depended partly on luck, partly on your ability to remember numbers and use this to gauge your opponents' possible hands, and largely on your ability to play with the cards you're dealt. This storm did not represent O'Brien's best hand.

If nothing else, Eugene Michael O'Brien, called Red because of his head of curly red hair, knew something about survival. His life had been difficult from his first gasp of air. When his mother had gone to the hospital to give birth to him, Red's father, a hard drinker with little money and no interest in raising children, had cautioned his wife, "You can either bring the kid home or you can come home, but both of you won't come home." The baby was shipped off to an orphanage halfway across the country, and he wouldn't meet his mother for thirty-seven years.

Childhood consisted of one move after another, from orphanage to orphanage, and in post-Depression America, before some of the child-protection laws were passed and when orphanages were institutions more like prisons than homes, O'Brien managed to get by. Every summer, when the school year ended, he was taken to a farm, where he was expected to work in what amounted to little more than child labor; one year, he lost two fingers in a power saw accident. His formal education ended when he was in fifth or sixth grade.

Somehow, he not only survived a Dickensian childhood; he retained a good-natured and gregarious disposition. He had taken his first job on the lakes when he was sixteen, and with the exception of a four-year stint in a glass factory, he'd worked on the freighters his entire adult life. He'd been married for six years, and the union produced a son, John, to whom Red was fully devoted. He saw very little of his son during the summer months, when he was away for long stretches of time, but that changed for the better when Red landed a job on the *Fitzgerald,* which often docked in Toledo, Red's hometown.

O'Brien loved working on the *Fitz.* He made many friends among his crewmates, and he enjoyed the hours that he whiled away in the rec room, playing poker and rummy. He got to know Ernest McSorley, also from Toledo, and the two would occasionally socialize during the off-season. O'Brien trusted McSorley's abilities as the *Fitzgerald*'s master. Like other crew members, he'd had his gripes about the *Fitz,* but in the gales of November, he was glad to be aboard the 729-footer. If he had to choose any boat to be out in the middle of a nasty storm, this was the one.

Shelter, for the *Edmund Fitzgerald* and the *Arthur Anderson,* was still at least four or five hours away. Hampered by a list and heavy seas, the *Fitz* steamed southeast with a disabling new problem: the wind had blown off the radar antennas on the pilothouse roof, leaving the ship, in essence, sailing blind.

At 4:10 P.M. Captain McSorley radioed the *Anderson* and reported the damage to Morgan Clark.

"I've lost both radars," McSorley said. "Can you assist me in navigation?"

Clark agreed without hesitation.

The assistance was critical. The *Fitzgerald* was about 3 to 5 miles east of Caribou Island, with a long journey still ahead. Waves were cresting at 10 to 15 feet, with winds at more than 60 miles per hour. For a damaged ship to veer off course in these conditions could be fatal.

Perhaps realizing that his ship was in grave peril, and not wanting to rely solely on the *Anderson,* which could lose its own radar as easily as the *Fitz* had, McSorley sent out a flurry of calls over the next hour. Shortly after talking to the *Anderson,* he also used his Radio Direction Finder to get a bearing on the Whitefish Point Lighthouse. The lighthouse, one of the oldest on Lake Superior, had been guiding ships to the shelter of Whitefish Point for more than a century.

It would now be crucial on the final leg of the *Fitzgerald*'s journey. However, the storm had knocked out the lighthouse's electricity, and after receiving an initial signal from it, the *Fitz* was unable to establish further contact.

McSorley radioed the Grand Marais Coast Guard station and asked whether the Whitefish Point radio beacon was working. Gary Wigen, standing in for the regular radioman, who had stepped out to aid in a boat launch, wasn't sure of the lighthouse's status.

"Stand by," he told McSorley. "We don't have the equipment here to tell if it is operating properly. I will call you back."

Rather than wait for the Coast Guard's response, McSorley sent out a call to "any vessel in the vicinity of Whitefish Point." He was answered by Captain Cedric Woodard of the *Avafors*, a 490-foot Swedish vessel that was just leaving Whitefish Bay. Between the snow squalls, Woodard could make out the outline of the lighthouse tower from his pilothouse window. The lighthouse, he informed his caller, was not functioning.

"Who is this?" he asked the unfamiliar voice on the radiotelephone. "Who am I talking to?"

"This is Captain McSorley."

Woodard was shocked. He'd known McSorley for fifteen years, had spoken with him often, and had communicated with the *Fitzgerald* on countless occasions. This voice didn't sound anything at all like McSorley's.

"I didn't recognize his voice at first," Woodard would say later. "It sounded like he had a cold or he was weary, [or] he had been up a long time. I didn't know which. It just wasn't his voice."

Woodard was further surprised when McSorley interrupted their conversation to call out to someone in the pilothouse.

"Don't allow nobody on deck!" he shouted.

What did that mean? No one in his right mind would have ventured out onto the deck in this weather unless something drastic was occurring. Woodard thought he heard McSorley shout something about a vent, but he couldn't make out what the captain was saying, and he didn't press the issue when McSorley returned to the call. McSorley, Woodard reasoned, knew what he was doing, and if he needed any help, he would have asked for it.

McSorley heard from Gary Wigen again, and the news was not good. Wigen had called the Sault Ste. Marie station and was told that the Whitefish Point lighthouse had suffered a power outage. A crew was working to restore its signal.

"Okay, thanks," McSorley replied. "We were just wondering because we haven't been able to get it for a while." McSorley concluded the conversation by promising to call back a little later.

Wigen's experience with McSorley was different from Woodard's. He found nothing unusual about the call, and he detected no worry in McSorley's voice. "After we heard that the *Fitzgerald* might have sunk, [and] everybody at the station had been talking about it," he recalled, "I was telling them that I had just talked to them just before people started getting worried about it, and I told them that they didn't sound like they was worried at all about anything. Everybody sounded like they were in real good spirits."

McSorley, in fact, was growing more desperate. Success in sailing through the storm depended upon his staying in control of the *Fitzgerald,* and with the radar out, water boarding his ship, and the Whitefish Point lighthouse inoperative, he was gradually but most definitely losing control of his ship's destiny. He had reached the point where his fate, as well as that of his ship and crew, depended upon assistance from others.

Water was now entering the *Fitzgerald* more freely than before, through hatch covers, the open vents, and other damage either topside or below the waterline. The *Fitz* had been gradually sinking lower in the water, and the storm, now hitting the ship full force, sent tons of green water over the spar deck.

Sometime around 5:30, the *Avafors* contacted the *Fitzgerald* again. Woodard told McSorley that the Whitefish Point Lighthouse's radio signal was still out, but that its light was operating again.

"I'm very glad to hear it," McSorley said, obviously relieved.

"It's really howling down here," Woodard went on. "What are the conditions like up where you are?"

"We are taking on heavy seas over our decks," McSorley told him. "It's the worst sea I have ever been in. We have a bad list and no radar."

"Are they both out?" Woodard asked, referring to the *Fitzgerald*'s two radar receivers.

"Yes," McSorley answered. "Both of them."

The good news about the Whitefish Point's light was short-lived. After operating for a brief period, the light shut down again, this time for what would prove to be the rest of the life of the *Edmund Fitzgerald*.

The *Arthur Anderson* passed through the area around Caribou Island without a problem, but even Bernie Cooper was impressed by the violence of the seas around him. The National Weather Service, he'd say later, had accurately predicted the weather conditions, but somehow those conditions didn't coincide with what he'd expected on the lake. In Cooper's words, the storm was "blowing a gagger," producing surprisingly heavy seas. "It got nasty, and nasty very quickly," he remembered.

The wind, Cooper noted, was blowing steady between 65 and 70 miles per hour, with gusts hitting 100, and quartering seas were breaking over the *Anderson*'s starboard side. He had not expected this intensity.

"Usually up on Lake Superior, it takes one to two hours for a sea to build up," he pointed out later. "I don't know what the captain of the *Fitzgerald* was thinking, but in my own thinking I figured we would be down a couple of hours above Whitefish before the sea got big enough to bother us, but the sea built in an hour and it was blowing."

Slightly more than ten miles ahead of the *Anderson*, the *Edmund Fitzgerald* struggled to stay on course. Without radar or a light from Whitefish Point, it had to rely on periodic calls from the *Anderson* for readings on its position. When Morgan Clark noticed the *Fitz* drifting a little to the left of the course to Whitefish Bay, he called the ship and pointed it out. Around 7:00 P.M., he called again, to let McSorley know that his ship was about 15 miles from Crisp Point—a mere 12 miles from Whitefish Point and safety.

"We haven't got far to go," he told the *Fitzgerald*'s captain. "We will soon have it made."

"Yes," McSorley responded. "We will."

"It's a hell of a night for the Whitefish beacon not to be operating," Clark offered sympathetically, knowing how unnerving it had to be for the *Fitz*, tired and wounded, not to be able to see at least some symbol of safety.

"It sure is," McSorley agreed.

The *Edmund Fitzgerald*, now sailing in blizzard conditions, needed about 60 to 90 minutes to make Whitefish Bay. Lake Superior, unwilling to negotiate, offered a quarter hour.

CHAPTER THREE

THE WRECK OF THE *EDMUND FITZGERALD*

BY EARLY EVENING, THE *EDMUND FITZGERALD* HAD LOST MOST OF ITS freeboard. It was listing even more heavily to starboard, riding low in the water and taking a terrible pounding from waves sweeping over its decks. Night had fallen, and for those trying to win the race against nature and time, darkness presented a new set of challenges. It was harder to gauge the height of waves, harder to see and estimate the damage they inflicted, and all but impossible to determine whether the hatch covers were still secure. No one on board the *Fitzgerald* would have dared to step outside for a closer, better look. They had only guesswork—bolstered with hope.

Captain McSorley surely knew that his ship was in the biggest battle it had ever faced—bigger, even, than that night in 1958, before McSorley had taken over, when the *Fitz* was on the lakes during the storm that sank the *Bradley*—but if he ever suspected that the *Fitz* was in mortal danger, he never let on to the *Anderson* or other ships on the lake.

"He gave no indication that he was worried or that he had a problem or there was something that he couldn't cope with," Bernie Cooper recalled. "There was no excitement or whatever. It was almost—well, this was a problem but it was under control. This is what you would assume from the way he talked, that there was no problem."

Part of this stoicism was pure McSorley, and part was long-standing tradition. From long experience, McSorley was rightfully confident in his ability to master a ship through a storm, and though he had been cautious enough to admit the damage to his ship to the *Anderson* and ask for its help, it was not in his nature to cave in under pressure. He would bring in his ship, even if he faced hell *and* high water. There was no need to alarm others as long as he had his ship under control.

Captain Dudley J. Paquette, master of the *Wilfred Sykes,* an ore carrier out on Lake Superior during the same November 10 storm, understood McSorley's apprehension and spoke of the stoicism found in pilothouses during storms on the Great Lakes.

"Silence is the usual response to heavy weather by the bridge watch," he said of the men in the pilothouse, peering out the windows at the stormy seas and fighting with the wheel, trying to keep their ship out of the troughs threatening to engulf and capsize them. "They pride themselves on being completely professional, and I'll say that I had never really seen or felt fear in a pilothouse before that night. It wouldn't have been noticeable to an outsider, but it was there during this trip. As captain, I did not dare show concern, of course, but I'll admit I'd never seen or been in anything like this in all my years of sailing."

Another former Great Lakes captain, talking to the journalist Robert Hemming for his book, *Gales of November,* agreed with Paquette's explanation.

"You don't get on the radio, where everyone on the lake can hear you, and talk about *possibly* sinking," this captain stated. "If you know for certain that you're going down, that's one thing; but to holler that you *might* be sinking is asking for trouble. If you make it in OK, you'll be the laughing stock of every boat on the Great Lakes—it ain't professional. What you do is hang on and make a run for it, and keep your mouth shut."

McSorley was making a run for it. The *Fitzgerald* was still plowing through the water, the *Anderson* was closing the distance between the two ships, Whitefish

Bay was up ahead, and the *Fitz* was still armed with top-notch communications equipment, if anything went wrong . . . The situation was extremely difficult but not impossible, and with any luck at all, McSorley and his men would be on land in a couple of hours, exhausted but safe, with an unbelievable story to tell anyone who would listen.

But the minutes, as Gordon Lightfoot would sing, were indeed turning to hours. The low-pressure system had moved off the lake, but its effects had not diminished. In fact, conditions were worse. Twenty- to thirty-foot waves, built up after a run down the lake, continued to smash the *Fitzgerald* from behind. Winds howled in excess of 60 miles per hour, with gusts as high as 90. Heavy, blinding snow fell.

Ten miles behind the *Fitz*, the *Arthur Anderson* contended with the storm on its own terms. The *Anderson* handled the conditions much better than the ship it was trailing, but as Bernie Cooper would later remember, Lake Superior seemed determined to swallow up his vessel.

"I had a hatch crane on deck. It stood about twelve feet above our deck, and a couple of these seas that came across buried my entire deck in about twelve feet of water," he recalled. "That old girl the *Anderson*, she came out shaking like a dog . . . shaking water off, water flying all over."

It was around 6:30 in the evening. A short time later, two more gigantic waves boarded the *Anderson*'s decks. The first rolled over the ship's poop deck, the second hit the bridge deck, nearly 35 feet above the water. The *Anderson* stood up to them, but these waves would haunt Cooper for years to come. By his calculations, if the heavy seas that hit his bridge deck continued down the lake, they would have reached the *Fitz* right about the time the ship disappeared.

"I don't know," he said, "but I've often wondered if those two seas might have been the ones. . . ."

If the *Anderson* was shaking like a dog, the *Fitzgerald* was more like a wounded dog looking for a place to rest and recover. It rode perilously low in the water, leaning heavily to one side and helpless against the relentless onslaught of the storm. It was running blind, dependent upon the *Anderson* for direction. The beacon of the Whitefish Point Lighthouse, still knocked out by the storm, offered no relief.

And the *Fitz* was out of options: it was either reach safe harbor in Whitefish Bay, or nothing.

Captain McSorley, standing at the windows of a very quiet, tense pilothouse, took a call from the *Anderson* at 7:10.

"There is a target 19 miles dead ahead of us," Morgan Clark told him. "You are ahead of us, so the target is nine miles on ahead." The math was simple. Ten minutes earlier, in an abbreviated conversation with the *Fitz,* Clark had informed McSorley that the *Fitz* was now running about ten miles ahead, and two miles to the east, of the *Anderson*.

"Well, am I going to clear?" McSorley asked the *Anderson*'s first mate. The last thing the *Fitz* needed to worry about was a collision with another ship. Stranger things had happened on the lakes.

"Yes. He is going to pass to the west of you."

"Well, fine," McSorley responded.

"Oh, by the way," Clark added, just as he was ready to sign off, "how are you making out with your problems?"

"We are holding our own," McSorley answered.

"Okay, fine," said Clark. "I will be talking to you later."

McSorley's were the last words heard from any of the souls aboard the *Edmund Fitzgerald*. Whether he believed them, or whether they were wishful thinking, will never be known. In all likelihood, in the darkness on the lake, with his ship cutting the distance to Whitefish Bay (though at an agonizingly slow pace), McSorley believed what he was saying. And why not? The *Fitz* had survived to this point, and it was positioned between two vessels that, in the worst imaginable scenario, could answer a mayday call.

But there would be no distress call. The first immense wave hit the *Fitzgerald* and completely overwhelmed it, pushing the ship's bow well beneath the lake's surface. The cargo hold, already burdened to its limit by the water taken on over the past several hours, flooded further. More than 26,000 tons of taconite pellets shifted forward, following gravity to the front of the ship. A second wall of water rolled over the ship, but it was almost anticlimactic—assurance that the *Edmund Fitzgerald*'s bow would never struggle back to the surface.

It all happened too quickly for anyone aboard to do anything but react to the moment. The pilothouse windows blew in, and inrushing torrents of water hurled everyone backward. The front of the ship, now angling downward toward the bottom of the lake, wavered unnaturally, sinking from the weight of the boarding water and rapidly shifting taconite pellets. At the back of the ship, the propeller continued to turn and drive the *Fitzgerald* forward. The middle of the ship buckled. The bow portion of the *Fitz* bent downward, laboring to drag the rest of the ship with it, while the stern section stubbornly held to the surface.

The ship plunged to the depths in dark, frigid water, its running lights still on, every pocket of air filling with water, from front to back of the vessel. The middle of the ship wrenched and twisted grotesquely. With metal tearing and grinding and compressing like an accordion, the sinking ship bellowed in protest hundreds of feet beneath the lake's surface. The *Fitzgerald* began to break apart. The weight of the water and cargo, now shifted as far forward as the hold would allow, added to the ship's downward momentum.

The bow rammed into the floor of Lake Superior with tremendous force, plowing through mud and silt, laying a 30-foot gash into the lake bottom. Although it was sinking in fairly deep water, the *Fitzgerald* was longer than the water was deep, and, as a result, its stern remained on the surface as the bow hit the lake floor. This did not last long. The stern finally surrendered, rising out of the water, the propeller still turning, before disappearing beneath the surface. Water flooded into the back of the ship, hitting the boilers and setting off a series of fiery explosions.

Throughout the tortured final moments of the *Edmund Fitzgerald,* the middle of the ship continued to twist and break. Hatch covers blew out, scattering taconite everywhere. The running lights flickered and went out. The ship's two lifeboats broke free and rose along with other flotsam, toward the surface. The *Fitz* finally broke apart, the torque in the middle of the ship twisting the stern until it was actually upside down when it broke away from the rest of the ship and dropped to the lake floor. The bow came to a halt. The little air remaining in the *Fitzgerald* escaped and bubbled upward.

Inside the remains of the *Edmund Fitzgerald,* twenty-nine men lay dead or dying, some from drowning, others from the explosion of the boilers. Within a matter of minutes, one of the Great Lakes' finest ore carriers—"The Pride of the American Flag"—had become a gravesite.

And no one on the surface had any idea of its fate.

The storm showed some slight signs of breaking at just about the time the *Fitz* lost its fight. The snow stopped and the skies cleared a bit. The lake still roiled with angry waves, and heavy gusts of wind rattled the *Arthur Anderson*'s super-structure, but for all aboard the freighter, relief was in sight. It had been one hell of a trip, and there was still a rough hour or so ahead, but Bernie Cooper, Morgan Clark, and the others on the *Anderson* could sense that the absolute worst was behind them.

Cooper, who had been out of the pilothouse when the *Anderson* had its last contact with the *Edmund Fitzgerald,* was back again, peering out the windows and into the darkness ahead. He could see running lights in the distance, belonging to three upbound saltwater ships—the *Nanfri, Avafors,* and *Benfri*—all leaving Whitefish Bay. What troubled Cooper were the lights he *didn't* see.

"Where's the *Fitzgerald?*" he asked Morgan Clark.

No one had actually seen the *Fitzgerald* for hours, not since its disappearance in the storm near Michipicoten Island. More recently, it had vanished from the radar, when the snowstorm and the heavy waves had flooded the radar screen with sea return and converted it into a mass of white.

But now, with the snowstorm dissipating and visibility on Lake Superior greatly improved, the *Fitzgerald*'s lights should have been visible between the *Anderson* and the tiny running lights dotting the horizon. At the very least, the *Fitz* should have turned up on the radar.

It was nowhere to be found.

Cooper fought off his fears of the worst. The *Anderson*'s last communication with the *Edmund Fitzgerald* had been only twenty minutes earlier, and, according to Morgan Clark, Captain McSorley had given no indication that the *Fitz* was in any immediate danger. Quite the opposite, in fact: "We are holding our own," McSorley had said. There had to be an explanation. Ships had a history of "going missing" in big storms, only to appear later on, battered but safe, in calmer waters. The *Fitz* had been struggling, and quite possibly it had suffered a blackout in the storm.

Cooper and Clark grabbed their binoculars and searched the horizon for a sign, perhaps a dark silhouette or some kind of light. For a few hopeful moments, wheelsman Robert L. May thought he saw two lights, a red one and a white one. The red light, he concluded, belonged to a radio antenna, maybe from Coppermine Point. He focused on the white light, but when he tried to point it out, neither Cooper nor Clark could see it.

May wondered if he was just seeing things. By his own estimation, he saw the light "just a fraction of a second," and, after thinking about it, he wasn't sure that his eyes weren't deceiving him. "When you are staring in the dark," he said later, "you can imagine an imaginary light."

"We should [have been] able to see his range lights," Clark said of the *Fitzgerald*. "Under normal conditions we [had] all kinds of lights on our vessel—cabin lights—and he had a lot more lights than we had . . . probably a hundred bulbs on the cabins and decks that we should [have been] able to see."

The radar screen offered no answers. The crew in the *Anderson*'s pilothouse could clearly make out the other three ships on the radar, and, for a couple of sweeps, they thought they saw a faint blip where the *Fitzgerald* might have been. These proved to be deceptive, disappearing as quickly as they turned up.

"We had something around six and a half, seven miles that the Captain and I discussed, but it would hold maybe two sweeps and then it would disappear," Clark remembered. "The next time it would show up and it would look like it was a contact, but it [had] changed too much of a position."

"We tried everything," Cooper testified later, at a Coast Guard hearing on the disaster. "I mean, you keep looking and we thought we saw something at six and a half or seven miles, and it seemed like there was a blip that would hit once in a while. . . . We were trying to half believe that that was maybe the *Fitzgerald,* and I doubt it was. I don't know because there was so much sea return. In fact, it [was] one of the worst sea returns I have ever seen on a radarscope."

Cooper asked Clark to work further with the radar while he radioed the *Fitz.* The radiotelephone picked up nothing but dead air and static.

This deepened Cooper's growing concern. He tried another ship in the area, and when that call similarly failed, Cooper reasoned that maybe the *Anderson*'s signal wasn't being picked up. This, too, proved to be a false hope: another attempt to call a ship brought back an instant response from the *William Clay Ford,* an ore carrier anchored in Whitefish Bay. The *Anderson* was coming in loud and clear. Was there any chance, Cooper wondered aloud, that the *Fitzgerald* had made it to Whitefish Bay? The *Ford* replied in the negative. No one had seen the *Fitzgerald* in the bay or on radar. Cooper, now really worried, contacted the other ships in the area, with similar results.

A grim sense of reality now settled over the *Anderson*'s pilothouse. In all likelihood, the *Edmund Fitzgerald* was gone. It didn't seem possible, but there was no denying the mounting evidence. Morgan Clark had been unable to come up with anything on the radar, even when he adjusted it to focus only on large targets. Repeated calls to the *Fitzgerald,* each more frantic than the one before, yielded no response.

"Everything told us that the *Fitz* had gone down," Clark later confessed. "Yet we couldn't believe it; she *couldn't* be gone."

Cooper called the Sault Ste. Marie Coast Guard station, using channel 16, the radio distress frequency. The Coast Guard, wanting to keep this emergency channel open, asked him to switch to channel 12, but when he tried to call back on that channel, Cooper couldn't get through. The Coast Guard station, he learned, was experiencing difficulties with its communications system; some antennas had been blown down by the storm. When he was eventually able to reach the Soo station, Cooper was in for another surprise: no one seemed especially concerned about the *Fitz*. There was another missing vessel out on the lake—a sixteen-foot outboard with two men on board—and the Coast Guard asked him to keep an eye open for it.

Cooper signed off and considered his options. The *Anderson* was closer to where the *Fitzgerald* had disappeared than any other vessel. Even though less than an hour had passed since the last communication between the two ships, the *Anderson* was unlikely to be of use to any possible survivors of the *Fitzgerald*. If they were in the water and had survived the rough seas, they would be reaching that critical time when hypothermia would mercilessly claim them, one by one. If they had escaped by lifeboat, they'd still be in great peril, tossed around on the lake, wet and freezing in the chill of the relentless wind. Death from hypothermia would take a little more time, but not much. Even if the *Anderson* stumbled upon the wreckage, it would be exceedingly difficult for a single rescue vessel to locate a lifeboat or individual men floating in the dark, choppy water. Men in lifeboats might have usable distress flares, but . . . Cooper shuddered at the prospects.

Thirty-eight minutes after talking to the Coast Guard, Cooper contacted the station again. This time around, he was more forceful in expressing his mounting fears about the *Edmund Fitzgerald*'s fate.

"This is the *Anderson*," he told the dispatcher. "I am very concerned with the welfare of the steamer *Edmund Fitzgerald*. He was right in front of us, experiencing a little difficulty. He was taking on a small amount of water, and none of the upbound ships have passed him. I can see no lights as before, and I don't have him on radar. I just hope he didn't take a nose dive."

CHAPTER FOUR

SEARCH FOR ANSWERS

THE FIVE MEN ABOARD THE HU-16 HUNG ON FOR DEAR LIFE. THE WIND buffeted the plane, pushing it around like a balsa wood model rather than a capable Coast Guard amphibious search plane. The cloud ceiling hung at about two hundred feet, forcing the plane down precariously close to the water. The plane would move ahead, drop, rise again to safety, push ahead and drop back down. At times, when it was banking, the HU-16 dipped so low that a wind gust could have put one of its wings in the water. One by one, the men on board made their way to the open door in the back and vomited. Below them, enormous white-capped gray seas raged in the night.

This mission had had an air of futility from the get-go. The men at the Traverse City Coast Guard station had been listening in on the conversations between ships in Whitefish Bay and on Lake Superior, and the Coast Guard at the Soo, and they were aware that the *Edmund Fitzgerald* was missing. All realized that, given the intensity of the storm and the passage of time, there was almost no chance for anyone on the *Fitz* to have survived in the lake's cold water, and all were upset that the Coast Guard had taken so long in dispatching them to the scene. They lost nearly a half-hour loading flares on the plane, and by 10:53 P.M., when they reached the area where the *Fitz* was believed to have sunk, the ship had been missing for three and a half hours.

Gary Rosenau, one of the five men on the HU-16, watched the radar and tried to help the pilot and copilot navigate the storm. The Coast Guard had dispatched a helicopter to the scene, and other aircraft, both Coast Guard and Canadian, were being prepared to join them. Rosenau, who'd spent much of his career on Lake Huron and flown in some heavy weather, couldn't believe the intensity of the storm. He could see on his radar screen the vessels anchored in Whitefish Bay as well as the ships on Lake Superior itself, and he silently wondered who in his right mind would sail in these conditions. When the HU-16 had passed near Caribou Island, the return on the radar had been such that Rosenau wondered if reefs were actually being exposed in the turbulence. The plane was being rocked around so badly that Rosenau, already double-strapped in his seat, had to wind his arms through his seat's armrests just to hold steady enough to read the radar screen.

Years later, he couldn't remember how long his mission had lasted that night. It could have been four hours, or it might have been six. It seemed much longer. He was, however, absolutely certain of one thing: in the extremely unlikely event that there had been someone on the water, there was virtually no chance they could have done anything to help.

"If there had been any people on the water that night, there's no way we could have found them," Rosenau remembered. "Even if we'd seen somebody wearing an orange lifejacket, I don't think we could have done anything, as much as we were being buffeted around."

The men on the HU-16 were prepared to drop a rescue canister to anyone they spotted on the water, but the maneuver would have been exceedingly difficult. The canisters were designed to drift to the lake by parachute, so the plane would have had to rise above the cloud cover, estimate the drop location, and hope for the best. In such high winds, the parachute would have taken the canister almost anywhere. As Rosenau put it three decades later, "I've seen one of those thousand-footers [ore carriers], riding high on ballast, without cargo, pushed sideways in a matter of seconds by the wind." He could only imagine what such winds would do to a canister.

The HU-16 continued to circle the area. Two men, safety-strapped into the plane, stood by the door and peered into the darkness below, each trying to find hope when they knew it had disappeared, along with the lives of twenty-nine men, hours earlier.

The search for the *Edmund Fitzgerald* and its crew was not the U.S. Coast Guard's finest moment. For openers, Captain Bernie Cooper had to all but plead with the Sault Ste. Marie station to take him seriously—"I considered it serious, but at the time it was not urgent," Petty Officer Philip Branch would testify in the Coast Guard hearings—and it seemed to take an eternity to get any sort of search-and-rescue craft deployed to the scene. Nearly two and a half hours passed between Cooper's first frantic call to the Soo station at 8:25 P.M. and the arrival of the HU-16. By that point, between three and three and a half hours after the loss of the *Fitzgerald,* the chances of finding survivors were almost nil.

The Great Lakes historian Frederick Stonehouse would indict the Coast Guard's rescue effort as "a conspiracy of ineptitude." He meant not the Guardsmen at work on November 10, 1975, but the Coast Guard's lack of appropriate search-and-rescue vessels.

"When the *Fitzgerald* was lost," Stonehouse wrote in *The Wreck of the Edmund Fitzgerald,* "all that the Coast Guard could muster was a buoy tender at Duluth, Minnesota (320 miles distant), a 40-foot utility boat and a harbor tug (both in a 'repair status' at the Soo), a collection of small motor lifeboats at Marquette and Grand Marais Michigan, and Bayfield, Wisconsin, and, of course, the grab bag of Coast Guard Auxiliary. All in all, it's a fine group for locating lost fishermen in the middle of summer, but a force absolutely inadequate to the real Coast Guard mission—rescue at sea!"

And this wasn't just any rescue at sea: this was a search for a massive, modernly

equipped ore carrier caught in one of the fiercest storms in recent memory, supposedly within twenty miles of Whitefish Bay.

After hearing the urgency in Cooper's voice in his most recent call, Philip
Branch tried to contact the *Edmund Fitzgerald* by VHF/FM radio. There was no
response. He then contacted a commercial radio station, WLC in Rogers City, to
see if someone there would try to reach the *Fitz*. When WLC, too, came up dry,
Branch placed a call, at 8:40, to the Coast Guard Great Lakes Rescue Coordination Center in Cleveland, to report "an uncertainty concerning [the] *Edmund
Fitzgerald*."

Meanwhile, Bernie Cooper and his crew progressed steadily toward safe harbor. The waves were still hammering away at the *Anderson,* but not quite as fe-
rociously as an hour or two earlier. High winds still rattled anything in their path
and whipped up waves that seemed to be coming from three directions, but the
storm center had moved far enough north and east to offer hope of an ending,
perhaps by daybreak.

The *Edmund Fitzgerald* weighed heavily on Bernie Cooper's thoughts. The
Anderson had passed not far from where the *Fitz* had probably gone down, but
he and his crew had seen nothing. Just before 9:00, the *Anderson* pulled into
Whitefish Bay, and Cooper radioed the Coast Guard at Sault Ste. Marie and officially reported the *Fitzgerald* as missing.

The search options were seriously limited. The *Naugatuck,* a 110-foot Coast
Guard harbor tug anchored at Sault Ste. Marie, was undergoing maintenance. It
had been pushed into "standby" status because of the severe weather, but the
present weather was *too* severe: the *Naugatuck* was restricted by its vessel clas-
sification from heading into open seas when winds exceeded 60 knots. The tug
was ordered to proceed to Whitefish Bay, but not beyond. Even this came to
nothing because the *Naugatuck* blew an oil-lube line on the way out and had to
return for repairs.

The weather was also too rough for the smaller Coast Guard patrol boats and
motor lifeboats to help in the immediate search, which left the Coast Guard little
choice but to reluctantly contact the big commercial vessels in the area, to see if
they would voluntarily join the search.

The closest of these vessels was a 767-foot ore carrier called the *Arthur M. Anderson*.

The call from the Coast Guard caught Bernie Cooper completely off balance. The *Anderson* was in Whitefish Bay, about two miles from Parisienne Island, when Coast Guard Commander Charles Millradt radioed and asked Cooper if he'd be willing to turn his ship around and search for the *Fitzgerald*.

"Do you know what you're asking me to do?" Cooper asked incredulously. How could he possibly ask his crew to go back out?

No way, Cooper said. He'd just been through a hell of an ordeal, and he wasn't about to leave the safety of Whitefish Bay for another round.

"You've got one on the bottom now," he told Millradt, "and if I go out there you'll have two on the bottom."

No one else was going out there. Cooper had spoken to the captain of the *William Clay Ford,* and he wasn't taking his freighter out, either. The storm was still too dangerous.

Millradt could do nothing but ask again, and Cooper, troubled by the idea that someone might still be alive and in need of help, showed signs that he might be persuaded to change his mind:

"I don't know," he said. "That sea out there is tremendously large. If you want me to, I can, but I'm not going to be making any time. I'll be lucky to make two or three miles an hour going back out that way."

The ultimate decision, Millradt understood, depended entirely on Bernie Cooper and his crew. The Coast Guard couldn't order the *Anderson* back out on the lake, and Millradt didn't need a weather bulletin to know that the going would be extremely hazardous. This was one of the biggest storms he'd ever seen—big enough, after all, to have defeated the *Fitzgerald*—but the nearest seaworthy Coast Guard cutter, the *Woodrush,* was anchored in Duluth, Minnesota, over 300 miles away. Millradt could only appeal to Cooper's honor as a sailor: if *he,* Bernie Cooper, were out there, hanging on for his life, wouldn't he hope someone would come looking for him?

"You'll have to make a decision as to whether you will be hazarding your ves- sel or not," Millradt told Cooper, "but you're probably one of the only vessels right now that can get to the scene. We're going to try to contact those saltwater vessels and see if they can't possibly come about and possibly come back also." Millradt then poked at Cooper's knowledge of recent history. "Things look pretty bad right now," he continued. "It looks like she may have split apart at the seams like the *Morrell* did a few years back."

Cooper didn't need a reminder of the *Morrell* story, though he might have wondered how the Coast Guard had reached the conclusion that the *Fitzgerald* had split apart. Only about half an hour earlier, he'd had to plead to get his sense of urgency across, and even then, he'd mentioned that he feared that the *Fitz* had taken a nosedive, not split apart.

"Well, that's what I've been thinking," Cooper admitted agreeably. "But we talked to him about seven and he said that everything was going fine. He said he was going along like an old shoe—no problems at all."

Millradt persisted, and Cooper finally relented.

"I'll go back and take a look," Cooper offered, "but, God, I'm afraid I'm going to take a hell of a beating out there."

Cooper hated the prospect of telling his crew that they were heading back out into the storm. Years later, he would recall one particular crewman, a man he described as a "gung-ho sailor," who'd talked about wanting to be out in a "real storm" and who was less than enthusiastic now that he'd had his chance.

"He was informed by the chief engineer that we were turning around and heading back out," Cooper said. "He went to his room, broke out a tape recorder, gave his last will and testament, sealed it in wax and put it in a jar so the world would know what happened to the *Anderson*!"

Millradt was less successful in trying to enlist other ships to join the search. He talked to the captains of seven ships, three American and four Canadian, an- chored in or around Whitefish Bay, and all but two turned him down. The

William Clay Ford, a 647-foot freighter owned by the Ford Motor Company, initially rejected him but eventually agreed to go out. The *Hilda Marjanne,* a smaller Canadian vessel owned by Upper Lakes Shipping, also tried to leave Whitefish Bay and assist in the search, but it didn't get far. After battling high seas for about half an hour, the ship's captain decided that the storm was too severe and the *Hilda Marjanne* returned.

The Coast Guard fared no better when contacting the three saltwater ships already out on the lake. Already regretting their decision to head out in the storm, the captains of the *Benfri, Nanfri,* and *Avafors* turned down requests to join the search party, all claiming that they couldn't change course without jeopardizing their vessels. The *Nanfri* did agree to reduce its speed and change its course slightly to the north, so it could make a cursory search when it passed through the area where the *Fitzgerald* was believed to have gone down.

"In my opinion, you could not turn the vessel," said Albert Jacovetti, the captain of the *Nanfri.* "With those high sterns, once you turn the vessel in the wind like that, she would just stop on you and go so far. You couldn't turn that stern up into the wind nohow, even if you had 20,000 horsepower."

Jacovetti had his doubts about how he and his crew could have assisted any survivors even in the event that the *Nanfri* had located a lifeboat or raft. "I don't know how you could have maneuvered your vessel to get anywhere near it, because the minute you stop a light vessel like that, she would have broken right off. I don't think you could have even dropped anchor there and done any good."

Captain Cedric Woodard of the *Avafors,* who'd spoken to McSorley earlier in the evening and worried about the *Fitzgerald*'s plight, later recalled: "There was nothing much we could do. We were having all we could do to keep in the sea or keep her going." Woodard had his own interests in the *Fitzgerald*'s fate: his son had worked on the ship for a while as a wheelsman. But the most he could volunteer was to keep an eye out for survivors.

"At the time we made no speed," Woodard continued, speaking of his attempts to push his ship through the storm. "I think there were times that we

went backwards, but it took us practically eight hours to go 12 miles, so you
know what kind of speed we were making."

Captain Don Erickson had just eaten dinner and returned to the bridge of the
William Clay Ford when he heard the first of Bernie Cooper's calls to the Coast
Guard about the missing *Edmund Fitzgerald*. The *Ford* was anchored in Whitefish Bay, and Erickson was hoping to wait out the storm before taking his ship
up the lake to Duluth.

It had been a trying day. The *Ford* had dropped off a load of taconite for a
steel firm near Detroit, and had encountered some rough winds early on the way
back. The ship had managed to lock through at the Soo, but it hadn't been easy,
and Erickson was happy to be anchored a couple miles off Whitefish Point,
where Michigan's lee shore sheltered his ship from the northwestern winds that
had been kicking up some menacing waves.

Erickson had been sailing since 1942, when he was seventeen. He'd put in
four years in the South Pacific during World War II, and after returning home,
he'd taken a job as an able-bodied seaman on a Great Lakes freighter. From that
point on, his was the typical story of advancing through the ranks until reaching
the top. In 1962, he'd assumed command of the *Henry Ford II,* then, three years
later, of the *William Clay Ford.* During his time on the lakes, he'd gotten to
know just about every captain in the business, including Bernie Cooper, whom
he respected as a captain and knew well enough to call a friend.

Now, listening to Cooper trying to convince the Coast Guard that something
terrible might have happened to the *Edmund Fitzgerald,* Erickson felt the same
disbelief that others felt when they heard the news. There had to be some explanation. Maybe the *Anderson* just couldn't see the *Fitz.* After all, Erickson himself had been in snow squalls so intense he could barely see the back of his own
ship. Still, the more he listened to Cooper's radio transmissions, the more concerned Erickson became. Cooper was having no success in contacting the *Fitz,*
and none of the other ships anchored in the vicinity, including the *Ford,* had
seen any sign of it.

When Chuck Millradt eventually contacted him about going out on the lake to search, Erickson turned him down flat. He'd heard Cooper do the same. Nobody wanted to head out into that storm, least of all the *William Clay Ford,* which would be going out on ballast and taking a battering.

Erickson had heard from Bernie Cooper earlier in the evening, when the *Anderson*'s skipper was calling the vessels anchored in the Whitefish Bay area and asking if they'd seen the *Fitz.* They'd also talked about going out and searching for the *Fitz,* both agreeing that it wasn't a good idea. Now, with the Coast Guard failing to recruit search ships, Erickson called Cooper again.

"Bernie, I'm thinking of going out there," he told Cooper.

"I was thinking about it, too," Cooper admitted. "If you go out there, I'll go out there."

It hadn't been an easy decision for either captain. They'd be endangering their vessels in what was all but certain to be a futile endeavor. Any sailor on the lakes would have sympathized with their reasoning, even if the people on shore wouldn't.

"They"—the general public—"think you can just go out, put something in the water, and pick them up," observed Dale Lindstrom, the *Ford*'s third mate that night. Lindstrom had been in the pilothouse when Cooper first attempted to contact the *Fitzgerald;* he'd overheard the conversations between Cooper and the other ships, and between Cooper and the Coast Guard; and he'd witnessed the difficult decision-making process taking place on both the *Anderson* and the *Ford.* Years later, he shook his head over the written accounts that suggested that Cooper and Erickson had quickly volunteered to head out on the search.

"Erickson didn't want to go, and I can't remember his exact words, but Bernie Cooper said something like, 'Hell, no, I don't want to go out there,'" Lindstrom remembered. "I'll go to my grave swearing this is the damn truth.

"When Erickson came up and I told him what was going on, he said, 'If they call, tell them no, we don't want to go out.' But then he sat in his room, and he opened the door and said, 'Dale, if they call us, tell them we'll go.' Bernie didn't want to go, either, but then he agreed, too."

"Everybody said no, including me," Erickson confessed. "But I talked to some of the guys on the boat, and I figured somebody had to go out there. The poor guys on the ship: it was possible that they got off and were in bad shape out there. They would need help."

The *Ford* and *Anderson* traveled on a parallel course to the search area. The Coast Guard HU-16 from Traverse City was already on the scene, flying low over the water and searching for signs of wreckage or survivors. The aircraft dropped flares to aid in the search, but no one aboard the *Ford* or *Anderson* saw anything but waves, which, if they'd had their way, would have swallowed up these two vessels the way they'd taken the *Fitzgerald* only a few hours earlier.

"I don't know if we could have ever, ever helped," Dale Lindstrom admitted when talking about the search-and-rescue mission nearly three decades later. "We would have died trying to get close to somebody. We would have had to put the boat between him and the seas. Maybe he could have grabbed a line or something. We weren't going to get anything in the water for them."

"They were out there with their ice lights and search lights on," Captain Erickson recalled, "and the Coast Guard was dropping flares and we were watching. I said, 'What the hell are we going to do if we see somebody floating in a lifeboat or raft or any other way?' You couldn't go alongside them to pick them up, and you couldn't launch a lifeboat. The Coast Guard said, 'Report to us and the helicopter will take care of it,' but I don't know how the helicopters would have picked anybody out of the water. We were out there now, but what were we going to do if we saw somebody?"

Captain Jimmie Hobaugh was at home in Duluth, getting ready to watch *Monday Night Football,* when he received a call saying that the *Edmund Fitzgerald* was missing in a storm on Lake Superior. At first, he didn't believe it. He'd seen the *Fitz* and knew of its reputation, and it didn't seem possible that that ship couldn't handle any challenge the lakes had to offer.

Hobaugh, a big, affable Oklahoma native, had spent his entire adult life on the sea, beginning when he joined the National Guard at fifteen. He'd been tossed out when his age was discovered, but, a few years later, after trying college and dropping out, he entered the Coast Guard, eventually attending officers' school and working his way upward until he had attained every rank in the Coast Guard. He'd worked on the oceans and the lakes, and had seen just about every type of sea condition imaginable. He'd been a group commander in Duluth for five years when he received his call about the *Fitz*. He was to recall his crew, take his buoy tender, the *Woodrush,* down to the area where the *Fitzgerald* was presumed to have sunk, and join in the search for the ship.

"Thank God it was a football night," he recalled, "because most of the guys were watching TV or listening or whatever. We pulled out in about an hour and forty-five minutes, with all hands except one third classman."

At first, Hobaugh couldn't understand why there was such a fuss being made about the storm. The waters in western Lake Superior were a little choppy, but nothing out of the ordinary. Unbeknownst to Hobaugh, though, just as the worst of the earlier storm was passing, a second, smaller one was moving in from the west; he and his crew had their hands full when they rounded Manitou Island and confronted both the remains of the *Fitz* storm and the newer storm. By the time they made it down Lake Superior and reached the last known position of the *Fitzgerald,* they were in seas that gave them a hint of what the *Fitz* had been through the previous evening.

"When the wind comes out of the northwest and hits the Canadian shore," Hobaugh explained, "it ricochets off and comes across and hits the U.S. shore, ricochets off and comes across. You had one sea from behind, and one from one side, and one from the other side, and no matter how you turned the ship, it was rough. The wind came out of the northwest and just pounded the heck out of us.

"In the ocean, you get those long swells that run across the entire Atlantic or Pacific. In the Great Lakes, it's a chop. You don't get all that long a period between swells. It's hammering at you all the time. A 25-foot chop just scares the hell out of you because it's not normal. It's interesting because at night you can't really see how rough it is. You just know you're rolling and bouncing around a lot."

*   *   *

The *Anderson* and *Ford* arrived in the area at about 2:00 A.M. The two Coast Guard aircraft—the HU-16, and a HH-52 helicopter—had already swept over the area, with no sightings of wreckage, survivors, or victims. The helicopter, equipped with a 3.8-million-candlepower searchlight, had no more success spotting anything than Bernie Cooper or Don Erickson had in looking out the pilothouse windows of their respective vessels. For all they knew, their boats had passed directly over the wreckage.

The two ships searched throughout the night while the Coast Guard called more vessels to join them. The storm continued to weaken, and by dawn's light, smaller craft were reasonably safe on the lake. For Bernie Cooper, the nightlong search for the *Fitzgerald* was almost as nerve-racking as his earlier adventures; vessels smaller than the *Anderson* would have been eaten alive.

By now, Cooper had conceded the worst. Too much time had passed since anyone had heard from the *Fitzgerald,* and no one, in or out of a life raft, would have survived a night on the lake in these conditions. It was strange, however, that nothing had been seen. An oil slick would have been extremely difficult to spot in the darkness and churning water, but not a single piece of wreckage or equipment from the *Fitzgerald* had turned up. On the other hand, given the weather conditions, there was no telling how far things would drift before they were discovered. Flotsam from past wrecks had been known to travel all the way across one of the Great Lakes during a storm.

Lake Superior presented its own set of rules. When things sank in Lake Superior, they tended to stay sunk, which was unfortunate for the families of those perishing in the lake's waters. The year-round icy-cold water temperatures neutralized the gases that made human bodies surface after drowning—hence the saying that "Lake Superior never gives up its dead"—and if the *Fitzgerald* had gone down suddenly and unexpectedly, as now suspected, it was likely that most, if not all, of the crew went down with it and would never be recovered.

Still, there had to be some kind of confirmation . . .

The *Arthur Anderson* and *William Clay Ford* worked tirelessly, covering an area that extended from fourteen miles west of Coppermine Point to fifteen miles north of Crisp Point, the search taking them into Canadian waters as well as U.S. waters. By morning, the *Ford,* operating under ballast and taking a pounding in the still-high seas, had dropped out, but other ships and aircraft had been dispatched; they would arrive throughout the day, and in the days to come, to help with the search.

The news spread quickly through the Great Lakes area, setting off hopeful—and, eventually, tearful—vigils among the families of the *Fitzgerald* crewmen and the shipping community in general. Some communities, like Rogers City, Michigan, which had been so deeply affected by the losses of the *Carl D. Bradley* and *Daniel J. Morrell,* could only pray that somehow the *Fitzgerald* would eventually turn up. By nature, shipping communities were tightly knit, their livelihoods dependent upon the materials they produced and the ships that hauled them. You saw these workers every day in the local restaurants or diners, you worshipped with them on Sundays, and their kids lined up next to yours in the school play. An accident at the plant or the loss of a ship in a storm could lay a shadow of grief over a town that would last, in this case, well into what would normally be a festive holiday season.

For the families of the twenty-nine men, the wait for news was a nightmare. Everyone, to a person, had always recognized such a loss as a horrible possibility. Commercial shipping, like commercial fishing, police work, or firefighting, has a built-in potential for disaster, and like the families of fishermen, police officers, and firefighters, shipping families hope that that potential never becomes real for their husbands, sons, and brothers. By the wee hours of November 11, when the anxious phone calls had been placed, and radios and televisions were tuned in for any information about the missing ore carrier, families were bracing themselves for the worst. Their lives, they feared, were about to change forever.

Father Richard Ingalls drove to the Mariners' Church of Detroit shortly after receiving a call about the disappearance of the *Edmund Fitzgerald.* Dawn had yet to break on Tuesday, November 11, and the cold, blustery air served as a

reminder of the nasty weather that had passed through the day before. Father Ingalls arrived at the church, parked his car, and walked into the unheated stone
structure.

He'd heard about the *Fitz* from Robert E. Lee, the curator of the Dossin Great
Lakes Museum. Lee had been up, listening to the calls and reports on the
Fitzgerald as they were filed by the ships in the area, and he'd called Father In-
galls to express his concern.

"There's trouble with the *Fitzgerald*," Lee said, repeating what he'd heard in
the radio transmissions. "Trouble," Lee and Ingalls knew, was a kind of verbal
shorthand used by sailors unwilling to state their actual fears in calls being
heard all over the area, by listeners eavesdropping on ship-to-shore communications.

"Both of us had been in the military," Father Ingalls would remember decades
later, "and we read between the lines right away. We expected the worst."

Father Ingalls asked Lee to keep him posted on any new developments, and
Lee called back a short time later. He briefed Ingalls on what he knew—which,
at that point, wasn't much. The ship had been missing since early the previous
evening, and by all indications, it had been lost in the storm. Twenty-nine men
had been on the *Fitz,* and while no one was saying as much, all were presumed
to have perished.

Father Ingalls left for the church as soon as he'd hung up and dressed. He had
been the rector of the Mariners' Church since 1965. Located in downtown Detroit a few blocks from the waterfront, the Mariners' Church had been a haven
for sailors and their families since 1849. It had been built from funds provided in
the will of Julia Ann Anderson, the daughter of an importer-exporter and the
widow of the commander of the Fleet of Detroit. Mrs. Anderson, an Anglican,
had specified in her will that the church would be called the Mariners' Church of
Detroit, and that it would be open to people of all faiths.

The church had been constructed on the site of the Anderson home, and it
had remained there until 1955, when it was moved two blocks east to accommodate the building of a civic center on its original site. Mariners' Church had

seen hard times, but, largely due to the efforts of Father Ingalls, it had been restored to its "English country Gothic" splendor. The church's maritime roots were evident everywhere, from the ships depicted on the stained-glass windows to the paintings and model ships displayed throughout the building.

If this was a place where the working class came to worship, it was also, in the wake of a disaster on the lakes, a place where widows, families, and friends gathered to mourn and seek solace. The church featured a four-story bell tower that housed an enormous one-and-a-half-ton bell, and since he had arrived at the Mariners' Church, Father Ingalls had been tolling the bell to commemorate all those lost on the Great Lakes. Now, with tragic news about the *Fitzgerald* ready to confront the friends and families of the twenty-nine lost men, Father Ingalls had a sad but appropriate chore to perform.

He ascended the bell tower's stairwell and, positioning himself beneath the giant bell, pulled down on the thick rope. The clapper struck the bell and sent its rich sound throughout downtown Detroit, down streets still largely deserted. He rang the bell twenty-nine times, pausing briefly after each ring while the bell's echoes offered their own mournful prayers.

When he'd finished, Father Ingalls returned to the nave of the church. He walked to the sanctuary and, keeping his overcoat on to protect him from the chill of the unheated building, knelt and began what he described as "a personal requiem for the twenty-nine."

With thanksgiving to God for their courage and strength, for the benefits we have received from their labors and for the blessed hope of their everlasting life, Father Ingalls prayed, *we hereby gratefully remember all the mariners of our Great Lakes who have lost their lives.*

People began arriving, one by one, in the church. Father Ingalls could hear the rustling of their footsteps behind him as he knelt in the sanctuary, and when he'd finished his prayers, he turned to address a small group of about twenty. They were reporters, and they had come after hearing the tolling of the bell. They wanted to know what Father Ingalls had learned about the *Edmund Fitzgerald,* and they asked him to explain the ringing of the church bell.

The search for the *Fitz* was still under way, Father Ingalls said, and in all likelihood, the reporters knew as much as he did about the accident, though he had little doubt about the tragic fate of the vessel's crew.

"That morning," he'd remember, "there was a sense that everyone was lost."

On board the *Arthur Anderson,* Captain Bernie Cooper and his crew continued a vigil of their own. Morning light brought increased visibility and calmer seas, but the tension and exhaustion from the previous two days were taking their tolls. What had started out as a routine trip from Two Harbors, Minnesota, to Gary, Indiana, had been transformed into a long limbo on the lake. There was still taconite in the belly of the *Anderson,* and the steel mill in Gary was still awaiting its shipment, but, so far from moving along into the final leg of its scheduled journey, the ship had yet to pass through the Soo Locks.

At 8:07 on Tuesday morning, November 11, Bernie Cooper's fears were confirmed: the *Anderson* discovered the first significant evidence that the *Edmund Fitzgerald* had sunk. Floating on the surface, nearly nine miles east of where the wreckage of the *Fitz* would eventually be found, were the badly mangled remains of Lifeboat Number 1.

Throughout the day, more debris was found and pulled from the lake by the *Arthur Anderson* and other search vessels, leaving absolutely no doubt about what happened to the *Edmund Fitzgerald*. The *Anderson* spotted the *Fitzgerald*'s second lifeboat an hour after discovering the first, and both of the sunken ship's inflatable life rafts were eventually recovered as well. The condition of the lifeboats and rafts spoke volumes, as did the recovery of twenty of the ship's cork life preservers: there was no indication whatsoever that any of these lifesaving devices had been used. In all likelihood, the *Edmund Fitzgerald* had sunk so suddenly that no one had the time to attempt an escape.

The condition of the lifeboats also offered mute testimony to the ship's violent final moments. Lifeboat Number 1 consisted only of the forward sixteen feet of a boat designed to hold fifty people. The boat, with "Edmund Fitzgerald No. 1" painted in three-inch lettering on both sides of the bow, had been torn in two, most likely while the *Fitzgerald* was sinking and the lifeboat broke loose from its moorings.

Lifeboat Number 2, though found in one piece, was heavily damaged as well. Its bow was split at the stem, a huge hole had been torn into its side, and the hull was buckled and dented. There was no chance that either lifeboat could have been used, even if the *Fitzgerald*'s crew had managed to escape the sinking ship and find the lifeboats in the surging seas. The lifeboats were retrieved and taken to the Sault Ste. Marie Coast Guard station.

The number of vessels and people involved in the search increased, with five U.S. ships (including three from the Columbia Transportation division of Oglebay Norton) and four Canadian vessels joining the *Anderson*. Fixed-wing aircraft and helicopters spent the day of November 11 crisscrossing the area, while search parties on foot combed the Michigan and Canadian beaches in search of bodies or flotsam that might have washed ashore. The *Woodrush* arrived from Duluth, and the newly repaired *Naugatuck* finally reached the area, too.

For all the intensive searching, very little of the *Edmund Fitzgerald* turned up. In addition to the lifeboats, life rafts and life preservers, eight oars or oar pieces, a piece of a sounding board, a wooden fender block, a wooden stool, a stepladder, eight flotation tanks from the lifeboats, a lifeboat rudder, and some other small items and scraps of wood were recovered. All were sent first to the Coast Guard station and, eventually, to Oglebay Norton.

The search continued until 10:12 P.M. on November 13, when the active search for the *Edmund Fitzgerald* was officially suspended. Aircraft from the Coast Guard station in Traverse City, Michigan, flew over the area every day for an additional week, and after that, once a week until the end of the year.

Not a single body was seen or recovered.

Debbie Champeau, a senior at Pius XI High School in Wauwatosa, a western suburb of Milwaukee, cringed when the voice over her classroom's loudspeaker ordered her to report to the school's front office. She knew she wasn't in any kind of trouble, and as she made her way down the school's empty halls to the office, she wondered what was going on.

The people in the office were of no help.

"Call home," she was instructed.

Her maternal grandmother answered the phone, but only added to the confusion when she told Debbie to come home immediately.

"What's the problem?" Debbie asked.

"Just come home."

The bus trip, involving the usual wait for the bus, plus another wait for a transfer, and all the riding in between, was tedious at best, but on this day, with the weather turning cold and all kinds of thoughts passing through her head, the seventeen-year-old wondered if she would ever get home.

She knew something was terribly wrong as soon as she walked in the front door and saw the looks on her grandmother's and mother's faces.

"Who died?" she asked.

On the afternoon of Tuesday, November 11, Florence Bentsen reported for work at her job in a St. Joseph card and gift shop. She'd had the previous day off, and she hadn't listened to the radio or watched the news on television, so she knew nothing about the loss of the *Edmund Fitzgerald*. Her son, Tom, was an oiler on the ship.

Shortly after she arrived at work, she was approached by Carol Greening, the store's owner.

"Are you okay?" Mrs. Greening asked.

Mrs. Bentsen assured her that she was fine.

"Has anyone called you?"

Mrs. Bentsen wondered what on earth was going on. Her boss had a "funny" look on her face, but she didn't offer any further explanation when Mrs. Bentsen told her that she hadn't received any unusual calls.

Florence Bentsen finished her shift and went home. Once again, she didn't turn on the news.

The next morning, Carol Greening called and told her to stay home. "I'm coming out to see you," she said.

It was during Mrs. Greening's visit that Florence Bentsen learned that Tom had perished on the *Fitzgerald*.

"The *Fitzgerald* went down on a Monday, and I didn't even find out until Wednesday," she recalled many years later.

The last time she'd seen Tom, on September 22, had ended on a down note. It was her other son's seventeenth birthday, and Tom had called from East Chicago, Indiana, to see if she and Bruce wanted to drive down for dinner. The *Fitz* was dropping off a load of taconite at Inland Steel, and Tom had received permission for his mother and brother to tour the ship.

The evening began to turn sour early, when the Bentsens' car broke down during the ninety-minute drive from St. Joseph. Then they drove to the wrong steel mill. When they finally met Tom, it was too late to go to dinner. Finally, the security guard refused to allow them to board the *Fitzgerald,* a fitting ending to a miserable evening.

Florence Bentsen would never forget that evening. She'd remember the forlorn look on Tom's face when they said their goodbyes in the parking lot, and she'd be troubled by the fact that he was working on the *Fitz* because he needed the field experience to complete his schooling for a third assistant engineer's license. He'd studied for four years to reach this point; at the end of the season, he'd be an officer starting off in what he hoped would be a long career on the lakes.

And now here she was, learning from her boss that her twenty-three-year-old son wouldn't be coming home again.

The loss of the *Edmund Fitzgerald* haunted Bernie Cooper, and it would continue to haunt him, off and on, for the rest of his life. He would replay the events of November 9–10 in his mind, never able to totally come to grips with what had happened to a ship that should have made it through the storm as capably as the *Arthur Anderson*. He would hear the sound of Ernest McSorley's voice, or First

Mate Jack McCarthy's, as they discussed the weather and the courses their two ships should take, or the damage to the *Fitzgerald* during its desperate, sinking run for Whitefish Bay. He wondered whether the *Fitz* had grounded on the Six Fathom Shoal, leading to some sort of structural failure. He remembered the conversation with Morgan Clark in which he'd expressed his concerns.

By the afternoon of November 11, the *Anderson* had left the search and was steaming toward the Soo Locks. Cooper docked in Sault Ste. Marie and placed a call to his employer, U.S. Steel. In a four-way conversation with three U.S. Steel officials, Cooper relayed the story of his trip down Lake Superior. Inevitably, the conversation turned to the Six Fathom Shoal and Caribou Island.

"He went in close to the island," Cooper declared, "and I am positive in my own mind . . . we had him on radar . . . we never had him visually, but we had him on radar all the time . . . and I am positive he went over the Six Fathom Shoal."

The more Cooper replayed the events in his head, the more convinced he became that the *Fitz* had suffered a mortal injury just before contacting the *Anderson* about its broken vents and lost fence rail.

"When we put down around Whitefish," he told the U.S. Steel officials, "and I got to thinking for sure that this *Fitzgerald* was gone, I wondered when he was making water if he had some cracks down below and making water, and not coming in through the vents, because he had both pumps on to hold his own."

Cooper realized, even as he offered his first in-depth narrative of the events, that he was going to be grilled about all this in the near future. The prospect worried him.

It worried U.S. Steel as well. There was bound to be a series of hearings and lawsuits over the *Fitzgerald*'s loss. Cooper would have to be cautious.

"I think we want you to say only what occurred as a matter of fact, to your knowledge—what was said to you, what conversations you had, what you did," the company attorney advised him. "I don't want you guessing as to what happened on this ship beyond the information that was directly related to you."

Cooper agreed that he didn't wanted to infer anything, but he was still concerned about how he would answer some of the tougher questions that might call for speculation, or might head to speculation.

"If they ask you for conjecture, don't volunteer any," he was instructed.

Cooper would be confronted with his own words within a matter of weeks, when he was asked to appear before a Coast Guard panel investigating the sinking and a transcript of his call to U.S. Steel was introduced as evidence. By that time, Cooper, heeding the advice of his attorneys, would be reluctant to speculate on the causes of the *Fitzgerald*'s demise, but his statements to U.S. Steel, offered when the events of November 9–10 were still clear in his mind, would come back to haunt him.

Without intending to, as the most credible "witness" to the *Fitzgerald*'s loss, he presented a scenario that would be debated for decades to come. In discussing Ernest McSorley's maneuvering around the Six Fathom Shoal, in what was supposed to have been a private conversation with the U.S. Steel officials, Cooper had broken an unwritten cardinal rule: a captain didn't openly question another captain's motives or actions.

Cooper believed what he'd said. He just never expected to be forced to defend it and live with it for the rest of his days.

The news media picked up the *Fitzgerald* story immediately. Front-page stories appeared in *The New York Times* ("Lake Superior Ship with 30–35 Missing"), *The Washington Post* ("All Hands on Ship Seen Lost"), *Chicago Tribune* ("Storm Rips Great Lakes Ore Boat; Fear 30 Lost"), and, in the *Fitzgerald*'s home port, the *Milwaukee Journal* ("Search Finds Ship Debris but No Sign of 29 Men"); Walter Cronkite addressed the story on the *CBS Evening News*. In the days following the ship's loss, even as the families of the *Fitzgerald*'s crew anxiously awaited final word on the sinking, reporters scrambled for every conceivable angle, filing reports on everything from the ship's history to November storms on the Great Lakes. Bernie Cooper remained silent, though reporters were able to find others, most notably Cedric Woodard of the *Avafors,* willing to talk for the record.

Predictably, there was no shortage of speculation as to the cause of the *Fitzgerald*'s demise, with two popular theories emerging. The first—the "two sisters" theory—had the ship's bow and stern lifted by water from two waves running close together, with the middle of the ship sagging until it split from a lack of support. According to the second theory, the *Fitzgerald* lost one or more hatch covers in the storm, and water flooding into the open hatches caused a fatal loss of buoyancy. These theories were distributed by the wire services to newspapers across the country.

The Coast Guard acted quickly to assemble an investigative panel. It was standard practice to file an official accident report after any shipwreck with a loss of life; now the Coast Guard quickly put together a four-member Marine Board of Investigation that would have the extremely difficult task of trying to determine a reason for the tragedy when there were no eyewitnesses or survivors to provide them with key testimony. The ship itself hadn't been located, and no one even knew for certain the final route that the *Fitz* had taken. In short, coming up with a final report was going to require detective work unlike any that the Great Lakes had ever seen.

However, it didn't take long to locate the *Fitzgerald*'s wreckage.

On November 14, less than twelve hours after the Coast Guard shut down its active search, a Navy Orion aircraft initiated a search for the sunken vessel, using a magnetic anomaly detection unit designed to pick up the presence of large underwater objects. The plane covered about 100 square miles of Lake Superior, focusing on the area where debris from the *Fitzgerald* had been recovered. It received an especially strong signal in a location roughly seventeen miles from Whitefish Bay. A light oil slick on the water seemed to indicate that this was the place. The pilot charted the location and reported it to the *Woodrush*, still in the area following its participation in the search for the *Fitzgerald*.

Jimmie Hobaugh, captain of the *Woodrush*, had been frustrated by a search that had yielded so little. Such a big ship should have left much more. "We were underway four nights and three days, searching for the *Fitzgerald*," he recalled, adding that he, like so many others, found it difficult to believe that the *Fitz* had sunk. "The only thing that we saw was a bubble of oil now and then."

Now, equipped with Egerton, Germershausen and Greer 250 side-scanning sonar equipment provided by the Coast Guard's Research and Development Center, Hobaugh and the *Woodrush* had a compelling new mission: to determine whether the large object detected by the Orion was indeed the wreckage of the *Edmund Fitzgerald*.

Developed in the 1960s, the side-scan sonar technique was very effective in locating sunken ships and aircraft in lakes and the deeper waters of the oceans. A torpedo-shaped "tow fish" would be lowered into the water, usually off a ship's stern, and would dangle hundreds of feet below the lake or ocean's surface, while the search ship would move it slowly across a carefully plotted search pattern. The tow fish would send pulses, usually in the 100–500 KHz range, in an angular path; that would bounce off the sea bottom and send back echoes that created an acoustic picture of the lake or ocean floor. That picture would be transmitted to a computer and monitor on the search ship, where shadowy images of the floor would appear.

The task was going to be a challenge for the *Woodrush*. Jimmie Hobaugh had the coordinates provided by the Orion, but a new storm system was brewing on the lake. Although not nearly as intense as the one of November 9–10, it wreaked havoc on the sonar. To obtain the needed images, the *Woodrush* had to move slowly and steadily in the water, holding a straight course and allowing the side-scanning sonar device to pass over an object located hundreds of feet below the surface; accomplishing this in choppy seas was no small accomplishment.

Still, within a few hours, Hobaugh and his crew were able to corroborate the Orion's findings. Something very large was on the floor of Lake Superior, in approximately 530 feet of water.

For the remainder of the day and over the following two days, the *Woodrush* fought the "poor sonic trace quality" resulting from the gathering storm, and tediously produced sonar images that answered some questions while creating others. The large presence, it turned out, was actually *two* large objects, each about 300 feet long, separated by a short distance. These two objects, Hobaugh reasoned, would account for a great percentage of the *Fitzgerald*'s 729-foot length. The sonar also revealed a "sonically rough area" in the space between the two large objects. This, Hobaugh believed, might constitute the *Fitzgerald*'s spilled cargo.

It was a good start, but the Marine Board of Investigation, now beginning its inquiry into the loss, needed more before officially concluding that this was the wreckage of the *Fitz*. Using any kind of underwater photographic equipment was out of the question—it was too late in the season, with weather too unstable and unpredictable to permit such an exploration. In addition, the board decided that the equipment used by the *Woodrush* was inadequate for exploring wreckage this deep. The only solution was to schedule another side-scan, this one using more sensitive equipment that would produce more detailed images.

The second visit to the wreckage site took place November 22–25. Once again, the lake was uncooperative, with high winds and choppy seas that made it clear that winter was setting in and any further exploration of the *Fitzgerald* would have to be postponed until the following spring. Still, with a Coast Guard investigation already under way, families of the victims restless for answers, insurance companies demanding some kind of explanation, and hungry news media looking for stories, there was plenty of pressure and motivation to continue, weather conditions be damned.

For three days, the *Woodrush* worked almost nonstop, making eighty passes over the wreckage and obtaining almost three hundred navigational fixes. Despite these efforts, the best conclusion anyone on board the *Woodrush* could draw was that the wreckage was "probably" the *Fitzgerald*.

After gathering as much data as possible from the sonar search, investigators shipped the information to Seaward, Inc., in Falls Church, Virginia. A model of the wreckage, based on analysis of the sonar images, was constructed and submitted to the Board of Investigation. The panel reviewed Seaward's analysis and concluded that the wreckage was "very probably" the *Fitzgerald*. That was as far as these efforts could go. It would take an actual visit to the sunken ship to do any better.

On Monday, November 18, the Marine Board of Investigation convened for the first time, on the ninth floor of the Federal Building in Cleveland. The four-member panel—Rear Admiral Winifred W. Barrow, and Captains Adam S. Zabinski, James A. Wilson, and C. S. Loosmore—proposed a lofty goal.

"This investigation is intended to determine the cause of the casualty, to the extent possible, and the responsibility therefore," Admiral Barrow announced to those attending. The investigation, he added, was intended to focus on proposing ways of saving lives and property in the future, rather than on assigning blame.

Of course, there were no survivors, no eyewitnesses to the sinking, no accurate logs of the ship's final journey, very few recorded radio or telephone transmissions between the *Arthur Anderson* and the Coast Guard in the immediate aftermath of the *Fitzgerald*'s disappearance, and no photographs or videos of the wreckage. The closest thing the board had to witnesses was the handful of men who had been in the *Anderson*'s pilothouse, and others who had limited contact with the *Fitz* during its final hours. Barring a stunning revelation sometime in the future, the best the board could hope to accomplish was an educated guess.

The board's four members were highly qualified to make just such a guess. Admiral Barrow had spent his entire career in marine safety and had served as chief of merchant marine inspection in Washington, D.C., before assuming his present command of the 8th Coast Guard District. Zabinski, known for his no-nonsense approach and fiery temperament, had been a master in commercial shipping prior to joining the Coast Guard; now he was a kind of traveling inspector, going out on Great Lakes freighters and observing them at work; he had also served on every recent Marine Board of Investigation, so that his presence gave a sense of continuity to all the investigations and accident reports filed on nautical accidents. Wilson had spent his career on the Great Lakes, where he had established himself as an authority on safety and inspection. Loosmore offered double credentials: a Coast Guard Academy graduate, he was licensed to practice law; he had also studied mechanical engineering at MIT and was only a thesis away from his doctorate.

Admiral Barrow ran a tight ship, as Thomas Murphy, an Oglebay Norton attorney, learned early in the proceedings.

"He was the straightest arrow the Coast Guard had ever seen," C. S. Loosmore said of his fellow board member. "On Friday, after the first week of hearings,

Admiral Barrow said, 'Well, we'll convene tomorrow morning at eight o'clock.' Mr. Murphy, who was representing Oglebay Norton, came up and said, 'Admiral, tomorrow is Saturday.' 'Yes, I am aware of that,' the Admiral said. And Murphy said, 'Tomorrow is Ohio State–Michigan.' Barrow looked at him like he was talking in Chinese. So Murphy, not leaving it alone, said, 'Well, you know, that's an extremely important event here in the Great Lakes'—inferring that Barrow didn't know that. Now Barrow was a fairly tall guy—I think he was six foot three or something like that—with this dark hair and this presence, and it was just wonderful to watch his attitude turn. He rose up to his full eighteen feet in height—or maybe he made Murphy three inches tall—and he said, 'Mr. Murphy, we're dealing here with a tragedy that has cost a major ship and twenty-nine lives. We will convene at eight o'clock in the morning.' I flat out loved it."

The investigators planned to call a host of witnesses to testify over the forthcoming weeks, including the *Anderson*'s captain and members of its crew, experts from the National Weather Service, former crewmen on the *Edmund Fitzgerald,* captains of other ships on Lake Superior during the November 9–10 storm, officials from Oglebay Norton, dock workers from Superior, Coast Guard personnel, and participants in the search for the *Fitzgerald*—all with the hope of piecing together a narrative of the *Fitzgerald*'s final voyage and sinking.

"We didn't know exactly what happened," James Wilson admitted. "Prior to the testimony, we didn't have anything, but we had these ideas. One was that she broke apart and sank, like the *Daniel J. Morrell*. That was probably the most obvious one. Then we wondered if she could have struck a pinnacle, because she was obviously near an island. And then the third theory was that something happened and she split apart on the way down. These were the three leading theories before we did the underwater search."

The board could make certain assumptions that would aid the investigation. They were all but certain of the location of the wreckage, and it was only a matter of time before the ship's remains were explored and photographed. The ship had foundered unexpectedly, meaning it had either suffered structural failure (an idea supported, at least to some degree, by the knowledge that the *Fitz* lay in two pieces on the lake floor), or had capsized or submarined. It had not caught fire and burned to the waterline, collided with another vessel, struck and sunk on shallow shoals, or suffered any number of other calamities that had claimed other Great Lakes ships in the past. This knowledge, basic as it was, would guide the board members in their questioning.

Nothing, however, was taken for granted. Too much was at stake, and not just the pursuit of the truth. There would undoubtedly be a series of insurance claims, civil suits, and other legal actions in the future, and while the board was willing to let others do its bidding in assigning blame in the *Fitzgerald* tragedy, it needed to be fair, open-minded, and thorough in its approach. Within a week of the sinking, the families of two victims had filed suit, the union representing the crew members had voiced opposition to the hearings, an army of lawyers had been hired to represent any number of parties, and, in general, there was a lot of scrambling to avoid blame. The Coast Guard itself was under fire, hearing grumblings that it had been less than efficient in its search-and-rescue operations.

The hearings were bound to be frustrating. No one wanted to be accused of conjecture—or, worse yet, of speaking ill of the dead—in implying any negligence or dereliction of duty on the part of the captain or crew of the *Fitzgerald*. Witnesses, some accompanied by their attorneys, were extremely cautious in their answers to the panel's questions. Quite often, board members found themselves repeatedly circling a topic, pressing witnesses for more detailed answers, or meeting off the record to hammer out particularly vexing or technical issues. Conflicting testimony was common.

Besides the re-creation of the *Fitzgerald*'s final journey, certain issues dominated the board's line of questioning:

1. Was the *Edmund Fitzgerald* a strong ship in good repair? With strong evidence of structural failure, the board needed testimony about the strength of the *Fitzgerald*'s hull, the recent inspections of the ship, the way the vessel worked in heavy seas, and whether it had sustained any damage in the past that might have weakened it in a way that contributed to its taking on water and perhaps even breaking apart on the surface.

2. Was the *Fitzgerald* loaded properly? Since the cargo holds were a ship's weakest point, the board needed to determine whether the loading process

might have been a factor in the ship's demise. Hogging during loading could have led to serious stress on the hull; or the shifting of cargo, brought on by improper loading, might have contributed to some of the *Fitzgerald*'s problems later in its final voyage.

3. Did the recent changes in the winter load lines create a hazard in late-season storms? Three recent changes in minimal draft requirements had permitted huge freighters like the *Fitzgerald* to carry larger cargos later in the season, when violent storms were common on the Great Lakes. The board needed to determine whether the reduction in minimum required freeboard increased the risk of heavy seas boarding a ship during a storm.

4. Was the *Fitzgerald*'s watertight integrity compromised by faulty hatch covers, or by improper dogging of the hatch covers? If the *Edmund Fitzgerald* foundered as the result of taking on too much water through its hatch openings—a common enough occurrence in the history of Great Lakes tragedies—the board had to learn as much as possible about the hatch covers and the procedures for fastening them down.

5. Was the *Fitzgerald* equipped with adequate safety and life-saving equipment, and if so, was the crew properly instructed in abandon-ship procedures? When the *Fitzgerald*'s lifeboats and life rafts were recovered, it was evident that no one had made any attempt to use them. The Marine Board appeared ready to concede that the *Fitz* sank quickly, with very little warning, but it seemed inconceivable that no one had attempted to abandon ship, that not a single body in a life preserver or floating on a life raft had been recovered.

Board member James Wilson later described the panel's process of questioning witnesses and piecing together of pertinent information as "a free-for-all." The four members, he pointed out, came from different parts of the country and had arrived in Cleveland the day before the hearings were set to begin. Less than a week had passed since the Coast Guard had officially abandoned its search for survivors and the *Woodrush* had located what was presumably the wreckage of the *Edmund Fitzgerald*. During that brief interval, the Marine Board had been formed, a preliminary list of witnesses had been drawn up, and each board member began sketching out questions for witnesses.

"Everybody'd been thinking about what they wanted," Wilson recalled. "Everybody had questions. Each person pretty much had an area that he wanted to explore, and sometimes we didn't agree with the other guy's questions."

Adding to the pressure was the fact that the hearings were under intense scrutiny. Attorneys representing Oglebay Norton, Northwestern Mutual, the estates of some of the *Fitzgerald* crew, and other interests attended the hearings, some asking questions of their own, and there was always a smattering of reporters looking for tidbits. C. S. Loosmore, the youngest of the board members, bore the brunt of the work, acting as the hearings' recorder in addition to his questioning of witnesses; when it came time for the report to be drawn up, he would be the one doing the writing.

Bernie Cooper's eagerly anticipated appearance before the board took place on Thursday, November 20, with a follow-up on December 10. Only ten days had passed between the loss of the *Fitzgerald* and Cooper's initial appearance, and his would be the first in-depth, public retelling of the events transpiring on Lake Superior during the storm of November 9–10. If anyone was able to provide the board with clues about how the *Fitz* had gone down, it would be this witness: not only had he had extensive contact with the *Fitzgerald* throughout the storm, right up until its disappearance from his radar, but also he was an experienced captain, capable of speaking authoritatively about Great Lakes vessels, storms, and how ships performed under stress.

Cooper's testimony managed to be both extremely detailed and agonizingly elusive. His riveting account of the *Anderson*'s experiences, beginning with the ship's leaving Two Harbors and ending with the futile search for the *Fitzgerald*, lived up to the expectations of the Marine Board—and the attending news media. Still, like a military officer testifying at a formal hearing, Cooper was reluctant to stray outside the facts; he had to be prodded before he provided any kind of speculation.

This was especially apparent when the board grilled him about the *Fitzgerald*'s movements around Michipicoten and Caribou Islands. The board had obtained a tape of Cooper's November 11 conference call to the U.S. Steel offices in Cleveland, during which he'd stated that he was certain that the *Fitzgerald* had passed too close to the treacherous shoals near the islands; in his testimony before the board, Cooper backed off from those statements.

"We were not plotting him," Cooper offered, somewhat defensively, with respect to the *Fitzgerald*'s course near Caribou Island. "All we can do is give you up to this point what we hauled down as an impression. It was my impression definitely—my mate and I both looked at this, and in the respect that he was in closer than I wanted to be is the absolute truth. I didn't want to be in that close to the island—and again, now, when you are using a small-scale chart, it changes in perspective. It definitely changes in perspective of what I was testifying about."

Cooper held his ground, even after the tape of his phone call was played into the record.

"You are talking about describing a conversation that I had when I had been up 48 hours and [was] tired," Cooper protested, when asked to describe his conference call with U.S. Steel. "There might have been something taken out of context, I don't know."

Aptly enough, Cooper's testimony exemplified the confusion on both the *Fitzgerald* and the *Anderson* throughout the tense final hours of their journeys on Lake Superior. Nothing seemed certain or easy to describe. Cooper excelled when he spoke of the weather and displayed his expertise in understanding its highly volatile changes, drawing laughter from those attending the hearings when he suggested that "there are two or three real good meteorologists along the lakes, especially when they agree with me."

However, this particular storm—which Cooper admitted was the greatest challenge he'd faced since the *Anderson* had been lengthened—proved to be devilishly difficult to understand. Cooper, like others testifying at the hearings, had been in other wicked storms on the lake, and this one, in terms of wind velocity, average wave height, and overall sailing conditions, didn't necessarily outdo some of the others. The early portion of the trip had been nothing at all, and even the early hours of November 10, when the *Anderson* and *Fitzgerald* switched courses to a more northern route, did not worry Cooper.

"You say, 'Why did we go out in a gale?'" Cooper said to Admiral Barrow. "Truly it was not a gale. It was a breeze. It was a fresh breeze."

Cooper described the building seas as the storm intensified during the day, but even there he found himself qualifying his statements about the overall intensity of the storm.

"I would consider it a severe local storm," he explained, "because it was intense, but it was not a vast, wide, two-day storm. To me, it looked more like a hurricane storm, which I am familiar with, plotting down in Florida."

The *Anderson,* Cooper pointed out, handled well in the storm. It rode smoothly—"It wouldn't roll an egg off the table," he said, quoting the ship's cook—and it held out strongly when it was hit by a couple of mountainous waves below Caribou Island. A few items—a wheelbarrow, an oil spill pan, a ring buoy, and a trash barrel—had been washed overboard, but, in general, the *Anderson* handled this storm as it had others in the past.

The *Fitzgerald,* six years younger than the *Anderson,* should have been able to deal with the storm. In Cooper's view, something traumatic must have occurred, yet whatever it was, it wasn't apparent to McSorley.

"I firmly believe that he had a damaged ship and didn't know how damaged she was," Cooper concluded.

Cooper, of course, only knew what McSorley had told him. He admitted worrying about the *Fitz* when McSorley reported a fence rail down—"a hogging situation would cause the fence rail to break"—but when McSorley didn't appear too worried about it, Cooper deferred to the more experienced captain's judgment.

"I watched him, but I wasn't concerned about him," Cooper testified. "I was more concerned about my ship getting down there and getting this thing over my stern. He's in the radar and he realizes that, but there is no problem."

In the days following the *Fitzgerald*'s sinking, Cooper had mulled over the events of the ship's final hours and had reached the conclusion that the *Fitz* must have suffered fatal damage somewhere around Michipicoten Island or the Six Fathom Shoal—serious damage below the waterline.

"I believe that she was cracked somewhere," Cooper told the Marine Board. "She was taking water fast enough because what he told me was that 'I have a list and I am taking water.' And I said, 'Have you got your pumps on?' and he said, 'Both of them.'

"So, from my experience on a previous occasion, I think what he did, he took that list, which seemed to be real fast, as far as I was concerned, and that water level would have reached a level of his draft and it would stay constant, no matter whether he had the pumps on it or not, if there was water coming in from below . . . from an opening in the hull. No matter how fast you pump, if water is coming in faster, you are not going to lower the water in the tank, because that water will stay at a constant level, with the same list."

But this was all offered in hindsight. While they were on the lake, battling the storm and heading toward Whitefish Point, Cooper was under the impression that McSorley had his problems under control.

"At no time did he initiate a call or state that 'I have got more than a problem,'" Cooper said. "When he told the mate that 'I am holding my own,' you have to assume he has no problems. He is only 15 miles from Whitefish. He is going home."

Although reluctant to state his case as forcefully before the Marine Board as he had presented it in his call to U.S. Steel, Cooper believed to his dying day that the *Edmund Fitzgerald* had either touched bottom or hogged in the turbulent seas around Michipicoten and Caribou Islands. The damage to the hull had allowed enough water to enter the *Fitzgerald* to cause it to lose freeboard and, ultimately, succumb to one or more huge rogue waves.

For the time being, though, everything was conjecture. As Cooper cautiously pointed out to the board, the answers might be found one day in the future, when the wreckage of the *Edmund Fitzgerald* was visited and explored.

The board's inquiries into the loading process produced nothing to indicate a problem when the *Fitzgerald* took on cargo in Superior. Both Donald Amys, the general foreman for Burlington-Northern, and Ed Dennis, who had supervised the loading on November 9, testified that all had gone smoothly. Dennis remembered the *Fitzgerald* because the weather was pleasant and Jack McCarthy was friendlier than most first mates overseeing the loading of their ships. Otherwise, there had been nothing to distinguish this loading from any other.

The board's questions about the replacement of hatch covers led to some troubling testimony. Ed Dennis couldn't specify when the *Fitzgerald*'s crew had begun replacing and fastening down the hatch covers, but other witnesses maintained that it wasn't at all uncommon for crews to fasten down only half of the hatch cover clamps, especially during the summer months, when the weather was good and there was no danger of encountering heavy seas. Witnesses also testified that a ship would sometimes leave the dock before the clamps had been dogged down, or that clamps might be removed before it arrived for unloading.

Andrew Rajner testified that there were times, while he was working as a first mate on the *Fitz,* when Captain McSorley directed him to fasten down every other clamp. It depended upon weather conditions and forecasts. If the weather changed during the trip, the crew would be instructed to fasten the other clamps—a process, Rajner estimated, that could be accomplished by three or four men within twenty minutes.

"If you were taking seas on the fore deck, could you do it?" Adam Zabinski asked.

"It could be a problem," Rajner admitted.

The implication of Zabinski's line of questioning was clear: if the *Fitzgerald* had left Superior on November 9 with only some of the hatch covers secured, it might have been impossible to fasten them later, when the weather had deteriorated and going out on the deck was dangerous.

No one believed that lifeboats worked, especially under extreme conditions. They were difficult, if not impossible, to launch, and even if they were successfully lowered over the side of a ship, the turbulent seas would capsize them almost immediately. It was one thing to conduct lifeboat drills on a warm, sunny afternoon, quite another to attempt to launch a lifeboat in the turmoil surrounding a ship's going down in a violent storm.

Virtually every witness brought before the Marine Board testified as much. No one seemed surprised that the *Fitzgerald*'s lifeboats had not been launched. The ship seemed to have sunk very quickly, and even if there had been a minute or two's warning, the crew probably would have disdained the lifeboats in favor of life rafts, which witnesses believed gave at least a fighting chance for survival.

Testifying before the board, former *Fitzgerald* crewmen expressed doubts that lifeboats could have been launched in the storm of November 10, 1975.

"In my opinion, you cannot launch a boat when there is any great sea at all," said Charles Lindberg, who had worked as a watchman and wheelsman on the *Fitz*. If the ship was rolling, Lindberg suggested, it would have been impossible to launch a lifeboat, and even in the event that one was successfully lowered over the side of the distressed ship, it was still facing long odds. "It would probably be smashed before it got to the waterline," Lindberg said.

Gerald Lange, a former first mate on the *Fitz,* shared Lindberg's skepticism, though he felt the lifeboats might have been launched. "If you had such heavy weather," he told the board, "you could get your boat probably over the side, but then she is subject to damage from the sea action."

Former *Fitz* watchman John Larson agreed. "I don't believe you could put a boat in that water," he testified, "because those seas would have damaged it or something. It would tip her over. I don't think you could handle a lifeboat even if you got it in the water."

Harry Hilgemann, a crew member on the *Arthur Anderson,* doubted that he would have so much as considered using a lifeboat if he'd had to abandon a sinking ship in the conditions he'd seen in the storm.

"I would have been heading for the inflatable rafts," he said, stating an opinion shared by most of those testifying. "In those seas, I don't believe it would have been possible to get a lifeboat over. With the life raft, if you could have inflated it on the deck and then go into it, I believe you could have had a pretty good chance."

John Larson also felt that survivors were better off on life rafts.

"After it is blown up," he said of the life raft, "it's got a cover on it and you would be out of the water. You would be protected from the exposure. That time of year, it is very important."

Perhaps the most unexpected source of lifeboat criticism came from the captain of the ship following the *Fitzgerald* on its final voyage. Captain Bernie Cooper, it turned out, had no more faith in the lifeboats than any of the crewmen.

"In rough weather, I don't think I would attempt to launch one," he confessed. When pressed for an explanation, Cooper dismissed lifeboats in favor of the rafts, which he suggested might work if inflated on deck and allowed to float free when the ship sank.

"I don't know," he said. "I just somehow or another . . . I guess I have just lost faith in lifeboats because of all the times I can remember and all the casualties I have read about on the Great Lakes. Any time there has been a seaway, that particular boat in trouble has never been able to get a boat off."

In its questions about the lifeboats and rafts, the Coast Guard panel also seemed to be exploring the idea that the crewmen might not have trusted the lifeboats because they weren't adequately trained and prepared to launch them. Those testifying estimated that it would have taken between five and ten minutes to launch a lifeboat, which would probably have been too long to save any lives on the *Fitzgerald,* if the ship sank as quickly as believed.

When questioned by the board about the frequency of lifeboat drills on the *Fitzgerald,* the former crewmen offered wildly different answers.

"We had weekly drills, and these drills were so noted in the pilothouse log," Gerald Lange tersely offered.

Charles Lindberg stated flatly that, aside from a fire and boat drill conducted when the *Fitz* was fitted out in the spring, he had never taken part in a drill under McSorley.

The contradictory testimony frustrated the board, leading to some rapid-fire and, in some cases, testy exchanges. Captain James Wilson barely kept his temper when questioning Larson about the *Fitzgerald*'s boat drills.

WILSON: We have conflicts in testimony, and you are here to help us. How often did you have lifeboat drills on the *Fitzgerald?* Why won't you tell us?

LARSON: Geez, I know when Paulson was there we had them maybe every five days, and McSorley was very lenient on it. He didn't have it very often.

WILSON: What do you mean, not very often?

LARSON: I can't say just how often.

WILSON: Don't you remember, or what?

LARSON: No. How often he had them, I can't say.

The tone grew even tenser, a short time later that same day, when Donald Hilsen, who'd worked as a watchman on the *Fitz,* was confronted by Adam Zabinski. Hilsen had testified that he could not remember McSorley ever holding a lifeboat drill. Zabinski, obviously frustrated, first by Larson's earlier statements and then by Hilsen's less-than-detailed testimony, struggled to maintain even a shred of decorum.

ZABINSKI: Mr. Hilsen, you indicated that the lifeboat station was the No. 1 boat. Was that on the port or starboard side?

HILSEN: There again, I can't be specific. I always get that mixed up.

ZABINSKI: Mr. Hilsen, who are you kidding? Any boat you ever went on— how many ships did you say you were on?

HILSEN: About 25.

ZABINSKI: Every ship you were on, Boat 1 was on one side, and Boat 2 was the other side, and don't try to kid me.

HILSEN: I am not.

ZABINSKI: Don't tell me you were on 25 ships and you don't know where No. 1 boat is. This is a serious matter here, and you have been evasive on every answer you have given, and I am fed up. Now you answer. What side is No. 1 boat on?

HILSEN: Port side.

ZABINSKI: Are you sure of that?

HILSEN: No, sir, I am not.

ZABINSKI: You're damn right you are not. You are not sure about anything. I don't know where you got your lifeboat certificate, but I will be darned if I don't check up on it.

Zabinski continued to hammer away at his witness, concluding his questioning with remarks that were both nasty and personal.

"There were 29 people, and you probably know a lot of them that are down in the bottom of Lake Superior," he challenged Hilsen. "You have to live with your conscience."

The Marine Board's frustrations were easy to understand. The Coast Guard required weekly lifeboat drills on all Great Lakes vessels, and the testimony that McSorley conducted regular drills could have been interpreted as covering up to protect the reputation of a respected mariner, or as an attempt to avoid making any statement that might be used later in a legal action. Since the *Fitzgerald's* logs were at the bottom of Lake Superior, there was no way of verifying any of the testimony.

Richard Orgel, a former third mate on the *Fitz,* pulled no punches in any of his testimony. He was not intimidated by the board or its line of questioning, and he stayed true to form when he addressed the issue of lifeboat drills. The drills, he suggested pointedly, were futile exercises.

"All these lifeboat drills," he said, "[are] always done on a nice sunny day, in daylight, in a harbor," he said. "It is a long way from the real thing."

The drills, he continued, were never conducted when the ship was out on open water, and even if that were to happen, there was no chance that a lifeboat would actually be lowered into the water while a trip was under way. In Orgel's opinion, the thought of launching a lifeboat in a storm wasn't realistic.

"The problems are just insurmountable," he told the board. "You want to remember now that the only people familiar with all those lifeboats are a couple of AB's [able-bodied seamen] and the mates. Now, you have cooks and firemen and engineers, and you have people that don't have any gear or clothes, and they are just wearing their going-uptown overcoats, perhaps. Then, with that type of equipment, you can imagine what it is like in a 25-foot sea."

Orgel's words, along with the testimony of the other witnesses, really brought one aspect of the *Fitzgerald's* last moments into sharper focus: either the *Fitz* went down so suddenly that no one had a chance to attempt an escape, or, perhaps even more disturbing, if the crew was aware of the ship's imminent demise, the men, like many of those on board the *Steinbrenner*—Lake Superior's most recent previous major disaster—had so little regard for the lifeboats that they didn't even try to use them.

The Marine Board of Investigation called its final witness on December 13. All told, the panel had interviewed forty-five witnesses over twelve days of hearings, and every conceivable angle of the *Fitzgerald*'s final two days had been addressed. Still, as anticipated, the testimony presented a mosaic of information rather than a clear, concise picture of how and why the *Fitzgerald* sank. The board made a point of soliciting speculation about what brought the ship down, but the only unanimous opinion was that the ship sank very quickly, offering no chance for a mayday call or escape.

"No doubt that they were all inside, and probably if something happened—if she broke in two or foundered or whatever she done—it happened all of a sudden," said Andrew Rajner. "If she rolled, it would be the same thing. It would be fast: You wouldn't have had time to grab a telephone or anything."

Delmore Webster reasoned that the *Fitz* must have plunged to the bottom of the lake. He agreed with Bernie Cooper that the *Fitz* might have grounded on a shoal and torn a hole in its hull, and that McSorley might have been unaware of the extensive damage to his ship.

"When you are in a heavy sea, you hear noises from the waves hitting against the deck," Webster explained. "It probably hogged and he didn't realize it. I think he punched a hole in it in several places, and I think he had the vent caps closed. It could have happened on the starboard side or maybe a little bit on the port side, and as he continued going, he realized it. He probably tried to pump his water out. He couldn't get his water pumped out. I really don't think he knew he was in peril, and I think the center of gravity overcame the center of buoyancy and they sank."

Gerald Lange defended McSorley's reputation. He had worked closely with McSorley, serving as first mate under him, and he knew McSorley well enough to say that the *Fitzgerald*'s captain wouldn't have taken foolish chances if he knew his ship was in danger.

"Captain McSorley was a professional sailor who knew his own capabilities, and knew the capabilities of his ship, and he operated accordingly," Lange declared. "He was cautious."

Lange had given the loss of the *Edmund Fitzgerald* a lot of thought, and unlike other witnesses, who declined to speculate deeply or in detail about the reasons for the sinking, Lange wasn't at all shy about expressing his opinions.

"First, I will say that I cannot accept the theory that the vessel broke in half. I have been through her bottoms and to me she was a well-constructed ship," he said. "In order to break a ship in half, you would have to have a sea in each end of the ship. You've got 700 feet of ship, and I cannot imagine a sea on each end of the ship. You would have to have 700 feet, one crest and another crest, and, well, I have never seen or ever heard of anything like that. You would have more than these two seas under that ship at all times, to my knowledge of weather observations.

"So, therefore, I can only say that I think he may have struck a shoal and he didn't realize how much damage may have occurred then and he continued on. The list probably came from water entering his ballast tanks more on one side, and I assume that he would have contacted the engineers to inquire about the list and they would look at their King gauges and see that the vessel is making water and immediately turn on the pumps to correct the situation, but in a sea that has been described—or what I have heard—[as] 25 or 30 feet high, it would be pretty hard to tell whether a ship is going down.

"It would probably be a gradual process and, judging from what I have heard in the telephone conversations that he had with various people, she was going along like an old shoe. I assume that he didn't realize that there may have been as much damage as there possibly could have been. Therefore, in my opinion, she either capsized, rolled, or she plunged."

As time would prove, these were only the first of a long list of theories. The men who had worked on the *Fitz,* who knew the ship inside out, and who knew many of the men who had perished in the sinking, still found it unimaginable that a vessel of that size, with a crew that experienced, could simply disappear in a storm.

"To my knowledge, that was the best crew that could have been on the *Fitzgerald,* with the mates, engineers, and the skipper," said Thomas Garcia, who had worked the decks of the *Fitz* and knew many of the lost crewmen. "The men throughout Oglebay Norton Company knew the *Fitzgerald* as 'The Mighty Fitzgerald.' She was the queen of our fleet. It was unbelievable when we heard she went down."

The Marine Board hearings, although useful for gathering information, had been maddeningly inconclusive. Besides listening to the testimony of its witnesses, the board had examined hundreds of charts, maps, documents and photographs, all leading to one inescapable conclusion: the board needed to see the wreckage of the *Edmund Fitzgerald* before it could even consider issuing a final report.

The panel considered its options. A free dive to the wreckage could be extremely dangerous, even if the diver used mixed gases and a protective suit: if the diver became entangled in the wreckage or disoriented in the lake depths of the lake—always a hazard in exploring deep-water shipwrecks—there was virtually no chance of bringing him back alive. In addition, such a dive would have to be brief, disallowing any thorough exploration of the wreckage. Using a small submarine would be less risky, but the Coast Guard ultimately rejected this option for much the same reason as they dismissed a free dive: since no one knew the condition of the *Fitzgerald*'s wreckage, there was a very real possibility of a submarine's being trapped by shifting wreckage or becoming entangled in it.

A cable-controlled underwater research vehicle (CURV), unmanned and maneuvered from the surface by remote control, presented the safest alternative. The CURV could be lowered to the wreckage area, where it could be manipulated at a painstakingly slow pace, videotaping objects directly in front of it. In addition to a pair of television cameras, the CURV unit was equipped with a 35mm camera for close-up stills, and it had a clawlike robotic arm capable of grasping or repositioning objects. The CURV had earned its stripes a decade ear-lier, when it recovered an H-bomb accidentally lost in 2,000 feet of water near Spain, and it was capable of diving to depths of 5,000 feet. A new model—CURV III—was owned by the U.S. Navy; it would be flown in from San Diego for the Lake Superior operation.

The exploration, Admiral Barrow announced during the final session of the Marine Board hearings, would have to wait until the following spring, when the ice on eastern Lake Superior had melted and the weather was more con-ducive to the extensive study that the Coast Guard planned. The public wanted answers, but the board wasn't about to sacrifice thoroughness for speed.

"The survey that we have in mind is one which cannot be accomplished in a single day or two days," Barrow stated.

In the meantime, the board would review the evidence and testimony it had received during the hearings. It would also conduct additional research. Each member would be riding a Great Lakes ore carrier and observing its operation. The board also hoped to obtain up-to-date soundings of the area around the Caribou and Michipicoten Islands. With any luck, these new soundings would indicate whether the *Fitzgerald* had touched down on previously uncharted—or incorrectly charted—shoals.

But answers to the mystery would have to wait.

Gordon Lightfoot paged through the November 24, 1975, issue of *Newsweek* and paused at a story entitled "The Cruelest Month." Pictured in the center of the page was the *Edmund Fitzgerald* sailing in its prime.

Lightfoot, a thirty-six-year-old Canadian balladeer known for such songs as "Early Morning Rain," "If You Could Read My Mind," "Sundown," and "Carefree Highway," had been drawn to the water since his childhood. "I have been fasci-nated by boats since I was seven and saw one being launched," he'd recall. "It slid sideways in the water, creating a great, powerful wave."

The *Fitzgerald* story, with its account of a giant ore carrier's losing battle with powerful waves, struck a chord.

"When the *Edmund Fitzgerald* went down," Lightfoot said, "I owned a sailboat. I imagined what that wave might have been."

He had written about ships and railroads in his folksinging past, but he was captivated by the prospect of telling a true story in one of his songs, especially a tale with the spiritual quality found in the story of the *Edmund Fitzgerald*.

"Shipwrecks are different than your coal mine or railroad disasters," he explained. "They have a different quality, a mystique and a mysteriousness. Witnesses usually don't live to tell the tale."

The *Newsweek* piece opened with a line that reflected the sense of mystery and timelessness that would boost Lightfoot's song, "The Wreck of the *Edmund Fitzgerald*," into the public's consciousness. "According to a legend of the Chippewa tribe," the article began, "the lake they once called Gitche Gumee 'never gives up her dead.'"

It was as good a place as any to start the song.

CHAPTER FIVE

THE MARINE BOARD REPORT

THE SUNNY SKIES AND CALM LAKE SUPERIOR WATERS GAVE NO INDICA-
tion of the tempest that had blown through only a few hours earlier. On board the
Woodrush, Captain Jimmie Hobaugh and Admiral Winifred Barrow discussed their
schedule for the day ahead, relieved that a storm wouldn't be disrupting their
mission.

Somewhere, far below the *Woodrush,* there rested two huge objects that
Hobaugh, Barrow, and a host of others hoped would prove to be the remains of
the *Edmund Fitzgerald.* Almost exactly six months earlier, the initial side-scan
sonar images had indicated the presence of these objects; a few days ago, a
follow-up side-scan had confirmed the previous findings and pinpointed the exact location of the wreckage. Now, on May 20, 1976, the CURV III was about to
be eased into the water. Everybody aboard the *Woodrush* waited anxiously,
hoping the CURV survey would answer the scores of questions that had been
nagging at investigators since the *Fitzgerald*'s disappearance.

The operation had been carefully plotted out from the moment the Coast
Guard learned that the CURV III was available for the survey. Hobaugh and his

ship and crew had become almost inextricably connected to the *Edmund Fitzgerald,* since the *Woodrush*'s involvement in the futile search-and-rescue mission to the sonar side-scan operations that had found the wreckage. In the months between the Marine Board's recess in December 1975 and the spring of 1976, Hobaugh devoted countless hours to preparing for the CURV operation.

"We spent all that winter going to San Diego, looking at CURV III, learning about its capabilities, and learning about what kind of ship to put it on," Hobaugh remembered. "My ship was perfect for it. I had a gun deck behind the stack that we could put the generator on—the gun had been taken off years before—and the buoy deck was big enough for all of us. We had a boom that we could use to pick up the CURV III, and we had room for the control shack and all the cable. We spent the entire winter planning how we were going to moor the ship so we could move and cover any object we wanted to look at."

When planning the operation, the Coast Guard had asked the National Weather Service to project a period in the spring when nature might provide a five- to seven-day window of opportunity for another side-scan and the CURV operations. The side-scan had gone as planned, but during the night before the first scheduled CURV visit to the wreckage, a storm lashed the *Woodrush* with 45-mile-per-hour winds and 8- to 10-foot waves. Anchored over the wreckage, Hobaugh and Barrow worried about the prospects for their first day's work with the CURV. It was as if Lake Superior wanted to hold on to its secrets about the *Fitz.*

Fortunately, the storm ended in six hours. The skies cleared and the seas calmed. Two mooring buoys had imploded after being dragged down during the storm, and had to be replaced, but otherwise the CURV was lowered into the water on schedule.

By comparison with the underwater apparatus used on future *Fitzgerald* explorations, the CURV operation was crude. The sledlike robot's propulsion motors stirred up sediment from the bottom of the lake, clouding the water and the black-and-white video images sent up to the *Woodrush.* The CURV's mercury vapor lights glared off objects in front of them, making it even tougher to identify the debris and twisted steel littering the floor of Lake Superior.

The men on the *Woodrush* stared quietly at their monitor screens, waiting for the CURV to reward them with something that would positively identify the wreckage as the *Fitzgerald*. The pieces came together gradually: a hatch cover half buried in the silt; what appeared to be taconite pellets strewn all about the debris field. For every decent image finding its way to the monitors there seemed to be a long, nerve-racking period during which nothing but darkness or suspended silt appeared onscreen. Huge chunks of mud and sediment, gouged out when the *Fitz* plowed through the lake bottom, gave a new shape to Lake Superior's floor. At times, it seemed as if the CURV were exploring the surface of another planet.

Then it happened.

A mountain of steel appeared on the monitor. The men on the surface held their collective breath as the CURV was maneuvered along the wall, and then upward. This was obviously the hull of a sunken ship, much of it buried in mud. The CURV continued its climb, and suddenly several black letters appeared. It took a few moments and further maneuvering of the CURV before the men on the *Woodrush* realized what they were seeing: the words "Edmund Fitzgerald" and "Milwaukee," upside down, indicating that the stern portion of the *Fitz* had come to rest in an inverted position.

No one had expected it. The side-scan sonar images seemed to indicate that both sections of the ship were standing upright, but there was no denying the silent evidence of those dark letters in the depths of Lake Superior.

The CURV moved upward until its lights fell on the *Fitzgerald*'s rudder and 19½-foot propeller, pointing unnaturally toward the surface of the lake.

The first big question had been answered.

The CURV made twelve dives to the wreckage between May 20 and May 28, producing 43,255 feet of television footage and 895 still photographs in 56 hours and 5 minutes of time at the wreckage site. The CURV worked methodically, moving back and forth over the ghostly presence at the bottom of the lake. Even though they were witnessing it firsthand, the crew on the *Woodrush* found it difficult to believe that the horribly twisted and battered images onscreen represented what had been one of the most powerful ore carriers in Great Lakes history.

The *Edmund Fitzgerald* had suffered an agonizing death. Much of the bow section was buried in mud. Gaping holes had been torn into the bow of the ship, and the grotesque twisting of steel at the end of the bow section spoke of the powerful forces that ripped the *Fitz* apart. Perhaps most telling of all, two hundred feet of the *Fitzgerald*'s middle section were simply gone. According to the CURV's measurements, the bow section was 276 feet long and the stern section 253 feet, meaning that a huge portion of the *Fitz* had disintegrated into the pieces cluttering the debris field between the two sections.

Not surprisingly, the CURV's exploration of the *Fitz*'s pilothouse proved to be the most compelling part of the dive. Windows were missing and the pilothouse itself had been crumpled by the explosive collision with the lake floor. The CURV moved right up to the windows and tried to peer inside, but very little was revealed, only the wires from the radiotelephone, now suspended forever in the water. Still, anyone who had ever spent time on a lake freighter could imagine the horror felt by those in the pilothouse during the *Fitzgerald*'s final moments, when a wall of water crashed through the windows and Captain Ernest McSorley, First Mate Jack McCarthy, and the others realized their inevitable fate.

To the great relief of those watching on the *Woodrush,* no bodies appeared on the monitors—in the pilothouse or elsewhere.

"We hooked up the video to every TV on the ship," Jimmie Hobaugh recalled, "so the entire crew was sitting there, watching everything that's coming up. The CURV III would swim up to a porthole, and everyone would just stop breathing. You never knew what you were going to see. You didn't know if you were going to see someone staring back at you. We looked in every porthole we could find—and the only ones that were accessible were the ones on the bow—and we saw absolutely nothing. We saw a roll of blankets in one, but it wasn't big enough to be a person. We also looked all around the pilothouse. All the wiring—the telephone wires and lines and everything else—were sticking up in the back of the pilothouse, but we didn't see anybody. We assumed that the only people who came off the *Fitz* were the people in the pilothouse—the master, the mate, and probably a wheelsman and watchman. They were probably pushed right out the back of the pilothouse when the water came flying through."

The photographs and television footage served the function of positively identifying the *Edmund Fitzgerald,* but they failed to answer the major questions of how and why the ship had sunk. The *Fitz,* it seemed, was destined to become one of Lake Superior's mysteries.

The Marine Board members spent more than a year sifting through the CURV III's photos and footage, trying to match what they were seeing with the information they'd gathered during their formal hearings. The wreckage was so badly damaged that it was impossible to draw conclusions about whether the *Fitz* had suffered a hull fracture or broke on the surface. Because the area around the hatches was so badly mangled, it wasn't possible to determine what kind of topside damage might have led to water flooding into the ship. The best the Marine Board's report could do was offer an educated guess.

The board members had dramatically shifted their focus of attention when the CURV III photographs came in. The *Fitz,* they decided, could not have broken apart on the surface.

"The bow section is upright, but it absolutely plowed into the ground," C. S. Loosmore noted, years later. "How do you get that? Neither one of those pieces has transverse stability if it's floating around by itself. If the bow had broken off and capsized, it would have capsized just as the stern did. The likelihood of the bow's capsizing, coming down exactly upright, and plowing thirty feet into the ground is zero. They had to be going full-bore when they hit the ground, and the only way that can happen is if this seven-hundred-foot ship, in five hundred feet of water, is hurtling down."

The condition of the wreckage, Loosmore added, also gave the board reason to consider causes other than structural failure for the ship's sinking.

"You don't see the sharp, brittle failure that you'd expect to see if the hull broke on the top," he said of the *Fitzgerald*'s wreckage. "This is a ductile failure, and you wouldn't have had that from a hull bending problem on the surface.

More importantly, we had all this wreckage in between [the two large sections], just torn to smithereens, and almost all ductile."

The actual writing of the report became Loosmore's duty—"He was the youngest, so he got stuck with it," Jim Wilson joked—but the process of deciding what to write was a group decision.

"Loosmore would set it up and write it," Wilson remembered, "and we'd say, 'I agree with this' or 'I don't agree with that'—that kind of thing. We got together in Seattle and went over it, face to face. If you had something the others didn't agree with, you'd have to defend it. It would be like a debate. We'd thrash it out."

According to Wilson, there had been no disagreement strong enough to warrant the writing of a dissenting opinion. All four members recognized a lot rode on this report. It would establish the *Fitzgerald*'s story for maritime history and, quite possibly, serve as the official record in monetary settlements or even litigation. Ultimately, they also acknowledged it was a report based on deduction. They had a wealth of material to work with, but in the end, they were still missing important information needed to render indisputable judgment.

The report, issued on July 26, 1977, was hotly disputed as soon as it was published. At 120 typed pages it was by far the longest and most detailed Marine Casualty Report in Coast Guard history, and the board admitted from the onset that it was impossible to provide a proximate—or final, indisputable—cause for the loss of the *Edmund Fitzgerald*. The best it could do was present the evidence and, through process of elimination, arrive at the most probable cause of the ship's sinking.

In its remarks, the Marine Board described some of the difficulties it had encountered in assembling its findings in a timely fashion: "This casualty presented the Board unique investigative challenges which delayed the submission of the report. Since there were no survivors or witnesses to be questioned, the Board went to considerable lengths to examine the wreckage located soon after the casualty."

The introductory remarks went on to mention the CURV's underwater survey of the wreckage, the photographs and television images produced, and the sketches of the wreckage that the board had commissioned after the CURV explorations. The report had been further delayed so that it could take into account a survey conducted by the Canadian Hydrographic Service, in which the depths of the waters around Michipicoten and Caribou Islands were measured to determine whether the *Fitz* might have bottomed out on a shoal.

After issuing its preemptive strike against the inevitable critics of the timeliness of its report, the Marine Board summarized its long-awaited findings in a few succinct sentences.

"The most probable cause of the sinking," the report offered, "was the loss of buoyancy resulting from massive flooding of the cargo hold. The flooding most likely took place through ineffective hatch closures. As the boarding seas rolled over the spar deck, the flooding was probably concentrated forward. The vessel dove into a wall of water and never recovered, with the breaking up of the ship occurring as it plunged or as the ship struck the bottom. The sinking was so rapid and unexpected that no one was able to successfully abandon ship."

The Coast Guard seemed resigned to the idea that the report would be controversial. The extensive media coverage, coupled with the enormous success of Gordon Lightfoot's song "The Wreck of the *Edmund Fitzgerald*," made the *Fitz* the most celebrated shipwreck story in Great Lakes history—the *Titanic* of the Great Lakes, as it was often called. In the more than a year and a half that had passed between the *Fitzgerald*'s sinking and the release of the Marine Board report, every shipwreck aficionado, former Great Lakes captain, amateur maritime sleuth, and news reporter seemed to have formed an opinion about what brought the big ship down, and there was no way that the Coast Guard's findings were going to satisfy them all. The board had considered several of the popular theories, and its report was careful not to entirely dismiss any of them.

The report reflected the Marine Board's countless hours of painstaking research and cautious reconstruction of the *Fitzgerald*'s final voyage. Entire sections were devoted to the ship's physical properties and history; the weather system that began in the Southwest and worked its way northeast until it was stationed over Lake Superior; the ship's last voyage, from its loading in Superior to its disappearance near Whitefish Point; the search efforts and the recovery of the *Fitzgerald*'s effects; and the CURV's underwater survey. The report included a series of charts and tables, a complete listing of the ship's officers and crew members, drawings of the *Fitz* and the underwater wreckage, and a rough sketch of the hydrographic survey around Caribou Island.

In its reconstruction, the Marine Board focused strongly on the conversations between Captains McSorley and Cooper, particularly the one during which McSorley had informed Cooper that the *Fitzgerald* had lost a fence rail and two vents and had developed a list. To that point, the *Fitz* had been running smoothly, with no reports of damage. The loss of the ship's radar, along with the *Fitz*'s slowing down to allow the *Anderson* to close the distance between the two ships, was also significant, especially since no formal track line charts of the two vessels' routes had been kept.

The report's expanded explanation of the accident followed basic logic from the evidence and testimony given during the hearings. The *Fitz* had departed Superior under good sailing conditions and had followed the usual shipping route, but, upon encountering deteriorating weather, Captain McSorley had changed course to a safer northern route. The ship continued without any reported difficulties until around 3:30 on the afternoon of November 10, when McSorley called the *Arthur Anderson* and reported the initial damage. The list had left the *Fitz* vulnerable to increasingly high seas, which eventually rushed over its decks and flooded the cargo hold through the hatch covers. McSorley, unaware of the extent of the flooding in his hold, continued on toward Whitefish Bay, even as the *Fitz* sank slowly, almost unnoticeably, into the water, until one or more massive waves pushed its bow beneath the surface and initiated a nosedive.

The Marine Board explained in great detail how it reached its conclusions. Rather than cite any single factor as decisive in the ship's sinking, the board argued that a series of events or situations combined to sink the *Fitz*.

For openers, there was the cargo itself—or, more accurately, the *size* of the load the *Fitzgerald* was carrying. In comparison with its previous downbound runs with taconite cargo, there was nothing unusual about the cargo, the tonnage, or the way the cargo was loaded. The November 9–10 trip was, in every respect, average and legal. What interested the Marine Board was the current winter load line regulations, which might have been a factor in the ship's loss.

The load line markings on the side of a ship indicated the depth to which the vessel might permissibly settle in the water when fully loaded. As a rule, ships were required to ride higher in the water as the shipping season latened, mainly to provide more freeboard when the lakes grew more unpredictable and choppy in the late fall and winter.

Big, powerful ships like the *Fitzgerald,* seemingly capable of handling any weather and sailing conditions, gave the U.S. and Canadian governments reason to reconsider and modify the old load line requirements, and on three occasions (1969, 1971, 1973) between the time the *Fitzgerald* was built in 1958 and when it sank, the load lines were altered, allowing ships like the *Fitzgerald* to take heavier cargos (at the cost of decreasing freeboard) later in the season. The load line alterations might have contributed to the *Fitzgerald*'s demise.

The Marine Board found this noteworthy: "Not only did the reduction in minimum required freeboard significantly reduce the vessel's buoyancy, but it resulted in a significantly increased frequency and force of boarding seas in the storm FITZGERALD encountered on 10 November. This, in turn, resulted in an increased quantity of water flooding through loosely dogged hatches and through openings from topside damage."

The topside damage received a good deal of attention in the report and would be a major focal point in future disputes over the cause of the sinking. The board concluded that the loss of the fence rail and two vents would not have been enough to sink the ship. The lost vents would have permitted water to enter the *Fitzgerald*'s ballast tanks, producing a list, and by all indications, this is what Captain McSorley believed to have happened. Not realizing the extent of the damage to his ship and the amount of water entering the *Fitz,* McSorley had only two of the ship's six ballast pumps working, most likely in the areas flooding from the lost vents.

Assuming the list had developed as a result of the topside damage reported by McSorley, the Marine Board looked for probable causes of the damage. To the amazement of the report's future critics, it decided that the damage must have been caused by "the vessel striking a floating object which was then brought aboard in the heavy seas." (The board did not specify or speculate as to what that heavy object might have been.) The *Fitz,* the report noted, had disappeared into a snowstorm about a half hour before the damage was reported, and the board reasoned that the reduced visibility, along with its disabled radar, might have hampered the *Fitzgerald*'s crew in seeing and avoiding the object. This object could have been responsible for additional unseen problems, such as damage to hatch combings near the front of the ship. If this were the case, the *Fitz* would have taken on more water than anyone was aware of.

These were the most controversial findings in the report. The loss of the fence rail indicated a major blow to the *Fitzgerald:* it would have taken a very large, powerful object—or the hogging of the ship—to break a sturdy fence rail. The Marine Board allowed that hogging or grounding was possible, but ultimately ruled it out. In trying to establish the *Fitzgerald*'s course, the board decided that it had passed safely around the treacherous shoals near Caribou and Michipicoten Islands, the most likely locations for groundings. The board also considered the idea that an unidentified object might have broken loose from the *Fitzgerald*'s deck and struck the railing and vents, but the only objects big and heavy enough to do such damage were hatch covers, the hatch cover crane, or the spare propeller blade. "If such extensive damage had occurred," the board decided, "a seasoned Master would have reported it. Such a report was not received."

The nonwatertight bulkheads might have also contributed to the *Fitzgerald*'s demise. The cargo hold was fitted with screen bulkheads dividing the load into thirds, and since these bulkheads were not watertight, any water flooding into the cargo hold would move freely from one compartment to another, affecting the ship's trim. This would have been especially hazardous near the end of the *Fitzgerald*'s run, when boarding water was pushing the bow deeper into the water. The water in the cargo hold would have moved forward in the direction of the downward-tilting ship, further decreasing buoyancy near the bow.

The board relied on its timeline of the *Fitzgerald*'s final voyage to bolster its theory of faulty hatch closures. Almost four hours passed between the first reports of damage and the probable time of the *Fitzgerald*'s sinking, and if the *Fitz* had lost one or more hatch covers, or had sustained a serious stress fracture near the Six

Fathom Shoal, it wouldn't have lasted as long as it did. Yet the ship sank very slowly, gradually slipping lower in the water until it eventually lost all buoyancy.

To support its theory, the Marine Board examined the *Fitzgerald*'s system of hatch covers, gaskets, combings, and clamps, although the report's conclusions were based more on deduction than on hard evidence. The wreckage provided little to go by. Hatch covers were strewn all over the place, and the overall damage to the *Fitzgerald*'s spar deck was so extensive that the board was unable to render a definitive judgment about the state of the hatches prior to the ship's sinking. However, the *Fitzgerald*'s most recent spar deck inspection, conducted ten days before, reported cracks and gouges around the combings of four hatches. The inspectors had deemed the damage minor, but the board wasn't so certain. There were no surefire ways of assurately assessing how deeply such damage would have affected the gasket seals in the hatch openings, but the Marine Board felt that, for one reason or another, the *Fitzgerald*'s weathertight integrity had been compromised.

"It is concluded," the report stated, "that the system of cargo hatch combings, gaskets, covers, and clamps which was installed on FITZGERALD and the manner in which the system was maintained did not provide an effective means of preventing penetration of water into the ship in any condition, as required by Coast Guard regulations."

The condition of the hatch clamps on the wreckage puzzled the board, just as it would challenge shipwreck sleuths for years to come. The CURV III survey had indicated that "only a few" of the *Fitzgerald*'s hatch clamps were damaged—a curious situation, to say the least. If all the hatch clamps had been properly fastened and secured, one would expect more to have been damaged when the hatch covers were ripped away by escaping air as the ship sank.

"In the opinion of the Marine Board, if the clamps had been properly fastened, any damage, disruption or dislocation of the hatch covers would have resulted in damage to or distortion of the clamps," the report declared. "It is concluded that these [damaged] clamps were the only ones, of those seen, which were properly fastened to the covers and that there were too few of these and too many unfastened or loosely fastened clamps to provide an effective closure of the hatches."

This was the most troubling statement in the entire report, if one subscribed to the hatch cover theory. Captain Ernest McSorley was aware of the weather forecast when the *Fitz* pulled away from the Superior harbor; knowing that there was rough sailing ahead, he should have demanded that every single hatch cover clamp be properly applied and adjusted. Anything less would have placed his vessel in jeopardy.

If, indeed, all the clamps were fastened down, were they in such a state that they couldn't be adjusted to make the hatches watertight?

Other questions arose from the board's hatch closure theory. The biggest one, perhaps, focused on the volume of water that could leak through the hatches if the covers were fastened down but not watertight. Could enough seep through—enough to sink a ship—in the time the *Fitz* was on the lake? If so, wouldn't someone have noticed it?

To test the theory, C. S. Loosmore constructed a model of a hatch combing, complete with a gasket, clamps, and cover. He then measured the flow of water through the slightest, quarter-inch gap between the cover and combing, when water covered the hatch. The results were telling—and surprising.

"It was a simple matter of some calculations to determine what the flow rate was, and once I knew the flow rate and the period of time [the water was entering the hatch], I could figure how much water came in. I calculated that if only something like one-third of the total number of openings was actually letting in water, the *Fitzgerald* would have lost five-and-a-half to six feet of freeboard by the time it turned and headed south at one or two o'clock in the afternoon on November 10. That's totally consistent with what was reported."

The *Fitzgerald* was not equipped with a sounding tube or other device to measure the presence or amount of water in its hold, and given the nature of the storm, it would have been exceedingly difficult, if not impossible, to reach the cargo hold from the access hatches on the spar deck. The Marine Board believed it would have been impossible to assess the flooding in the cargo hold until the water had reached the top of the taconite itself.

"Who would have noticed it?" C. S. Loosmore wondered, when questioned about it long after the report was issued. "You've got the pilothouse in front, the engine in the back, and these tunnels in between. There is no direct access or flow-reading system—no way of knowing how much water's in the cargo hold. There's *always* some water in there. This boat's bouncing around. People aren't walking around and peeking into a hatch. There's no draft-reading system, either, nothing that determines if a vessel's lost any freeboard."

The gradual loss of freeboard, Loosmore contended, might have been a reason for McSorley's reporting larger waves than were being reported elsewhere.

"Nobody was reporting waves of the same stature that the *Fitzgerald* ran into," Loosmore observed, "and the reason is poor old McSorley was standing closer to the water than he'd been standing over the last thirty years."

The board rested its hatch-cover case on the belief that the cargo hold had flooded over a long period of time, perhaps beginning as far back as the *Fitzgerald*'s earliest encounter with the storm. At first, water could have entered the hold in relatively small amounts, but as the storm intensified and the *Fitz* had to contend with massive waves sweeping over the spar deck, the volume of water entering the cargo hold would have increased exponentially. This, along with water boarding the ship as the result of the topside damage, led to the end.

The Marine Board examined other possible causes for the ship's listing and sinking, most notably the possibility of the *Fitzgerald*'s grounding on a shoal; suffering a stress fracture that might have led to serious flooding outside the ship's hold; or breaking apart on the surface before it sank. Any of the three alternatives was possible, but the board ultimately dismissed them.

"The topside damage and list could have been caused by a light grounding or near grounding on the shoals north of Caribou Island," the report conceded. "Although their testimony is not fully consistent, both the Master and the Watch Officer on ANDERSON indicated that FITZGERALD passed within a few miles of Caribou Island and that they had a conversation concerning the closeness of FITZGERALD to the shoals of the island."

As James Wilson later explained, the board just couldn't accept the argument that the *Fitz* had struck a shoal and suffered a fatal fracture below the waterline.

"When we looked at the ship on the bottom," he said, "the first thing we noticed was that the after section was inverted. The fact that the stern was inverted turned out to be better luck than if it had been the other way around, because we could see that the stern was undamaged. If she had hit something, why didn't it tear into the after section? The after section of the ship was riding lower than the forward."

The board also accepted the testimony of a naval architect, William Cleary, testimony about how the *Fitzgerald* would have traveled in the event that it had actually touched bottom in shallow water.

"If she had hit something and it hadn't penetrated the cargo hold," Wilson said, "she makes it to Whitefish Bay. If it penetrates the cargo hold, she goes down fast."

After presenting its findings, the Marine Board drew its final conclusions and made recommendations about how this kind of disaster might be prevented in the future. While absolving everyone of guilt due to negligence, dereliction of duty, or inappropriate behavior, the board, troubled by some of the testimony, still listed a number of measures that could be taken to improve Great Lakes shipping and the safety of the big ore carriers. The recommendations focused on ways of improving a ship's watertight integrity, above and below the hatch openings, as well as improving the ways a ship could be abandoned in high seas.

Perhaps, as James Wilson noted in retrospect, thirty years after the loss, there was a terrible irony to the tragedy that the Marine Board certainly couldn't state in its report, and that maritime historians might find difficult to believe: the twenty-nine men on the *Fitzgerald* might have been lost *because the ship was so modern and strong*. Lifesaving equipment, as well as lifeboat and life raft drills, weren't high-priority items in an industry in which the loss of a powerful ship seemed inconceivable.

"A long time ago, if a ship sank the sailors had a pretty good chance of survival," Wilson noted. "Why? Because they'd all been in a shipwreck before. They had a lot of experience. I don't think it's possible now, because they're not worried about it. You don't have the sinkings. You have a false sense of security. You're really in a quandary because, as it gets safer, it becomes a higher risk."

C. S. Loosmore, like Wilson, remained adamant in his belief that the *Fitz* was brought down by water entering its hold through its hatch covers, but he differed from the report on one significant point.

"If you look at the underwater pictures that we took of the wreckage," he said, referring to the CURV photographs, "you can find hatch combings, and along those hatch combings you will see those clamps—the C-clamps. You'll find one of those clamps hanging down undamaged, and then you'll see another one hanging down undamaged, and then you'll see one just torn apart. I believe that the only way that could have occurred would have been if those undamaged clamps were not torqued down. They probably were not even flipped up and pushed down into the little buttons. I think the *Fitzgerald* sank because they didn't put the hatch clamps down. My opinion of what sank the *Fitzgerald* and the conclusions of the board are not the same."

The problem, Loosmore explained, building on James Wilson's earlier speculations, might have been the sense of security that comes from spending so many uneventful years on the lakes. Loosmore recalled a conversation—ironically, with Wilson—that brought the idea into focus for him. While investigating the loss of the *Fitz,* Loosmore and Wilson rode on an ore carrier from Detroit to the Soo Locks. The seas, Loosmore noted, were calm. At one point during the trip, while the two board members were standing in the pilothouse, Loosmore directed Wilson's attention to the chart table behind the navigation station.

"Where's the edge on the chart table?" he asked Wilson. On saltwater vessels, the chart tables have a rim around their edges to keep objects from sliding or rolling off in heavy seas.

"You don't need it," Wilson responded.

"What do you do when the ship rolls? Doesn't your pencil jump off?"

"The ship doesn't roll," Wilson said.

Wilson, a lifetime veteran of Great Lakes shipping and inspection, had been through a lot, and he felt safe on the massive vessels that hauled cargo from port to port in some pretty inclement weather. The Great Lakes could be treacherous, but they weren't the South Pacific or the North Atlantic. Such sentiments, Loosmore felt, were the rule rather than the exception.

The captain and crew on the *Fitz* were highly experienced, confident in their ship's capabilities. Securing every single clamp on every single hatch cover was a tedious, time-consuming process, and with the *Fitzgerald*'s track record, there was no reason to suspect that the ship couldn't travel down the lake, in the typical storm the National Weather Service was predicting at the time of the ship's departure from Superior, with only some of the clamps fastened down.

"They knew they had all those hatch clamps, but they didn't need them," Loosmore stated, rejecting the speculation that McSorley might have been trying to save overtime expenses by ordering only some of the clamps fastened down. "I think they were complacent. They had done this kind of thing with no damage, no problem at all, for years and years."

The first formal dissent arrived in September at the offices of the National Transportation Safety Board in Washington, D.C., in the form of a long letter by Paul E. Trimble, president of the Lake Carriers' Association.

"The lake shipping industry, proud of its safety record through the years, completely rejects the Coast Guard theoretical cause of the FITZGERALD sinking," Trimble wrote. The Lake Carriers' Association, representing fifteen shipping firms with 135 vessels working on the Great Lakes, disputed the Coast Guard's theory of ineffective hatch covers, arguing that it was much more probable that the flooding inside the *Fitzgerald* had occurred as the result of the ship's grounding somewhere near the Six Fathom Shoal.

"The lake shipping industry and its professional naval architect advisors can find NOTHING in the available factors to support the Coast Guard's thesis that the sinking resulted from poor hatch cover procedures," Trimble went on. "We can't identify one such factor, whereas, such factors do support shoaling as the cause of the sinking."

Cynics might have agued that Trimble and his group had an interest in rejecting the Marine Board's report, but Trimble was a former vice admiral of the Coast Guard and he presented a compelling case. The hatch covers and clamps currently used in the shipping industry, Trimble pointed out, were vastly superior to those used in the past, and it would have been wrong for the Marine Board to assume that the *Fitzgerald*'s crew had been sloppy in securing them. The board had concluded that water had entered the *Fitzgerald*'s hold over a long period of time, under deteriorating weather conditions; but, using the Marine Board's own timeline, the Lake Carriers' Association argued that the *Fitz* had encountered the worst of the weather during only a small portion of its journey. Further, Captain McSorley hadn't mentioned any problems with hatch cover damage or loss during his conversations with the *Anderson* or other ships.

It was much more likely, Trimble argued, that the *Fitzgerald* had water flooding into its ballast tanks as the result of a hull fracture. McSorley had contacted the *Anderson* shortly after passing through the Six Fathom Shoal area, reporting that he had a fence rail down, he'd lost two vents, and the *Fitz* had developed a list. The *Fitz* could easily have handled water entering the ballast tanks through the eight-inch vent openings, so the list had to have originated from another source.

"Within the time frame involved," Trimble suggested, "such a list can be readily explained by holing of the vessel's ballast tanks caused by striking Six Fathom Shoal."

Once again, Trimble enlisted the Marine Board's own report to bolster his claim. According to the report, no course for the *Fitzgerald* had been charted. it was known that the *Fitz* had passed within a short distance of the shoal—closer, Captain Bernie Cooper had testified, than he wanted his ship to be—and the hydrographic survey of the area conducted by the Canadian Hydrographic Service had revealed a shoal even shallower than six fathoms in the area.

"This verified shoal," Trimble wrote, "was in the track of the FITZGERALD, as observed by the ANDERSON, thus making shoaling even more certain as the start of the fateful events leading to the sinking."

In the opinion of the Lake Carriers' Association, the *Fitz* had suffered a hull fracture below the waterline—a fracture that, in all likelihood, worsened when the *Fitzgerald*'s hull was working in heavy seas. The *Fitz* sank lower and lower in the water, until the bow was driven beneath the lake's surface by huge waves washing over its decks.

It was a persuasive argument—certainly as valid as the Marine Board's conclusions—and it would become the most accepted alternative to the official report. The Lake Carriers' Association letter exemplified the passion with which the *Fitzgerald*'s sinking would be debated in the future, as well as the frustrating near certainty that a final answer would never come. As in so many arguments, facts could be manipulated or ignored to support a cause. In dismissing the theory that the hatch covers were at fault, the Lake Carriers' Association was willing to ignore convincing evidence that at least one hatch cover might have been lost while the *Fitzgerald* was still on the lake and heading for Whitefish Bay. In addition, the letter waved off the notion that the hatch covers might not have been properly closed and secured, even though Trimble was willing to concede that this practice "might have been observed on one or more vessels in other than heavy weather conditions."

If nothing else, the Lake Carriers' Association letter challenged the National Transportation Safety Board to reexamine the Marine Board's report and draw its own conclusions. In fact, an NTSB representative had attended some of the Marine Board's hearings shortly after the loss of the *Fitzgerald* and, at the time of Paul Trimble's letter, the NTSB was in the process of putting together a lengthy report of its own.

Released on May 4,1978, the NTSB report managed to support *and* reject the earlier Coast Guard findings. Both reports argued that the *Fitzgerald* sank as the result of massive flooding of its cargo hold, but the NTSB disagreed with the Marine Board concerning how that flooding had occurred.

"The probable cause of this accident was the sudden massive flooding of the cargo hold due to the collapse of one or more hatch covers," wrote James B. King, the chairman of the NTSB panel. "Before the hatch covers collapsed, flooding into the ballast tanks and tunnel through topside damage and flooding into cargo hold through non-weathertight hatch covers caused a reduction of freeboard and a list. The hydrostatic and hydrodynamic forces imposed by heavy boarding seas at this reduced freeboard and with the list caused the hatch covers to collapse."

The four-member NTSB panel had before it the same evidence, testimony, photographs, and video evidence used by the Marine Board's panel, and, in general, its report was very similar to the Marine Board's. The accounts of the *Fitzgerald*'s final voyage, the weather and conditions on Lake Superior, and the search efforts were almost identical. The NTSB, like the Lake Carriers' Association, had a hard time accepting the Marine Board's conclusion that massive flooding of the cargo hold was possible only through poorly secured or faulty hatch covers, even with the *Fitzgerald*'s loss of freeboard and waves washing over the decks. The flooding, the NTSB believed, had to be more sudden and catastrophic.

"The hatch cover failure would have been severe enough to allow rapid massive flooding of the cargo hold," the NTSB report declared. "Since there were no watertight bulkheads within the cargo hold, the flooding water would have progressed throughout the hold in minutes, causing the vessel to sink bow first to the bottom of the lake. Upon impact with the bottom, the midship portion disintegrated and the stern section rolled over, coming to rest upside down."

This scenario, like the others, could neither be proved nor refuted. The *Fitzgerald*'s hatch covers were in such a state that it was impossible to make a definitive judgment based on them alone. A couple had fallen inside hatch openings, but most were missing or were found in the debris apart from the wreckage. The Number 1 hatch combing was badly damaged, which could have happened when a hatch was blown off or washed away, or when the *Fitzgerald* struck the lake floor. Other combings were damaged, but to a much lesser extent. Since the Number 1 hatch was closest to the front of the ship, it stood to reason that the loss of that hatch cover—and subsequent flooding—would have most rapidly pushed the bow of the *Fitzgerald* deeper into the water.

Finally, there was the conversation between Ernest McSorley and Captain Cedric Woodard of the *Avafors,* during which McSorley had shouted, "Don't allow nobody on deck" to another *Fitzgerald* crewman. That, along with the unusual tone that Woodard detected in McSorley's voice, made one wonder what, exactly, was happening on the *Fitzgerald,* particularly on its spar deck. Woodard thought he'd heard McSorley shouting something unintelligible about a vent, but was it also possible that one or more hatch covers might have worked loose at that point?

The NTSB report featured a wrinkle—a dissenting opinion—that only intensified the debate. In his dissenting opinion, Philip A. Hogue agreed with the Lake Carriers' Association's conclusion that the *Fitzgerald* had probably grounded on the Six Fathom Shoal.

"The most probable cause of the sinking of the SS EDMUND FITZGERALD," Hogue wrote, "was a shoaling which first generated a list, the loss of two air vents, and a massive flooding of the cargo hold resulted in a total loss of buoyancy from which, diving into a wall of water, the FITZGERALD never recovered."

In building his case, Hogue quoted the Marine Board report extensively, agreeing that the flooding of the cargo hold had taken place over a period of hours, and that Captain McSorley probably never fully understood the peril he was in. Hogue also agreed with the NTSB majority opinion that faulty hatch covers were not, in themselves, sufficient to have caused the flooding that overwhelmed the *Fitzgerald*. And, like the Lake Carriers' Association, he referred to Bernie Cooper when he presented his case for shoaling.

"On p. 2140 [of the Marine Board's testimony transcripts], Captain Cooper stated, 'I have never known a ship to lose a fence in a seaway,'" Hogue wrote. "'The only solution I can have to a fence rail breaking is—you can't break one by sagging a ship, but you would have to bend the ship, hog it up the middle, to put such a tension on the fence rail that you would break it.'"

Hogue saw the loss of the fence rail as a key to the mystery of the *Fitzgerald*'s sinking. If the *Fitz* had touched down on a shoal near Michipicoten or Caribou Island, it might have hogged and lost its fence rail. More significantly, the hogging might have caused a hull fracture, which would have explained the list that the *Fitzgerald* so quickly developed.

Although he didn't go into detail about the *Fitzgerald*'s ballast pumps, Hogue seemed to believe that the pumps, each capable of pumping out 7,000 gallons of water per minute, might have delayed the inevitable loss of buoyancy for a few hours, even if they could not remove water from the cargo hold itself. In Hogue's scenario, the *Fitz* limped along, taking in more water than it pumped out, listing significantly and taking on quartering seas until it could finally take no more. Hit by a massive wave that drove the bow below the surface, the *Fitzgerald* plunged to the bottom of the lake.

The argument that the *Fitzgerald* sank as the result of structural failure on the surface did not go away. Those subscribing to the idea that the *Fitz* broke apart on the surface compared the sinking to the earlier losses of the *Carl D. Bradley* and *Daniel J. Morrell*. The two ships had been older vessels, constructed out of metals less durable than the steel used on the *Fitz,* but what if the *Fitz* was already weakened by problems with its hull before it left port on November 9, 1975? Could the ship, after being battered for hours by high seas that worked its hull more strenuously than ever, have suffered a massive structural failure and, breaking in two on the surface, sunk so quickly that the crew had no time to react and abandon ship?

A number of witnesses, including Captain Bernie Cooper, had stated that they believed that the *Fitz* holed somewhere near the Six Fathom Shoal, and the Marine Board had considered this before rendering its final decision. The board had also heard testimony from hull inspectors and experts on ship construction. The most damning testimony, however, was the testimony that *wasn't* given before the board—a statement that might not even have been heard had this witness not become upset by the way Oglebay Norton seemed to be dragging its feet in offering compensation to the families of the victims.

George H. (Red) Burgner had worked as a steward on the *Fitzgerald* between 1966 and 1975, and on Oglebay Norton vessels for fourteen years before that. In addition to working on the *Fitz* during the shipping season, Burgner, a resident of Superior, worked as a ship watcher on the *Fitzgerald* during the winters between 1966 and 1973, when the ship laid up for the winter at the Fraser Shipyards in his hometown. Although Burgner had worked on the *Fitz* in 1975, bone spurs on his heel had sidelined him later in the season.

On December 13, 1977, Burgner gave a sworn statement in Minneapolis to the law firm of DeParcq, Perl, Hunegs, & Rudquist, which was representing the families of two of the lost crewmen, Blaine Wilhelm and Allen Kalmon. He offered his insights and opinions on a wide variety of *Fitzgerald*-related topics, including the abilities of Ernest McSorley and Jack McCarthy, and the way the ship was maintained. Those disputing Burgner's testimony tried to present him as a disgruntled employee, or as trying to cash in on all the attention going in the *Fitzgerald*'s direction, but, according to Burgner, Oglebay Norton didn't want him testifying in front of the Marine Board of Investigation.

"Don't say anything to anybody," Burgner claimed he was told by company officials at the time of the Marine Board hearings. "We don't want you up here. We don't even want your name mentioned."

In his deposition, Burgner said he had called Oglebay Norton's vessel personnel manager shortly after the sinking, to tell them what he knew about the *Fitzgerald*'s maintenance history and the ship's condition at the time of the disaster. After ordering him not to speak to anyone about what he knew, the company official asked Burgner (who had recently retired to Texas) to meet him at a hotel in Dallas. Burgner agreed.

In Dallas, Burgner met with an Oglebay Norton attorney and the vessel personnel manager. He told them that he believed the *Fitzgerald* had a loose keel, and that that might have led to structural failure and caused the sinking. Once again, he was asked to keep his opinions to himself.

"It's a good place for you down in Texas," they told him. "If nobody brings your name up, we're not gonna mention it, either. And if you get any contacts from anybody, don't say anything to them until you contact us first."

Burgner testified that his main concern was for the families of the *Fitzgerald*'s lost crewmen. He'd personally known a number of the men, and if Oglebay Norton took care of their families, he was willing to keep his suspicions to himself.

"They said they'd do it, and I went home figuring that that's what they were going to do," he testified.

Oglebay Norton had reason to hope Burgner wouldn't testify at the hearings. Within days of the sinking, Burgner contacted Irmengard Kalmon, the wife of Allen Kalmon, and told her that he knew what had really caused the *Fitzgerald* to sink. Burgner believed the *Fitz* had been poorly maintained, and had sunk as the result of structural failure brought on by a weakened keel. This condition, Burgner said, was known to McSorley and others.

Burgner kept his secret for two years, until he learned that Mrs. Kalmon hadn't been given her claim for damages. When one of Mrs. Kalmon's lawyers phoned, Burgner agreed to meet him and tell him what he knew. When Oglebay Norton learned of this development, a company attorney contacted him and asked him to refrain from talking to the other lawyer. Burgner, who was supplementing his income by delivering trailers, was trying to work out a time when he'd be off the road and free to talk to Mrs. Kalmon's attorney.

"Go ahead and deliver trailers," the Oglebay Norton attorney advised him. "Don't even wait for him." When Burgner objected, the company attorney backed off. "Let him go ahead and ask you a few questions, and when he does, call us. [But] if you're gonna take off, we'd suggest that you just take your trailer and go."

The Minnesota attorney representing Mrs. Kalmon corroborated Burgner's story. "The steamship company was really worried about this guy," the attorney said. "They were frantically trying to find him. They called his wife. They called motels along the way."

Burgner met with Mrs. Kalmon's attorney, and a short time later, he was flown to Minnesota to videotape his testimony.

Burgner's deposition represented by far the most critical statement issued to that point on the events leading to the accident. Burgner testified favorably about McSorley and McCarthy's knowledge and abilities, but he also made it clear that he felt McSorley was a company man who "beat hell" out of the *Fitzgerald* in nasty weather in order to deliver his cargo on schedule. Not only did McSorley rarely anchor his ship and wait out a storm; he rarely slowed down in heavy weather, thus exposing his ship to greater pounding from the seas. Comparing McSorley to his predecessor, Peter Pulcer, Burgner character-ized McSorley as not inclined to push his crew to do proper routine mainte-nance, whereas Pulcer always insisted on the maintenance regardless of his crew's feelings.

"Captain Pulcer pushed his mates," Burgner testified. "[If] something had to be done, he got the mates and they got the crew to do it. McSorley was not that way."

McSorley, Burgner claimed, would delegate authority to his mates when routine repairs were required, but he wasn't inclined to follow up and see that the work was done. "If they did it, all well and good," Burgner said. "If they didn't do it, he used to gripe about it, but not to the persons that he should have."

This attitude, Burgner insisted, led to low morale among the crew.

Burgner testified at length about what he'd seen below the *Fitzgerald*'s decks and why he felt the keel had been weakened as a result of poor repairs or maintenance. The ship, he claimed, had never responded well to heavy seas after the load line requirements had been changed. Like other witnesses testifying before the Marine Board, Burgner believed that the *Fitz* had too much action in heavy seas, and he corroborated the previous testimony that McSorley wasn't comfortable with it.

"She had an awful lot of movement to her or action to her," Burgner said of the *Fitz*. "To all of us on the ship at the time, that wasn't ordinary."

Burgner went on to say that he'd discussed the matter with McSorley and that McSorley was openly concerned about the way the *Fitz* worked in nasty weather.

"He didn't make a secret of it," Burgner testified. "He was scared of it. Don't get me wrong, McSorley was a good skipper. In a sense, he could handle the ship. But he was scared of it. Captain Pulcer was also a good skipper. He handled it in a different way, but he wasn't scared of it."

The *Fitzgerald*'s crew, Burgner maintained, would complain about how the *Fitz* was "just falling apart"—sometimes in the mess hall when Captain McSorley was within earshot. One morning in 1975, Burgner overheard a conversation between McSorley and Ransom Cundy, William Spengler, and Eugene O'Brien, during which the three crewmen expressed concern that hull plates were coming loose from the *Fitzgerald*'s keel. The three had been scraping mud out of one of the ship's tunnels, and they had noticed that they could jam a shovel between the keel and some of the ship's plates.

According to Burgner, McSorley said he didn't care. "All this son of a bitch has got to do is stay together one more year," McSorley supposedly said. "After that, I don't give a shit what happens to it."

Shocking as it was, Burgner's testimony might have been dismissed as the words of a malcontent eager to make his reputation at the expense of another, or as someone who just didn't care for McSorley. Naysayers were quick enough to write him off as such, and at the Marine Board hearings, witnesses had lined up, one by one, to testify about McSorley's competence as the *Fitzgerald*'s master. However, Burgner's story about the damage to the *Fitzgerald*'s hull and the repairs to it checked out, at least to some extent. Obviously, with the *Fitz* in wreckage, there was no way to verify Burgner's claims, but the ship's repair records indicated that work had been done on the problem areas he cited.

Whether the repairs, mostly patches welded to the shell plating, were sufficient to ensure the *Fitzgerald*'s safety depended upon whom you were talking to. Such repairs were hardly out of the ordinary, and as long as a ship passed inspections and didn't experience any problems with leakage around the repairs, they were generally considered sufficient. Burgner took exception to this idea. If the keel—the backbone of a ship—worked loose from the plates, the strength of the ship's hull could be compromised, especially during bad weather, when the vessel was taking a beating in heavy seas. The welds could crack from the tension.

Burgner's testimony supplied plenty of ammunition to those who believed that the *Fitzgerald* broke suddenly on the surface. According to this argument, the *Fitz*, twisting in the massive waves, suffered the same effect as a piece of wire that has been bent, straightened out, and re-bent until it breaks. The weakened areas of the *Fitz* would have suffered a widening of the cracks, allowing water to enter the ship's tunnels or tanks to such an extent that it couldn't be pumped out. In the meantime, additional stress weakened the hull even more until, in one catastrophic moment, the *Fitz* split apart and sank.

So, by the end of 1977, a handful of credible theories, based on strong evidence and careful consideration of expert testimony, had been delivered to the public.

Other theories would follow, but for the time being, these would stoke the debates over the causes of the *Edmund Fitzgerald*'s demise.

Still, far too many questions remained. The families of the victims needed closure, even as maritime historians and enthusiasts pondered the different theories, never quite satisfied with the published reports.

The public wasn't finished with the *Edmund Fitzgerald*—not by any stretch of the imagination.

CHAPTER SIX

TARNISHED GRAVESITE

THE MYSTERIOUS CIRCUMSTANCES SURROUNDING THE LOSS OF THE *Edmund Fitzgerald,* coupled with the enormous success of Gordon Lightfoot's musical account, created a snowball effect that surprised everyone connected to the ship. For the families and friends of those lost, private grief became a source of public inquiry. For Bernie Cooper, Don Erickson, Jimmie Hobaugh, and others, whom fate had involved in the *Fitzgerald* story, passing time only reminded them that they were trapped in history, bound to a tragedy that would shadow them for the rest of their lives. Even Gordon Lightfoot, who'd written his song as a tribute to fallen sailors, was surprised by the way "The Wreck of the *Edmund Fitzgerald*" redefined his career. It was now the centerpiece of every concert, the song he would be remembered for. Rather than fade from memory, like so many shipwreck tragedies of the past, the *Edmund Fitzgerald*'s story gained momentum in the years following the loss of the ship and its crew.

The first written accounts of the *Fitzgerald*'s final voyage were now being published, and they helped stoke the public's interest. Robert E. Lee, the curator of the Dossin Great Lakes Museum in Detroit, and the man responsible for calling

Father Richard Ingalls with the news of the *Fitzgerald*'s loss, published first, with *Edmund Fitzgerald 1957–1975,* in 1977. The forty-eight-page book, packed with photos, paintings, drawings, and maps, offered an outstanding look at the ship's background, though it was probably too technical for casual readers. Lee's account of the *Fitzgerald*'s final trip and sinking drew heavily on the Marine Board report, as did Frederick Stonehouse's *The Wreck of the Edmund Fitzgerald,* published later that same year.

Stonehouse, a highly regarded Great Lakes historian and a resident of Marquette, Michigan, had already published several books about Lake Superior shipwrecks; he had had no intention of writing a book about the *Fitz* until the growing mass of information about the disaster convinced him that "there was more to the loss of the *Fitzgerald* than I had at first believed." His book, revised and updated on a number of occasions in years to come, was greatly opinionated, presenting a no-holds-barred criticism of the Coast Guard's search-and-rescue mission. More reader-friendly than the Lee book, *The Wreck of the Edmund Fitzgerald* included portions of the Marine Board and National Transportation Safety Board reports, as well as Paul Trimble's letter of rebuttal.

Other writers included *Fitzgerald* chapters or sections in their books, each with a slightly different approach. Julius F. Wolff's encyclopedic *Lake Superior Shipwrecks* (1979), addressed almost every known shipwreck on the lake since the nineteenth century. His coverage of the *Fitzgerald* included the first published account of Red Burgner's negative remarks about Ernest McSorley and the maintenance of the *Fitz,* setting off another round of debates over the causes of the catastrophe, Burgner's credibility, and the wisdom of sullying Ernest McSorley's reputation as a seaman.

Perhaps the most ambitious project of all, undertaken by the journalist Robert J. Hemming, attempted to reconstruct the conversations that took place on the *Fitz* during its last trip. Hemming interviewed many of the lost crewmen's family members, as well as a number of the principal figures involved in the search-and-rescue mission. He pored over the Marine Board report and transcripts and talked to men who earned their livings on the lakes, all in an effort to place the reader aboard the *Fitzgerald* as the ship battled the storm while making its way down Lake Superior. His account, published in 1981 as *Gales of November,* spent very little time on reports and theories, instead presenting a highly dramatic rendering of the *Fitzgerald*'s final two days.

The appearance of all these books had a mixed effect on the families of the victims. The media attention immediately following the loss of the ship had been overwhelming, thrusting ordinary people into a spotlight they would have preferred to avoid. The publicity, legal issues, and commercialization of the shipwreck seemed to place a new focus on the story, moving the attention from the twenty-nine men on the ship at the bottom of the lake to a marketplace capable of exploiting and selling the story regardless of the families' wishes.

The publications presented a dilemma. Each new book opened old wounds, yet each new book kept the story alive. No one wanted a single crew member— or the *Fitzgerald* story—to slip from memory, yet what one family member might consider a tasteful narrative wound up offending another. Each had a strong opinion about how the story should be told, yet the events that so deeply affected them seemed to have a life of their own—a life that could exceed the families' influence and grasp.

And, as they would learn, this was only the beginning.

It was inevitable that the wreckage would be revisited. The CURV III expedition had been woefully incomplete, producing tantalizing television images and photographs that offered valuable information, which, over the long haul, begged for further explanation: *The big ship is in two huge pieces, with debris scattered over acres of the bottom of Lake Superior,* the images seemed to say. *You know that much. But you don't know why. And you must know why.*

Had it touched bottom in the shallow waters near the Six Fathom Shoal? In early 1976, while the Marine Board was adjourned and awaiting the CURV exploration and results, divers had explored the area around the shoal, searching for evidence of broken or disturbed rocks, scrapes of paint, or any other sign that the *Fitz* had bottomed out, but nothing turned up. The CURV III had gone over the exposed bottom of the stern and had found neither tears in the hull nor any dents, scrapes, or missing paint. The bow, buried in more than twenty feet of mud and spilled taconite, was saying nothing.

Had the Fitz lost buoyancy because of flooding in the cargo hold? The hatches and hatch covers provided nothing definitive to support the Marine Board's conclusions. The CURV III materials showed what looked like damning evidence—the undamaged clamps, the mangled combings, at least one cover standing on end inside the hatch opening—but none of this was conclusive, especially when the photographs and images captured only a very small area per frame, forcing investigators to piece the photos together painstakingly to create an overall picture of the wreckage.

Another exploration, using better technology, was necessary if there was to be any hope of finding answers to the prickly questions.

Such an expedition would not be easy to mount. The Coast Guard and National Transportation Safety Board reports satisfied the need for an official explanation, even if the two reports conflicted in their conclusions; the U.S. government wouldn't be sponsoring any more explorations of the wreck. The Canadian government was similarly disinclined to go any further, and since the *Fitz* rested in Canadian waters, privately funded explorers or organizations would have to show Canadian officials a reason to grant the necessary permits to visit the wreck. If a private group did obtain permission to dive the wreck, the expedition promised to be a costly one. Hiring a boat and crew and obtaining the advanced equipment necessary to improve upon the CURV exploration, required deep pockets.

The French underwater archeologist and explorer Jacques Cousteau, internationally known for his explorations of shipwrecks and innovations in diving technology, was just such a deep-pocketed person, and on September 24, 1980, two members of his famous *Calypso* crew visited the *Edmund Fitzgerald* in a two-person submarine.

Unfortunately, the dive turned out to be nothing special. Cousteau and his crew were already busy with an ambitious film project for the National Film Board of Canada, making a documentary retracing the routes taken by early French explorers on the St. Lawrence River. Cousteau was in the area to accept an award in Detroit, and he entrusted the visit to the *Fitzgerald* to his son, Jean-Michel.

The submarine's trip to the *Fitz* lasted about half an hour and involved an examination only of the bow section of the wreckage. The two divers on the mini-sub, Albert Falco and Colin Mounier, noted the extensive damage to the bow and concluded that the dents must have been caused by a series of collisions between the bow and stern sections as the *Fitz* was breaking apart on the surface.

This scenario had a historical precedent. While the *Daniel J. Morrell* was breaking apart on Lake Huron, heavy seas had caused the ship's two broken sections to collide violently, the stern section swinging around and slamming into the bow portion until the two pieces finally separated. The *Calypso* crew believed that this had also happened with the *Fitz*.

Still, there was something very unsatisfactory about the *Calypso*'s findings. Falco and Mounier concluded that the *Fitz* had not sunk quickly, as generally believed; instead, the ship broke apart and stayed afloat for a while before the two pieces sank slowly together. Falco and Mounier pointed to the proximity of the bow and stern sections to support their claim: if the *Fitzgerald* had broken in two while it was sinking, they proposed, the two sections would have been spaced farther apart.

This conflicted with what little was known about the *Fitzgerald* or about other ore carriers known to have broken on the surface. The crew of the *Fitzgerald* had not transmitted a mayday call, which they certainly would have done if the ship had remained afloat for any length of time after it had broken up. The *Fitz* had been equipped with three VHF/FM 25-watt radiotelephones, two operating on the ship's power, the other running on batteries. The frequent calls between the *Fitz* and other vessels during its final hours on the lake indicated that the phones were in good working condition, and, even if the ship's power had been lost when the ship broke apart, as had happened in the case of the *Daniel J. Morrell,* the men in the *Fitzgerald*'s pilothouse still would have had the battery-operated phone at their disposal.

The conclusion about the proximity of the two sections was equally difficult to accept. In its report, the Marine Board had used the proximity of the bow and stern sections to support its *rejection* of the idea that the ship had broken on the surface; also, in the cases of the *Morrell* and the *Carl D. Bradley,* the ships' two sections had been spaced much farther apart than the pieces of the *Fitzgerald*. How the *Calypso* explorers could reach exactly the opposite conclusion was anybody's guess.

In any event, the *Calypso* crew had never claimed to be making a serious, detailed scientific study. The famous boat's trip to the *Fitz*, although news-worthy, offered less insight in the long run than the CURV mission four years earlier.

Nearly a decade passed before anyone explored the wreckage again. Interest in the *Fitz* continued to simmer, especially every November, when radio stations played the Gordon Lightfoot song more frequently, and the Mariners' Church of Detroit held its annual service remembering the lost crewmen.

The service had evolved over the years: the *Fitzgerald*, Father Richard Ingalls discovered, had touched a lot of people in unexpected ways, and these people wanted to gather and pray at the Mariners' Church when the service was held each year on the Sunday closest to the November 10 anniversary. The ceremony, which originally consisted of Father Ingalls's tolling the bell and mentioning the *Fitzgerald*'s crew during his regular Sunday service, grew to include members of the shipping community and the community at large, with an honor guard of mariners assembling around a large model of the *Fitzgerald* during the service, and voluntary bell ringers, chosen from the community at large, assisting with the bell service. Chairs now had to be placed in aisles and at the back of the church to accommodate all those who came.

The public's unflagging interest in the *Fitzgerald*, along with maritime histori-ans' desire for more answers about the ship's loss, led to another exploration of the wreckage in 1989, this one using a Remote Operated Vehicle (ROV), which, like the earlier CURV, allowed researchers, scientists, and technicians to view the wreckage through the eyes of a device manipulated from the surface of the lake. The technology of underwater exploration had made great strides since the CURV took the first footage of the wreck; the current dive to the *Fitz* would find researchers from Deep Diving Systems International, a firm out of Falmouth,

Massachusetts, testing its new towed survey system (TSS), which promised to deliver three-dimensional images of the wreckage.

Organized by Michigan Sea Grant, a joint research program involving the University of Michigan and Michigan State University, the 1989 expedition attracted international media attention as soon as it was announced. Television and newspaper reporters flocked to the scene, eager for new information on the Great Lakes' most famous shipwreck. The National Geographic Society announced plans for using the footage in a television special. The U.S. Fish and Wildlife Service provided a research ship, the *R. V. Grayling,* to use as a base of operations. This was no spur-of-the-moment drop-in like the *Calypso* visit nine years earlier, and people lined up to be a part of the project.

Brent Biehl, a Paradise, Michigan, businessman who'd made his way to Whitefish Point the night the *Fitz* went down, was hired to locate and mark the wreckage for the expedition's crew. It was an experience he would never forget. Biehl had used a chain saw to cut through fallen trees when he went to Whitefish Point on November 10, 1975; he remembered the intensity of the storm and how it had flooded the area a thousand feet beyond the shoreline.

"Storms create excitement if you live up here," he told reporters fourteen years later, "and if the waves get to a certain point, you know something might happen. But we didn't know we'd lost a freighter until the next morning."

The story had haunted him ever since; now, in locating and marking the *Fitzgerald* wreckage, Biehl found himself making a connection as much personal as professional. Biehl and his son took a boat to the site and, using a depth finder, located the wreckage. They lowered a line with an attached anchor and manipulated it until it caught on the wreckage. They then tied a buoy to the line, marking the exact location for the *Grayling*.

Biehl was thrilled by his contribution, illustrating how the *Fitz* had touched so many people around the Great Lakes over the passing years. "The water was blue green and the rope was yellow," he remembered. "The sense of having the rope in your hands and knowing that at the end of it lay the *Edmund Fitzgerald,* this ghost ship, [was] quite a feeling. After being out in the storm that night, it was like coming full circle for me."

A storm delayed the beginning of the exploration, just as a storm had threatened the opening of the CURV operation the spring after the *Fitz* went down. Yet, as before, the lake surrendered.

Besides its advanced photographic capabilities, the TSS offered great flexibility in studying the wreck. The ROV—a robot tethered to a sled similar in appearance to the CURV sled—swam around the wreckage with much greater mobility than the more awkward CURV, and while those manipulating it did have to be careful to avoid snagging its 300-foot umbilical cord on the wreckage, the ROV moved about freely, taking wide-angle and close-up pictures.

The first dive commenced on August 23, and for the next three days, the ROV cameras recorded the most stunning footage of the *Fitz* seen to that point. The crew on the *Grayling* waited in nervous anticipation, their eyes fixed on the ship's television monitors, as the TSS made its way downward, its lights cutting through utter darkness. No one knew what to expect—what portion of the ship would be appearing first, what condition the wreckage would be in, or whether the new technology would deliver the clear images that it had been designed to capture—but their fears were quickly put to rest when the TSS's lights finally caught, faintly, the *Fitzgerald*'s radio tower.

"When the first flickering images of the long dead vessel appeared on the monitor, all conversation stopped cold," wrote Fred Stonehouse, aboard the *Grayling* as an observer. "A silence every bit as deep as that surrounding the sunken steamer engulfed us. It seemed that even the activity of breathing was suspended."

The suspense aboard the *Grayling* heightened as the ROV moved about the pilothouse, edging up to the smashed-out windows and peering inside. The pilothouse structure had been extensively damaged, and items inside had shifted and scattered when the *Fitz* plowed into the lake floor. The radiotelephone cords hung loose in the water. A few items of clothing appeared on the monitors, sad reminders of the men on board. No bodies, however, came into view.

The ROV swam alongside the pilothouse, revealing one major surprise: the starboard pilothouse door was open. The CURV scan had somehow missed this, and when the ROV moved in to survey the doorway more closely, it was evident from the undamaged hinges, doorknob, and frame that the door had not been forced open by escaping air when the ship went down. A troubling question now arose: was it possible that one or more of the men in the pilothouse, aware that the *Fitzgerald* was about to sink, had attempted to abandon ship? Although it wasn't standard practice, some masters and mates liked to leave a door open during storms so they could hear foghorns, whistles, and other sounds through the usual noise of the storm—and it was entirely possible this was done on the *Fitz,* which was running without radar—but the possibility that the men had more warning than previously believed was disturbing.

Visibility in the water was excellent, and the images sent back to the *Grayling* revealed a grotesquely damaged ship virtually unchanged since the time of its sinking. The ship's white paint remained mostly untouched by rust or corrosion, and silt had yet to form a filmy skin over the wreckage. The letters "EDMUND FITZGERALD" were clear and easy to read.

A few other surprises cropped up during the ROV's examination of the bow. The window in the back and another on the side of the chartroom were intact, although all the other windows had imploded during the sinking. Tons of taconite covered the wreckage—much more than previously observed—which suggested that the stern section might have floated upside down for a brief period, dropping its cargo on the bow section before falling to rest. The extreme damage to the bow all but proved that it had sunk before the stern, hitting the lake floor so violently and so fast, as to crumple the hull "like tin foil," as one of the *Grayling* crew observed.

Perhaps the biggest surprise, a large hole on the starboard bow, led to excited discussion.

"It got everyone's attention," Tom Farnquist, director of the Great Lakes Shipwreck Historical Society and one of the organizers of the dive, told the press. "The way the metal was ripped . . . didn't look like bottom damage. It looked as if it had been ripped outward, not punctured inward."

Fred Stonehouse was also puzzled by the gaping two- to four-foot hole.

"I find that terribly inexplicable," he told reporters. "It's almost like you cracked an eggshell. In this case, it's half-inch steel."

The expedition produced five hours of the best footage yet of the wreckage, but in the end it, too, like the surveys before it, was inconclusive. The expedition had been designed more as a test of newly developed underwater technology than as a thorough, scientific study of the *Fitz,* and the footage added more frustration to those seeking answers about the ship's demise.

"The mystery is intact," Tom Farnquist announced.

To many following the *Fitzgerald* story, Tom Farnquist was a controversial figure who, through ambition and sheer will, had inserted himself into the story and become one of its major characters. His formidable interest in and knowledge of Great Lakes shipwrecks drove him in ways that led to the highest praise and most damning criticism imaginable. Depending upon whom you were talking to, Farnquist was either a rock-solid Great Lakes historian and museum director, or he was a museum director and scuba diver who illegally removed artifacts from ships and placed them in the Shipwreck Society's museum. There seemed to be no middle ground in the discussion.

The lakes meant everything to Farnquist. He'd submerged himself in them as a young scuba diver, when he visited shipwrecks and studied the sunken history of Lake Superior. He'd honored them in 1978, two years after the loss of the *Fitzgerald,* when he cofounded the Great Lakes Shipwreck Historical Society. He'd preserved them in 1985, when he helped open the Great Lakes Shipwreck Museum in Whitefish Point, a nonprofit operation serving thousands of visitors annually. He'd made a name for himself as one of the foremost authorities on the *Edmund Fitzgerald,* leading three separate expeditions to the wreck site.

His critics, however, saw what they felt was a darker side, and they questioned his motives and decisions as an explorer and historian. He'd removed objects from shipwrecks and placed them in the shipwreck museum. The state of Michigan filed suit and the Department of Natural Resources obtained a search warrant. Farnquist claimed that the episode reflected an oversight in filling out the required paperwork, that Shipwreck Society divers removed the artifacts to protect them from poachers. His detractors said otherwise. As far as his enemies were concerned, Farnquist was a figure to be watched in the future.

"Law enforcement officials for the Department of Natural Resources in Michigan stated that 'although the letter of the law may have been violated, the spirit of the law was not,'" he pointed out. "A settlement between the state of Michigan and the Historical Museum had been reached, in which the artifacts belonged to the state and the artifacts in question were loaned back to the Shipwreck Society for long-term display."

In fairness to Farnquist, the retrieval and presentation of shipwreck artifacts would always be a sensitive issue, with historians' and underwater archeologists' intentions continually under question and scrutiny. As the best-known and most recent Great Lakes shipwreck, the *Edmund Fitzgerald* presented a tantalizing challenge. The ship had lost an anchor in the Detroit River in 1974, which had been retrieved in 1992 and was now a popular display at the Dossin Great Lakes Museum. Even seemingly insignificant artifacts from the *Fitz*—taconite pellets, for example—held special value. Farnquist and the Great Lakes Shipwreck Historical Society had no specific designs on artifact retrieval from the *Edmund Fitzgerald,* but one couldn't have blamed them if they did.

Like many others, Tom Farnquist dreamed of visiting the *Fitzgerald* wreckage. For a sport diver, it was the ultimate Great Lakes adventure; for the historian, it represented a unique opportunity to study a great mystery. The ROV expedition had been a great beginning, but the unanswered questions left him with even more questions about the *Fitzgerald*'s demise.

He found his opportunity in an unusual source. Dr. Joseph MacInnis, a Canadian physician who was also a highly regarded underwater explorer, had been approached by the International Joint Commission—a six-member committee assembled by the Canadian prime minister and President Bill Clinton—with the idea that MacInnis develop an educational project on the effect of chemical pollution on the Great Lakes and the St. Lawrence River. How did pollutants such as PCBs make their way into the food chain, and how did that endanger people's health?

MacInnis was an ideal candidate for finding a way to make such a project appealing to the general public. He had visited the *Titanic* in 1991, and his best-selling book, *Titanic: In a New Light,* along with the television special and IMAX movie coming out of the same expedition, had been immensely popular. MacInnis had the name recognition necessary for developing and funding the project proposed by the International Joint Commission, and he was creative enough to make the end result interesting.

The ideal project, MacInnis felt, would benefit most by having a team of scientists and researchers diving the Great Lakes and St. Lawrence River in a series of loosely connected smaller projects, including studies of how toxins affected the zooplankton population in Lake Superior or the beluga whales in the St. Lawrence River. The project, "Great Lakes '94," would take place over a six-week period during the summer of 1994.

The *Edmund Fitzgerald* might not have seemed closely connected to the other aspects of the project—indeed, by MacInnis's own admission, the promise of good underwater footage of the *Fitz* was really a carrot he could dangle in front of the potential viewers of his proposed educational program. "Frankly, people are not terribly interested in toxic chemicals," he conceded. "But they certainly are fascinated with the *Fitzgerald.*"

MacInnis saw the *Fitz* as representative of a much larger story.

"In many ways, the *Fitzgerald* story is our relationship to the Great Lakes writ large," he wrote in his book, *Fitzgerald's Storm.* "It contains elements of heroism and humility as well as ignorance and arrogance. It features people who look at life with wonder and others who are so busy stripping things apart that life's fascinating complexities are reduced to trifles not worth bothering about."

MacInnis's challenge, as he saw it, was in finding a way to make his television audience draw that connection. After all, two large countries shared these waters.

"We're hoping public interest in the *Fitzgerald* carries over to a broader appreciation of the health of the Great Lakes basin, which is home to 40 million people," he announced optimistically.

The Harbor Branch Oceanographic Institute of Fort Pierce, Florida, backed the project, supplying its 168-foot research ship, the *Edwin Link,* as the study's on-water headquarters. Harbor Branch also donated the use of its three-person minisub, *Clelia*, for the actual dive to the wreck. The twenty-two-foot sub represented another major advance in technology in the exploration of the *Edmund Fitzgerald*. The front of the sub was clear Plexiglas, affording the crew a clear, panoramic view of the sunken vessel. Powerful mercury vapor lights, similar to the ones used to explore the *Titanic,* promised to bring out the colors of the *Fitz* and everything around it in stunning detail, while high-resolution cameras recorded the exploration for posterity. The sub's sonar side-scan would provide another kind of picture: the topography of the floor of the lake and the debris scattered around it. The *Clelia's* ability to hover assured its crew a good, steady view.

MacInnis and Harbor Branch Oceanographic assembled a crack team of researchers, scientists, and technicians to run the operations, the dozens of participants coming from both the United States and Canada. Students in the High School Aquanaut Program, sponsored by the University of Connecticut, were enlisted to help chart the underwater wreckage. There was no shortage of people eager to work on the project.

Tom Farnquist was one such interested party. Farnquist bought into the MacInnis project with $10,000 of the Shipwreck Society museum's finds, a sum that assured the Society a dive to the wreck. An exceptional speaker and public relations man, Farnquist also became one of the project's spokespersons.

The first of the *Clelia's* dives to the *Fitzgerald* took place on July 3, 1994. The yellow minisub was lowered into Lake Superior and the three explorers aboard became the first to visit the *Fitz* since the *Calypso* dive nearly fourteen years earlier. Over the next three days, the *Clelia* made six dives. The *Fitzgerald,* now showing hints of rust, was more battered than previously believed, and each visitor was awed by the sheer size and scope of the wreckage.

"The size is incredible," said Jene Quirin, a board member of the Great Lakes Shipwreck Historical Society, who became the first person to photograph the *Fitzgerald.* "You're creeping up on this large piece of machinery that at one time was alive. It's almost like coming upon a dinosaur, sitting there in the quiet and darkness in this eerie setting. It was, at one time, on the surface, alive."

Those examining the wreckage reached an entirely different conclusion from the crew of the *Calypso:* the *Fitzgerald* had taken a nosedive and hit bottom at high speed, the bow crashing into the floor of the lake while, in all likelihood, its stern was still on the surface.

"This thing had to have hit the bottom butt-hard," said Tim Askew, Jr., the minisub's pilot. "This stuff is just everywhere."

"It struck with incredible force," added Tom Farnquist. "I think it drove itself to the bottom with the screw still going . . . I don't think the crew had any idea what was happening."

New evidence, captured on film or witnessed by the crews on the *Clelia,* certainly seemed to support this view. A close-up examination of the lake floor revealed evidence of a tremendous impact. ("It really looked like a moonscape in a lot of places because the chunks of clay were so jagged and angular and really untouched after the impact," said Quirin.) The stem of the bow—the strongest point on a ship—had been bent at a right angle, further indicating the force with which the *Fitzgerald* hit bottom. The engine telegraph in the pilothouse was set at "all ahead full," meaning the *Fitz* had been running at full speed at the time of its sinking.

As before, no one reported seeing human remains and, as before, the ship offered no conclusive evidence of what had caused it to sink.

"We still can't say why the ship went down," Joseph MacInnis told the press at the conclusion of the expedition, "but we've found things that have never been seen before."

MacInnis felt confident that his group had collected enough new evidence to show how, if not why, the *Fitzgerald,* sank.

"We think we will be able to reconstruct exactly how the ship went down," he said.

Three weeks after MacInnis, Frederick J. Shannon led a crew on still another visit to the *Fitzgerald.* Shannon, a former policeman and private investigator, proposed a unique approach to studying the *Fitz:* he would investigate the wreckage as if it was a crime scene.

Shannon probably knew as much about the *Fitz* as anyone, including his rival

Tom Farnquist. Shannon had become obsessed with the *Fitz* shortly after it went down, and he'd gone to extraordinary lengths to learn as much as possible about the ship and its story. He'd compiled a massive file of books, magazine and newspaper articles, official reports and documents, and photographs of the *Fitz,* and he'd interviewed an impressive number of mariners and experts, including Captain Bernie Cooper, in his quest to learn all there was to know about the *Fitz.* Shannon hoped to use what he learned to write a book and produce a documentary film.

Shannon's obsession was even further intensified by his feud with Tom Farnquist. At one time, the two had been colleagues joined by their mutual interest in the famous shipwreck, but a bitter disagreement over Shannon's use in lectures of underwater footage owned by the Shipwreck Society had led to a split that resulted in nasty public bickering, finding them taking potshots at each other in the press.

Shannon had watched Farnquist and the Shipwreck Society bask in the publicity surrounding the MacInnis dive, knowing full well that, soon enough, he would have his chance. Funding his project with $75,000 of his own savings, Shannon assembled a competent team to command a mother ship and a two-person minisub, and if his team lacked the sheer numbers and academic credentials of the earlier MacInnis exploration, it didn't lack in the skills necessary to pull off the planned three-day operation.

In a total of seven dives over three days, Shannon recorded thirteen hours of footage of the *Fitzgerald* wreckage. Perhaps predictably, his findings differed from Farnquist's: Shannon shared the Cousteau group's opinion that the *Fitz* had broken apart on the surface. As part of his research, Shannon had interviewed Red Burgner, and he accepted the former steward's theory that the *Fitz* might have split apart when the weakened hull cracked in the storm. Shannon found no evidence of shoaling when he examined the relatively intact bottom of the *Fitz*'s stern. Further, Shannon reported finding the ship's propeller jammed into the rudder, evidence that the vessel had not gone down under full power, as previously believed. The open door of the pilothouse, along with an open door to the wheelsman's cabin, hinted that the crew had warning of the ship's impending doom and might have attempted to escape.

"All former theories are shot. They can go back in the closet," Shannon announced victoriously after seeing the wreckage. "The extreme tearing pattern reveals evidence that the separation was not instantaneous. There are deep dents and buckles in the hull, but they don't indicate the boat struck a shoal."

The *Fitzgerald,* Shannon maintained, had been "overworked and hadn't been in up-to-par condition for over a year"—a position that Red Burgner had presented in his earlier deposition. The *Fitz,* Shannon noted, had made 748 trips over its seventeen years on the lakes, and the sheer number of trips, coupled with the hugeness of the loads the *Fitz* had carried during its record-breaking runs, were bound to place great stress on the ship's hull. Shannon couldn't pinpoint exactly when the structural failure had occurred, but he was certain that the ship was not in one piece when it hit the bottom of Lake Superior.

For all the fanfare that accompanied it, the Shannon expedition wouldn't be remembered for its conclusions about the *Fitzgerald's* sinking; Shannon's theories, no more or less valid than anyone else's, would be added to the growing list and subjected to the usual discussion and debate. Instead, the expedition would be remembered for its gruesome discovery of human remains, and for Shannon's photographs and footage of those remains, which he suggested he might release in his forthcoming book and documentary.

Up to now, no one had seen any of the bodies of the crewmen—or at the very least, no one was saying he had. Most were presumed to be entombed in the stern section; the men in the pilothouse, it was supposed, had been expelled into the lake when water gushed through the pilothouse windows and flooded the ship. The *Fitzgerald's* massive wreckage was scattered over a large area, and given the less than ideal conditions, it was very possible that the CURV, ROV, and minisubs had passed over a body without seeing or recording it.

This afforded some comfort to the families of the lost crewmen, who didn't need their grief compounded by the knowledge that their loved ones might be lying out in the open, exposed to the prying eyes or camera lenses of future underwater explorers. It also came as a relief to those visiting the wreckage, who held their breath every time a camera or light approached a window or porthole. No one had consciously sought to find any of the bodies.

Nor, for that matter, had Shannon sought to do so. The discovery of the greatly decomposed remains, partially hidden by debris on the floor of the lake near the starboard bow, had been accidental. The *Delta,* the sixteen-foot minisub that Shannon was using, was on its fourth dive, moving about the bottom of the lake and taking video footage of everything in its path, when a body, clad in coveralls and wearing a canvas lifejacket, was discovered. Shannon made no effort to disturb or further examine the remains, and he immediately notified the Canadian government of his discovery. He also offered to provide a videotape of the remains in the event that someone would be interested in trying to identify them.

"We were not looking for bodies and really didn't anticipate finding any," he insisted, when addressing the media about his discovery.

Still, in making the announcement—and in mentioning that he'd seen such personal effects as shoes, sandals, and a belt near the stern section—Shannon set off a firestorm of angry reaction and criticism that would affect any future exploration of the *Edmund Fitzgerald.* Until that point, the victims' families might not have been happy about people poking around an underwater gravesite, but they had expressed very little organized opposition to it. As long as the explorations were conducted legally and tastefully, with full respect for those who'd lost their lives on the ship, the explorations were tolerated. The families, like the maritime historians, hoped for answers.

The discovery of the body changed everything. Although the remains were in such a condition that it would have been impossible to make a positive identification without retrieving them—and, in fact, some questioned whether the body actually belonged to a *Fitzgerald* crew member—the families cited the discovery in petitioning the Canadian government to declare the ship off limits to future exploration. In addition, after hearing Shannon mention the possibility of publishing photos or footage of the remains, family members pushed legislators to pass new laws prohibiting such displays.

News of Shannon's discovery made national headlines, overshadowing the good work his expedition had accomplished, and placing him, perhaps unfairly, in the role of bad guy. Shannon and his crew were aware that they were exploring a gravesite, and while he might have done himself a greater service if he'd kept quiet about his discovery, rather than discussing it openly with the media, it's also noteworthy that he never sold a photograph or video image to any of the tabloids or magazines more than willing to pay large sums for them. When he had concluded the last of his visits to the *Fitzgerald,* Shannon left a memorial behind the ship's pilothouse: a plaque with the names of the twenty-nine crewmen, along with Bernie Cooper's name and the names of the crew that had participated in the exploration.

None of it mattered to Shannon's detractors. All that really mattered was that he'd seen and photographed a body. In the eyes of his enemies, he had desecrated a grave.

The passage of time did nothing to douse the fiery emotions dividing Tom Farnquist and Fred Shannon. Both cared deeply about the *Fitz*—there was no disputing that—but that passion had mutated into something ugly and hurtful. Farnquist still held his position as executive director of a museum filled with Great Lakes relics that attracted a growing number of visitors each year. Shannon possessed an impressive archive of information on the *Fitz,* which he still hoped to parlay into a profitable book and film documentary. Both gave lectures and film presentations on the *Fitzgerald,* and if some of their ideas and conclusions about the ship were disputed by camps loyal to one or the other, no one doubted their authority on the topic.

This might have been enough for some, but as time had shown (and might always show), people could get extremely territorial over the *Edmund Fitzgerald.* Farnquist denied that he was involved in a turf war with Shannon; he was, he insisted, simply trying to carry out the wishes of the dead crewmen's family members. He did admit that, in the wake of the dispute over Shannon's discovery of the body, he had much stronger feelings about Shannon. The issue, he said, had become a contentious battle between Shannon's vision and the wishes of the family members.

All this was brought into sharp focus when, a short time after visiting the wreckage, the Shipwreck Society, at the request of the *Fitzgerald* family members, began mounting an effort to remove the *Fitz*'s bell and place it in the museum. The bell, Farnquist said, would become a permanent memorial to the men who perished. A new bell, bearing the names of the *Fitzgerald*'s captain and crew, would be mounted on the wreckage.

On the surface, it looked like an honorable endeavor. The relatives of the men entombed on the *Fitz* had held services and put up headstones for their loved ones, but for many, true closure had never been attained. Most accepted the terrible truth that, in all likelihood, the remains of their loved ones would never be retrieved and brought to the surface for burial on land. The families had come to view the *Fitzgerald* as a type of burial ground, and rather than worry about the improbable return of the crewmen, they turned their attention to seeing that it would be permanently honored as a gravesite, free from the curiosity of sport divers and the clutches of those who would remove artifacts—perhaps even their loved ones' personal effects—from the ship. The bell, engraved with the names of the *Fitzgerald*'s crew, would act as an unofficial headstone.

The bell removal and replacement required some legal and public relations maneuvering. Since artifacts could not be legally removed from the *Fitz* without formal permission from the Canadian government, the Shipwreck Society needed to prove that retrieval of the bell amounted to more than the procurement of an important artifact for the museum—an object destined to attract visitors willing to lay down cash to see the heart of the Mighty *Fitz* on display.

Farnquist and the Shipwreck Society played their hand beautifully. A petition stating the families' wishes was drawn up: once the original bell had been removed and the replacement bell put in place, the families hoped that the *Fitzgerald* would be closed to further exploration.

Fred Shannon seethed when he learned of the plans.

"This is the most unethical, self-serving, sneaky approach to artifact removal I have ever heard of," he charged, hinting that, if necessary, he would file a lawsuit to block the Shipwreck Society's plans. The removal of the bell, Shannon insisted, would probably be a messy process involving the use of explosives or other measures that could damage the wreckage.

Farnquist dismissed Shannon's charges as "a last-ditch effort by a desperate man." The removal of the bell, he assured the press, would be accomplished by a diver equipped with a state-of-the-art deep-pressure suit, working under the watchful eye of a Canadian navy submarine.

"It would be a very clean and delicate, but easy process," Farnquist stated. "We would never undertake such an effort without having a detailed plan to assure the ship wouldn't be harmed."

The debate underscored the territorialism infecting any discussion of the *Fitz* between the two men. Shannon hoped to revisit the *Fitz* and shoot additional footage of the wreckage. The families' wishes to close off the site from future exploration, if accepted, would shatter those plans. On the other hand, Shannon had every right to question Farnquist's motives. Regardless of how Farnquist and the Shipwreck Society chose to present their case to the press, there was no denying that the Shipwreck Society and its museum stood to profit from the bell's retrieval, at the cost of ruining exploration of the *Fitzgerald* wreckage by future historians.

The Shipwreck Society proceeded with its plan. Ruth Hudson and Cheryl Rozmon, two relatives of lost crewmen, drafted a letter that was sent to the *Fitzgerald* families. By late April 1995, they had accumulated more than eighty favorable responses, and had won the support of the Canadian navy and the National Geographic Society. The bell would be replaced in a series of dives between June 22 and July 5.

Shannon countered by filing a lawsuit seeking to block the bell recovery project, and in the last week of April, a Michigan judge temporarily barred the removal of the bell or any other artifacts from the *Fitzgerald,* pending the outcome of a May 16 hearing. The lawsuit attacked the Shipwreck Society's plans from several angles. First, the suit contended that a portion of the *Fitzgerald* wreckage rested in U.S. territorial waters and was subject to the Michigan Great Lakes Bottom Lands Act, which prohibited the removal of artifacts from shipwrecks if doing so acted against the public interest. Second, the suit argued that the removal of the bell would destroy the *Fitzgerald*'s "historical, educational and scientific value." Finally, the removal of the bell threatened Shannon's plans for filming the ship in the future, which in turn, compromised his book and documentary projects. According to the suit Shannon had "a right to see the *Edmund Fitzgerald* in its complete state, without damage, at any time."

Shannon hoped the court would see Farnquist and the Shipwreck Society as being more concerned with benefitting the museum rather than as a way of honoring and preserving the memory of those lost in one of the Great Lakes' most fabled disasters. Unfortunately for Shannon, the court rejected all of his arguments. The *Fitzgerald* rested in waters right on the U.S./Canadian border, but Judge Lawrence M. Glazer ruled that the wreckage was in the jurisdiction of the Canadian government.

Shannon was unable to prove that the bell recovery project posed a threat to the structure of the *Fitzgerald,* mainly because the Shipwreck Society had no plans to use explosive devices in the removal. Instead, the bell would be cut away by an underwater torch, which could mean cutting the stanchions holding the bell in place and little else. It mattered little to the court that to cut away and remove anything from a ship was, from a purist's standpoint, to deface a historical artifact. If the removal of the bell was acceptable to the owners of the *Fitzgerald,* the Canadian government, and the families of the deceased, it was acceptable to the court.

This left Shannon with the task of defending the weakest of his arguments. Since Canadian authorities had yet to ban further exploration of the *Fitz,* Shannon bore the burden of showing how the removal of one small piece from the massive wreckage could harm the marketability of his book and documentary projects. The argument was doomed to fail. Entrepreneurs had been capitalizing on the *Fitz* for the better part of a decade, often to the dismay of the family members, but to this point no one had stood in open court and argued for the right to use the *Fitzgerald* as a moneymaker.

Judge Glazer listened to Shannon's attorney, Michael Rizik, present his case, but he had little patience for it. Rizik tried to explain that the bell's removal would damage Shannon's credibility if he showed footage of the ship without its bell.

"He sees a strong likelihood that the book may not sell as well because he wants more photographs, and without the bell this book may suffer," Rizik argued. "The same thing is true for the film."

Rizik's next words may have cut closer to the heart of the dispute than anything else said during the entire proceedings.

"Believe me, Judge," he said, "this is an adversarial setting. There is no love lost between my client and Mr. Farnquist."

The judge ruled in favor of Farnquist, and on July 4, 1995, after formal permission to raise the bell had been secured from the Canadian government and the Northwestern Mutual Life Insurance Company, the HMCS *Cormorant,* a 245-foot Canadian ship, transported a crew to the site of the wreckage. The carefully planned operation, overseen by the Shipwreck Society, the National Geographic Society, and the Canadian navy, would take place over several days, and would be part underwater archeological expedition and part prayer vigil. *Fitzgerald* family members waited on a nearby yacht while the diver, Bruce Fuoco, cut the bell loose and supervised its rise to the surface. When the bell was hoisted to the deck of the *Cormorant,* Jack Champeau, brother of third engineer Buck Champeau, reached out and pulled the rope.

"On the night before I left for Vietnam, Buck came to see me in my room," Champeau remembered. "He told me not to worry. He said even if something happened to me, if I was missing, he would come to Vietnam and find me and take me back. I know that I cannot find Buck down there and take him back with me, as much as I would like. So I am doing the next best thing."

Tom Champeau, another of Buck's brothers, hoped for finality in the bell-ringing. "More than anything," he offered, "I think a lot of the families want to say, 'This is it, this is the end of it.'"

In an editorial published on the day of the bell recovery, the *Cleveland Plain Dealer* spoke in favor of making the bell recovery a springboard to declaring the *Fitzgerald* a gravesite off limits to divers.

"The *Fitzgerald* isn't a coral reef or a wreck from the 1800s or some other sightseeing venue," the editorialist wrote. "It is a tomb and the only difference between it and other crypts is that it is 535 feet below the lake. Those hapless sailors would never have chosen such a resting place. Fate brought them there. They deserve to rest in peace."

On July 7, family members attended a formal dockside bell presentation service on the Lower St. Marys River, and a banquet hall in the Keewadin Casino in Sault Sainte Marie. The ceremony, which featured the tolling of the bell twenty-nine times in memory of the *Fitzgerald*'s crew, celebrated not only the retrieval of the bell but also its installation in the Great Lakes Shipwreck Museum. In a legal document signed by three officers of the Great Lakes Shipwreck Historical Society, two trustees of the Mariners' Church of Detroit, and forty-six family members, the *Fitzgerald*'s bell was "donated to the custodianship and conservatorship of the Shipwreck Society, to be incorporated in a permanent memorial at Whitefish Point, Michigan, to honor the memory of the twenty-nine men of the *S.S. Edmund Fitzgerald,* who lost their lives on November 10, 1975."

According to the terms of the document, the museum was responsible for maintaining the bell according to the wishes of the families. It was not to be sold, moved, or used for commercial purposes, and if the museum failed to honor those terms, the bell would be transferred to the Mariners' Church of Detroit for safekeeping.

For all its legalese, the document was easy to understand. The bell belonged to the families of the men lost on the *Fitzgerald,* and not to any individuals, corporations, or museums. The legal skirmishes over its recovery were over. It was now time to move on.

But the legal issues and commercial exploitation of the *Edmund Fitzgerald* did not end there, any more than the memory of the ship and its fallen crew members faded with time. The *Fitz* possessed staying power, and the international fascination with the ship grew. The annual services at the Mariners' Church became standing-room-only events, attended by people from all over the United States. Books, plays, videos, postcards, paintings, songs, and newspaper and magazine articles assured the families that the *Fitzgerald* would never be forgotten, just as playing cards, ashtrays, coasters, and even a brand of *Fitzgerald* beer raised eyebrows and hackles, proving that free enterprise would stretch all conceivable limits on taste and fortune.

The restoration of the ship's bell turned out to be more of a headache than anticipated. The Shipwreck Society had turned the bell over to Michigan State University for restoration, and workers there had removed the oxides and stains that had accumulated on it in the depths of the lake. The Shipwreck Society, however, wasn't satisfied. The bell's finish was dull, and it didn't look new. So, without consulting with the families, the Shipwreck Society had the bell professionally polished and lacquered, giving it a bright, shiny brass finish that made it look newer than new. Some of the family members were not impressed. "If I'd known he was going to do that to the bell, I never would have signed those papers," one relative complained.

The Michigan State University restoration workers, who'd spent hundreds of hours on the bell, were also outraged.

"We restored an artifact," said Ed Mahoney, an associate professor in the university's department of maritime and underwater resource management department, "[but] they wanted a monument or tourist attraction."

Tom Farnquist and the Shipwreck Society saw it differently. Removing the bell from a ship built in 1958 was hardly comparable, from a historical perspective, to taking something off a much older vessel.

"The *Edmund Fitzgerald* bell was not an artifact," Farnquist stated. "It was raised as a memorial. We're talking about a modern day freighter."

According to Farnquist, the family members had complained about the bell's appearance when they saw the original restoration, and the Shipwreck Society had set out to make it more acceptable as a memorial. The bell was polished; its stand was painted black, instead of the original gray; and the bell's old, grimy rope had been replaced with a new one. The old rope, Farnquist said, had been replaced for ceremonial purposes, and he promised that it would eventually be returned to the bell.

The bell, Farnquist, and the Shipwreck Society were back in the news in early 1996, when Farnquist announced plans to place the bell on display at "Underwater Canada '96," a festival being held in Toronto at the end of March. The large symposium brought together divers and historians from Canada and the United States, and Farnquist felt that allowing the bell to be displayed could be a nice gesture of gratitude for the government's help in retrieving it. It wouldn't hurt, either, in the continuing efforts to convince Canadian officials to make the *Fitzgerald* a sanctioned gravesite. By the terms of his contract with the *Fitzgerald* families, he was not permitted to move the bell or use it for commercial purposes without their consent. Farnquist assumed that he would have no trouble there, since Underwater Canada was a not-for-profit organization, and since he was only going to be moving the bell to one city, and for a very brief period of time.

Unfortunately for those making the plans, the family of Buck Champeau objected to moving the bell. Mary Soyring, Champeau's sister, worried that setting a precedent by moving the bell might eventually turn the bell into a "traveling trophy." Her family was the only one to oppose the exhibit, but it was enough. The Shipwreck Society abandoned the plan.

"We thought it would be a good idea, but we will not go against the wishes of even one family member," Farnquist said.

Although far from pleased with all this, the families dealt with the ceaseless capitalizing on the *Fitzgerald* as well as they could. The ship's story and its image were in the public domain, and they were powerless to stop the commercial exploitation of a tragedy.

They did, however, push the Canadian government to act on declaring the *Fitzgerald* an official gravesite.

Over the years, they'd heard all kinds of disturbing rumors about divers descending to the wreckage. Some, they heard, had retrieved taconite pellets and were selling them to collectors. Others were grabbing anything they could bring back to the surface. One rumor had an entrepreneur designing a glass-bottomed submersible, which, for a price, would take passengers to the wreckage.

Most of this *was* only rumor, but the success of two sport divers gave reason to worry. In 1975, it was generally accepted that the wreckage lay too deep for scuba divers. However, recent developments in diving gear and the use of mixed gases were permitting deeper dives, and it was probably inevitable that someone would attempt to reach the *Fitz*.

Just such a dive occurred less than two months after the raising of the *Fitzgerald*'s bell had supposedly put an end to visits to the wreckage.

On Labor Day weekend, 1995, only weeks after the bell retrieval, the Orlando diver Terrence Tysell and the Chicago diver Mike Zee, wearing tanks that weighed about 320 pounds each and using mixed gases, spent about six minutes at the wreck site, setting records for the deepest scuba dive on the Great Lakes and the deepest dive to a shipwreck. The descent took only six minutes, but at that depth, there was little time for exploration. Both men gripped the rails on the *Fitzgerald*'s bow, but neither made any attempt to explore or enter the vessel. Instead, the two shot video footage of the wreckage from a distance, using hand-held lights for illumination, before they began the slow, three-hour process of returning to the surface, their progress monitored by a four-man crew in a boat overhead.

News of the expedition shocked and angered the *Fitzgerald* family members, who had hoped that the bell retrieval would be the last time anyone would visit the wreck.

"If I could talk to these men, I would ask them why they violated my son's grave," Ruth Hudson, the mother of Bruce Hudson, protested. "It's his burial ground, and the burial ground of all the others. No one has a right to disturb it."

The divers saw it differently. What they'd done was perfectly legal—pleasure divers were not bound by the same permit regulations that archeological divers had to follow—and they hadn't disturbed anything on the ship. They had been planning the expedition for several years, mainly because they were attracted by the challenge of visiting the Great Lakes' most famous shipwreck.

"The main thing I'd love to tell these folks is we did it to pay our respects," Tysell insisted.

The dispute reignited the old arguments pitting underwater explorers and sport divers against the relatives of the dead. Divers had been exploring shipwrecks—including wrecks with human remains still on board—for many decades. Underwater science and archeology were accepted academic disciplines, considered necessary not only for historical and scientific study but for examining important ecological issues, as had been the case with the earlier MacInnis exploration. The National Geographic Society, which had contributed heavily to the bell retrieval effort, intended to publish color photographs of the wreckage in its magazine, yet Tom Farnquist, who stood to profit from the pictures and accompanying article (which he wrote), loudly objected to others' visiting and photographing the wreckage. The difference, he said, was family disapproval: the wreckage was a gravesite, and they had a right to determine how it was explored.

The issue was partly resolved when the Michigan legislature passed a law banning the publication or public display of human remains in Michigan waters without the permission of the next of kin. Violators of the 1997 law could be charged with a felony punishable by a $5,000 fine and/or two years in prison. The law, however, was only a symbolic victory for the families of the *Fitzgerald* victims: it did not apply to the Shannon footage, which had been taken before the law's passage, or even to the *Fitzgerald,* which wasn't in Michigan waters.

If anything, the new law stirred up even more controversy. The media, otherwise sympathetic to the families, weighed in with reservations about how the law might affect reporting of disasters in the future. The law exempted photographs and video footage taken for law enforcement, scientific, archeological, or medical purposes, but there was something unsettling about the way those exemptions could be defined. The law, its detractors believed, was setting a dangerous precedent. It was too broad and was almost certain to be challenged in court.

"There are two flaws with the legislation," a *Grand Rapids Press* editorial argued. "First, it's not easy to distinguish among scientific, personal, or for-profit research. . . . Second, the bill draws the line on photographing bodies at shipwrecks and mine disasters, but how soon before it's expanded to include other deadly events?"

"The legislature is always on shaky ground when it tries to legislate good manners and good taste," declared Dawn Phillips, a legal representative of the Michigan Press Association.

The legislation spelled still another setback for Fred Shannon, who was planning explorations of the *Carl D. Bradley* and *Daniel J. Morrell* in the near future. Victims were still missing from both shipwrecks and presumably were entombed in the wreckage. If the Michigan law was adopted by other states bordering the

Great Lakes, he could be stymied in what he believed to be valid, important explorations.

Shannon denounced the new law as a violation of the First Amendment.

"We already have rules and regulations and laws needed to protect these sites," he noted. "I think it's a violation of basic freedom to prohibit us from making observations and reporting what we see."

Pat Gagliardi, the original sponsor of the Michigan bill, waved off Shannon's position. All lawmakers wanted to do, he said, was grant the families of those entombed on the *Fitzgerald* and other shipwrecks the same legal protection they'd have in cemeteries on land.

"We don't want to take away anyone's First Amendment rights," he insisted. "We're just trying to do something that morally makes a lot of sense."

July 17, 1999

The 290-foot Coast Guard cutter *Mackinaw,* stationed above the site of the wreckage of the *Edmund Fitzgerald,* had the honor of serving a function unique to the Great Lakes: for the first time in the history of the lakes, the wreckage of a commercial freighter was going to be formally consecrated as a gravesite, and the *Mackinaw,* carrying friends and families of the lost crewmen, was about to function as a church, with Father Richard Ingalls conducting the services.

Rows of folding chairs lined the after deck of the *Mackinaw.* Canadian and American flags stood on either side of a podium near the stern railing. In front of the podium, a small replica of the *Fitzgerald*'s bell waited silently on a table. Two large wreaths, one donated by Gordon Lightfoot, and thirty long-stemmed red carnations rested on two tables nearby.

The service would be the closing of a circle as well as the formal consecration of a gravesite. Captain Don Erickson, who had commanded the *William Clay Ford* during the early search for the missing *Fitzgerald,* and Captain Jimmie Hobaugh, who had brought the Coast Guard cutter *Woodrush* from Duluth to join the search, had been invited to participate in the service. Both had been

inextricably connected to the *Fitzgerald* for life, both reluctantly bound by cir-
cumstance to a tragedy that became the defining moment of their careers.

By now, many of the family members knew each other well. They had spoken
to one another on numerous occasions over the years, often to discuss the best
way to preserve their loved ones' memories and the sanctity of the lost ship in
which they were interred. They had run into each other at the annual services at
the Mariners' Church, or at gatherings such as the bell retrieval and the celebra-
tion a few days later. Like all small communities, they had their leaders and their
followers, their spokespeople and those who preferred to remain quiet. Grief
had brought them together, and since the event that had brought them together
was one of historical significance, they endured the hard kind of grief that never
goes away. Every November 10 would see to that.

They came to the *Mackinaw* with their children and their children's children, as
well as with spouses, brothers, sisters, and other relatives. They carried lawn
chairs and coolers and heavy clothes for the cool air on the water. Many brought
scrapbooks and albums packed with photos of their loved ones, articles about the
Fitzgerald, postcards and letters they'd received from the men, and other memen-
tos that they'd saved and brought out from time to time as a means of drawing
their loved ones close one more time, or as a way of educating children who otherwise knew the men only as the names in stories repeated over the years.

And when they met on board the *Mackinaw,* they greeted each other as family.

Like members of a large, extended family, they'd had their disagreements and
squabbles, and some were much closer than others. They'd lived through the
Fitzgerald story so many times, in their minds and in the retelling, that they
could speak it in a kind of shorthand. All were haunted by questions with no final answers, even when they voiced strong opinions that temporarily divided
them: they could quibble over points of law or action, but the two enormous,
silent hulks of steel 530 feet below them always brought them back to the beginning.

The consecration itself had a political air. The Canadian authorities had continued to drag their feet over formally declaring the *Fitz* off limits to further exploration until the families had once again mobilized for a cause that seemed

destined to remain in legal limbo. If the Canadian government wouldn't make the *Fitzgerald* a sacred gravesite, they would. Maybe the consecration would move the officials to action; if not, at least the wreck would have been declared sacred by a higher authority. Maybe divers and explorers would honor that.

The *Mackinaw* had pulled out of Sault Ste. Marie at 8:00 that morning, with 133 civilians on board. The trip to the site took more than five hours; at times, it seemed as if the weather was going to cause problems. The skies darkened and the wind whipped the flags on the *Mackinaw*'s stern. But the sun was out and the lake had calmed to two-foot waves by the time the *Mackinaw* was directly positioned over the wreckage, at 1:30 P.M.

Father Ingalls began the ceremony half an hour later. One by one, participants approached the podium—the Great Lakes captains, now retired, who had encountered this lake under the best and worst of circumstances; the attorneys who had fought for the *Fitzgerald* families and helped organize the ceremony; the public affairs officer from Canada's Consulate General; two family members, Ruth Hudson and Cheryl Rozman, who had worked on the organization of the consecration ceremony and now acted as spokeswomen for the other family members. Each had prepared a statement or prayer. Some in attendance held hands; others wept quietly. Father Ingalls had designed the service to be both a consecration of a gravesite and a continuation of the annual commemoration services offered at the Mariners' Church, a remembrance begun in the early morning hours of November 11, 1975, when he rang the church bell and prayed for the souls of the *Fitzgerald*'s crew for the first time.

The ninety-minute service offered numerous references to the sea, dating back to the New Testament and Jesus' choice of fishermen as disciples. Wearing a specially designed crucifix forged in the shape of an anchor, Father Ingalls recalled a story of stormy seas that had threatened another vessel nearly two thousand years earlier.

"'And when He was entered into a ship, his disciples followed him,'" Ingalls read from the Gospel of Matthew. "'And, behold, there arose a great tempest in the sea, insomuch that the ship was covered with the waves; but He was asleep.

And his disciples came to him, and awoke him, saying, "Lord, save us, we perish." ' "

The seas, Ingalls reminded the families, had then grown calm. The men on the *Edmund Fitzgerald* might not have been spared the violence of their own storm, but they were now in another kind of calm—eternal peace.

Father Ingalls referred to "contemptuous rogue waves that break hearts and crush great hulks of steel," and to the parable that said "Hope deferred makes the heart sick," but this was not an occasion dedicated only to mourning.

"May we all thank God that we are permitted this extraordinary opportunity to have the service of 'Burial at Sea' to bring full flower our Memorial for the Twenty-nine of the stately big *Fitz,*" he prayed.

After consecrating the site, Father Ingalls repeated a tradition that would continue as long as his church commemorated the loss of the *Edmund Fitzgerald:* a necrologist read the names of the twenty-nine men, and one by one, a family member, or a proxy for a family member, approached the replica of the *Fitzgerald's* bell and gave the rope a tug. After ringing the bell, each participant picked up a carnation and dropped it onto the surface of Lake Superior. A piper dressed in Scottish garb played "Amazing Grace" and "Flowers of the Forest," and two buglers concluded the ceremony with "Taps."

For those aboard the *Mackinaw,* there was hope in the sense of finality. After finishing "Taps," one of the buglers faced the families and played "Reveille," an upbeat finale that underscored the remarks offered by Robert N. Dunn at the end of the ceremony.

Dunn, a Chicago attorney instrumental in the planning of the service, expressed the hope that the consecration of the site would permit the *Fitzgerald's* crew to rest in peace. He then paraphrased a poem by a poet whose name he didn't know:

And so, let us remember the love and the strength of the men of the Edmund Fitzgerald *when we say: "They are gone." Gone where? Gone from your sight is all.*

They are just as large in your hearts and prayers as when you last saw them. And just at the moment when you are saying, "They are gone," there are old friends and loved ones saying, "They are here, safe and happy with us!"

And when your ship sails over the horizon toward that other shore, the sun will shine brightly on you, and you will hear their glad shouts saying, "Here they come!"

The ceremony ended and the *Mackinaw* headed back to Detroit, where the family members would say their goodbyes until the next time they had occasion to gather. Reunions based on tragedies—even reunions like this one, which was supposed to have been somber yet joyous—always left a dull ache afterward, and this would be no exception. Some of the family members would see one another within a few months, when another anniversary arrived and they'd gather in Detroit or Whitefish Point. For others, the next big meeting would be a little more than a year away, when the twenty-fifth anniversary came around and there was bound to be another round of commemorations accompanying a spike in the public interest in the *Fitzgerald* story.

The *Mackinaw* arrived at the Sault Ste. Marie locks after a pleasant trip down the lake. The Coast Guard cutter was locking through when a number of people aboard took notice of a long ore boat locking through beside them. The huge vessel, like the *Mackinaw,* had been downbound on Lake Superior, and its crewmen were probably enjoying one of those pleasant summer days when the lake stretches out before you in a beautiful expanse of blue and you just know why you've chosen to make your living on the water.

The ship was the *Arthur M. Anderson.*

POSTSCRIPT

PAM JOHNSON WALKED TO THE EDGE OF LAKE SUPERIOR AND STEPPED IN. Cold water filled her shoes and worked its way up her bare legs. She looked out across the water on this cold, blustery November evening and thought about her father, Bob Rafferty, who had perished on the *Edmund Fitzgerald* exactly twenty-five years earlier. His body—his DNA—remained in these waters, and he would be here, buried at sea, long after Pam herself had passed on.

She had been living in Fort Benning, Georgia, when her mother called with the news about the *Fitz*. She was eight months pregnant, living with her husband on an Army base, and she felt disconnected from the terrible events that had taken place so far away on the upper Great Lakes. She had seen an article about the *Fitzgerald* buried deep in her newspaper, when she was looking for the movie listings and thinking about going out for the evening with her husband. Her father had worked on a number of ships, including the *Fitz,* so she didn't immediately make the connection. When her mother called and mentioned the *Fitzgerald,* she'd blurted out, "Is my daddy dead?"—a strange feeling for her, since she never called her father Daddy and she had never considered the idea of his not being around. She was about to bear him another grandchild and all of a sudden she felt as if she were five years old again.

Twenty-five years was a long time, and Pam's children were now grown. She'd lived all over the place, including some time in Germany, as she followed her husband wherever his career took him. They'd finally settled in Kansas and, with no children to take care of anymore, she'd eventually taken a job making meals for the elderly. She loved the work, just as her father, who'd spent a career cooking for men on the long ore boats, had loved his. He'd been a crusty sort of guy, as so many boat stewards were, and she'd laugh whenever she thought about how sloppy he could be around the kitchen at home. One time, while he was doing dishes, the cat had dropped a dead mouse at his feet; he'd used a dishtowel to pick up the mouse by the tail, and after he'd deposited the mouse in the garbage, he'd gone back to the dishes, using the same towel.

Some of Pam's fondest memories of her father involved food. Bob Rafferty was a big, husky man, and he loved the chili dogs they served at a now-defunct hot dog joint in Toledo. His wife, Brooksie, couldn't stand the things, so he'd take Pam with him on some of those occasions when he had a hankering for a good dog. For Pam, it was one of those father-daughter memories that seemed to have a texture—the warmth of the building when they walked in from the cold, the swivel stools at the counter, the steamy front windows.

She's been too busy with her own itinerant life to become very involved in the annual *Fitzgerald* memorials, until recently. She'd written Gordon Lightfoot not long after his song came out, and he'd written a nice letter back, and she'd eventually met him when he gave a concert in Salina. She'd kept track of the *Fitzgerald* news, had spoken to some of the family members, and had helped Bob Hemming when he was working on his book about the *Fitz,* but she'd never made the trip from Kansas to the annual ceremonies at the Mariners' Church in Detroit or the Great Lakes Shipwreck Museum at Whitefish Point.

Tom Farnquist had been instrumental in getting her out to the twenty-fifth anniversary commemoration. He'd helped her with her travel arrangements, and he'd been kind to her when she arrived in Michigan. She'd seen his museum and, of course, the *Fitzgerald*'s bell. After the anniversary service ended with the ringing of the bell, she'd come out here to Whitefish Point.

The water was bone-chilling cold, and she tried to imagine what it must have felt like to her father, when the *Fitz* was plunging to the bottom of the lake. It was the kind of thought you tried to avoid, but it was unavoidable; it was the kind of thought that tormented every family member or friend of anyone who had died a sudden, violent death. Fortunately, time had a way of holding those thoughts to only occasional appearances.

Pam pulled out a tiny shampoo bottle—the kind they give you in hotels. It was empty. She unscrewed the cap and, bending over, dipped the bottle into the lake. Grains of sand mixed in with the water, clouding it before settling at the bottom.

She would take this bottle, along with the sand in her shoes, back to Kansas. She now had a part of Lake Superior and, with it, a part of her father.

Tim McCall initially learned about the *Edmund Fitzgerald* when he was an eighth grader in Indianapolis, working on a project entitled "What a Disaster!" His class broke into groups, each group to study and file a report on subjects ranging from natural disasters to such historical events as World War II and the Holocaust. The *Titanic* was up for grabs, as was the *Edmund Fitzgerald.* Since he knew almost nothing about the *Fitz,* McCall chose the lost freighter's story for his project.

McCall, who was born on August 10, 1985, nearly a decade after the *Fitz* went down, was mesmerized by the mystery and drama of the story, and he wasn't content with simply completing his class project and moving on; he decided to do what every fourteen-year-old kid does in his free time: start a Web site.

"I didn't think enough people knew about it," he stated shortly after the Web site celebrated its fifth anniversary on April 25, 2005. "I wanted to teach people about it."

Oddly enough, while there were a number of sites offering information about the *Fitzgerald,* there wasn't a single one devoted exclusively to the ship. The name Edmund Fitzgerald had already been appropriated by a firm producing shipwreck and lighthouse documentaries, so McCall wound up calling his Web site *ssefo.com*—short for *S.S. Edmund Fitzgerald Online.*

By his own admission, the early permutation of the site was "a mess," but with the help and encouragement of his parents, McCall developed it into a dynamic, useful source of information that included a history of the ship and its last voyage, photographs, a list of the crew members, crew profiles, the lyrics to the Gordon Lightfoot song, and a bulletin board encouraging people to share their ideas about the *Fitzgerald* and the different theories about its sinking. In time, relatives of the lost crewmen visited the Web site and contacted McCall, leading to a series of interviews that were eventually added to the site.

"My age was an advantage," McCall remembered, noting that Web site visitors were always surprised when they learned that the site had been founded and was being operated by a teenager. "Obviously, I had no ulterior motive. I don't make a dime on the Web site."

Not that McCall's youth shielded him from some of the *Fitzgerald* story's downside: he was exposed, quickly enough, to the petty bickering and territorialism that has tarnished the shipwreck from the beginning. He was threatened with a lawsuit, and, on one occasion, had to shut down the bulletin board when a visitor posted a vicious message about one of the crew members.

He persevered through it all, through his high school years and his attendance at Indiana University, where he enrolled in a pre-med program. The *Edmund Fitzgerald,* McCall's family and friends came to realize, was far more than a phase or passing interest to McCall; with more than 100,000 visitors per year, the Web site and its young founder were becoming important figures in the *Edmund Fitzgerald's* future.

John O'Brien was seventeen years old and attending college in Columbus, Ohio, when the police knocked on his apartment door on November 11, 1975.

"We're looking for John O'Brien," they told the startled teenager.

Thoughts raced through O'Brien's head. What had he done? Had something happened to his car? Had someone stolen it or wrecked it?

"That's me," he managed.

"You need to call this number," one of the cops told him, handing him a slip of paper. "It's an emergency."

The telephone number was his mother's back in Toledo.

O'Brien didn't have a phone in his apartment, and all kinds of ideas had run through his head by the time he'd reached a phone and called home. He never would have imagined the news he received from his mother: "Your dad's boat came up missing."

Thirty years later, O'Brien looked back on the anxious days that followed. He'd immediately returned to Toledo, and for the next several days, he and his family hung on to withering hope, no one quite believing that the *Fitzgerald* had sunk or that Red O'Brien would never be heard from again. John had visited the *Fitz* with his father, and had even hoped to work on it—or a ship like it— someday. Red O'Brien had never uttered a word of concern about the ship's safety. Even as the hours added up and reason insisted that there was little to hope for, the family held on. "I know your dad," somebody would tell John. "He's probably on an island someplace. I'm sure he made it."

In a strange way, the loss of Red O'Brien opened up the future for his son. John was an exceptional student, starting college at sixteen and graduating two years later. Despite the fact that both of his parents had taken great pride in his scholastic achievements, John failed to share their enthusiasm, and he might have remained in Ohio, trying to determine the course he wanted his life to take, had the *Fitzgerald* reached its destination on November 11, 1975.

The death of Red O'Brien gave John a sense of freedom. His mother had re-married and still lived in Toledo, but without his father around, John no longer felt as rooted to the area. He vacationed in Florida, fell in love with the southern part of the state, and packed up and moved. In time, he became very successful in a string of businesses, and between that and the real estate he accumulated over the years, he enjoyed the kind of life his father had wanted for him.

"I've been very blessed," he says, sitting back and reflecting on the turns his life has taken since the loss of the *Edmund Fitzgerald,* "and I've got to give my dad a lot of credit for it. He was one to say, 'What do you want to be? Get an education. Don't be like me, working on a boat. Go to college, go to college.'"

These weren't just hollow words, spoken by a father hoping his son would fare better in life than he did. Red O'Brien set up a trust fund, built from years of savings, to assure his son the education he never had. The monthly stipend from the trust fund was available only as long as John remained in school.

"It made me stay in college," John admits, "because college was a job. I was getting paid. Here was my dad, a guy with limited education, working on the lakes, yet he had the insight to do these things. A lot of people have great ideas, but they don't do anything about it. He was different. He went out and did it. He was very motivating for me. He got me moving."

John was only four years old when his parents divorced, and the split cut even more into the limited time he had with his father. His mother was always gracious about adjusting visitation hours to accommodate Red's limited time in Toledo, and when father and son did get together, even if for a few hours, Red O'Brien made a special point of seeing that John stayed mentally sharp.

"We never went anywhere without doing math in the car," John remembers. "He would give me all these quizzes. We were always doing math."

John doesn't spend too much time thinking about the *Fitzgerald*. There are photographs of his father in the house, as well as photos of the ship; a *Fitz* magnet occupies a spot on the refrigerator. John's three daughters have heard the ship's story, though his seven-year-old twins are too young to fully appreciate it. John and his wife traveled to Whitefish Point and Detroit for the twenty-fifth-anniversary ceremonies honoring the *Fitzgerald*'s crewmen, but, by John's own admission, such pilgrimages aren't necessary for his coming to terms with events that happened so long ago.

He has few regrets. He and his father enjoyed a good relationship while Red was alive, and John will see that his father's memory is kept alive in his children and, eventually, grandchildren.

"I'm really sorry that I never had the experience of being with my father as I got older," he says. "You know, when you're seventeen, you haven't really appreciated your dad yet. He's going to be there forever. I wish he could have seen all the things that we accomplished. It's really too bad because I'm sure my father would have been somewhere near me when he retired.

"One of my favorite singers is Jimmy Buffett. He sings a lot about the water, the ocean, and stuff like that, and we live the Jimmy Buffett lifestyle. We have the ability to take three months off in the summer and go down to the Florida Keys, where we can fish and go diving. My dad would have loved that, too.

"My dad was a nondrinker and nonsmoker, and he was in perfect health. He could have lived to be seventy-five, eighty years old. So I did get a little shortchanged there, but you have to live with the hand you're dealt."

THE CREW OF THE *EDMUND FITZGERALD*

Ernest Michael McSorley, 63, Master, Toledo, Ohio

John Henkle McCarthy, 62, First Mate, Bay Village, Ohio

James A. Pratt, 44, Second Mate, Lakewood, Ohio

George John Holl, 60, Chief Engineer, Cabot, Pennsylvania

Michael Eugene Armagost, 37, Third Mate, Iron River, Wisconsin

Edward Francis Bindon, 47, First Assistant Engineer, Fairport Harbor, Ohio

Thomas Edgar Edwards, 50, Second Assistant Engineer, Oregon, Ohio

Russell George Haskell, 40, Second Assistant Engineer, Millbury, Ohio

Oliver Joseph Champeau, 51, Third Assistant Engineer, Milwaukee, Wisconsin

Frederick J. Beetcher, 54, Porter, Superior, Wisconsin

Thomas Bentsen, Oiler, 23, St. Joseph, Michigan

Thomas Dale Borgeson, 41, Able-Bodied Maintenance Man, Duluth, Minnesota

Nolan Frank Church, 55, Porter, Silver Bay, Minnesota

Ransom Edward Cundy, 53, Watchman, Superior, Wisconsin

Bruce Lee Hudson, 22, Deckhand, North Olmsted, Ohio

Allen George Kalmon, 43, Second Cook, Washburn, Wisconsin

Gordon F. MacLellan, 30, Wiper, Clearwater, Florida

Joseph William Mazes, 59, Special Maintenance Man, Ashland, Wisconsin

Eugene William O'Brien, 50, Wheelsman, Township, Ohio

Karl Anthony Peckol, 55, Watchman, Ashtabula, Ohio

John Joseph Poviach, 59, Wheelsman, Bradenton, Florida

Robert Charles Rafferty, 62, Temporary Steward (First Cook), Toledo, Ohio

Paul M. Riipa, 22, Deckhand, Ashtabula, Ohio

John David Simmons, 60, Wheelsman, Ashland, Wisconsin

William J. Spengler, 59, Watchman, Toledo, Ohio

Mark Andrew Thomas, 21, Deckhand, Richmond Heights, Ohio

Ralph Grant Walton, 58, Oiler, Fremont, Ohio

David Elliot Weiss, 22, Cadet (deck), Canogha Park, California

Blaine Howard Wilhelm, 52, Oiler, Moquah, Wisconsin

THE WRECK OF THE *EDMUND FITZGERALD*

by Gordon Lightfoot

The legend lives on from the Chippewa on down
Of the big lake they call Gitche Gumee.
The lake it is said never gives up her dead
When the skies of November turn gloomy.
With a load of iron ore 26,000 tons more
Than the *Edmund Fitzgerald* weighed empty;
That good ship and true was a bone to be chewed
When the gales of November came early.

The ship was the pride of the American side
Coming back from some mill in Wisconsin.
As the big freighters go it was bigger than most
With a crew and good captain well-seasoned;
Concluding some terms with a couple of steel firms
When they left fully loaded for Cleveland
And later that night when the ship's bell rang
Could it be the north wind they'd been feeling?

The wind in the wires made a tattletale sound
And a wave broke over the railing,
And every man knew as the captain did too
'Twas the witch of November come stealing.
The dawn came late and the breakfast had to wait
When the gales of November came slashing.
When afternoon came it was freezing rain
In the face of the hurricane west wind.

When suppertime came the old cook came on deck saying
"Fellas, it's too rough to feed ya."
At 7 P.M. a main hatchway caved in he said
"Fellas, it's been good to know ya."
The captain wired in he had water coming in
And the good ship and crew was in peril;
And later that night when his lights went out of sight
Came the wreck of the *Edmund Fitzgerald*.

Does anyone know where the love of God goes
When the waves turn the minutes to hours?
The searchers all say they'd have made Whitefish Bay
If they'd put 15 more miles behind her.
They might have split up or they might have capsized,
They may have broke deep and took water;
And all that remains is the faces and the names
Of the wives and the sons and the daughters.

Lake Huron rolls, Superior sings
In the rooms of her ice water mansion.
Old Michigan steams like a young man's dreams;
The islands and bays are for sportsmen;
And farther below Lake Ontario

Takes in what Lake Erie can send her,
And the iron boats go as the mariners all know
With the gales of November remembered.

In a musty old hall in Detroit they prayed
In the Maritime Sailors' Cathedral;
The church bell chimed 'til it rang 29 times
For each man on the *Edmund Fitzgerald*.
The legend lives on from the Chippewa on down
Of the big lake they called Gitche Gumee.
Superior, they said, never gives up her dead
When the gales of November come early.

GLOSSARY

access tunnels—long tunnels running beneath the spar deck on either side of the cargo hold, allowing crewmen to move between the front and back of a ship during inclement weather

aft (or after deck)—back, or stern, section of the ship

ballast—added weight, usually lake water, to lower the ship in the water and add stability

ballast pumps—pumps used to remove water from a ship's ballast tanks

ballast tanks—large, watertight storage tanks below the cargo hold, on the starboard and port sides of the ship, in which ballast is stored

ballast tank vent—pipe running from a ballast tank to the spar deck, allowing air to be removed from the ballast tank

bow—front or forward section of a ship

bow thruster—small propeller, located in the ship's bow, used to help in maneuvering

bulkhead—partition used to divide sections of a ship's hull

captain (or master)—commander, or chief officer, of a ship

capsize—roll onto a side or turn over

chief engineer—crewman in charge of the ship's engine

de-ballasting—the process of pumping, or expelling, water from a ship's ballast tanks

draft—depth of a ship's hull beneath the waterline

fathom—a measurement of depth, equal to six feet

first mate—the second in command of a ship

flotsam—floating debris or wreckage

fore (or foredeck)—forward, or bow, section of a ship

founder—to fill with water and sink

freeboard—distance between the waterline and the spar deck

green water—solid water, rather than spray, washing over the decks of a ship

grounding—striking bottom, or running completely aground

hatch combings—raised rims around the hatch openings, upon which the hatch covers are fitted

hatch covers—large, flat sheets of steel that cover the hatch combings and prevent water from entering the cargo hold

hatches—openings in the ship's spar deck, through which cargo is loaded

hogging—the bending down of the front and back of a ship, with no support for the middle

hold—the large area of a ship in which cargo is stored

hull—main body of a ship, upon which the decks and superstructures are built

keel—backbone of the ship, running the entire length of a ship, upon which the framework of the ship is built

keelson—reinforced "ribs" of a ship, attached to the keel

knot—a measurement of speed, in nautical miles per hour, 1.15 statute miles per hour

list—a ship's leaning or tipping to one side

pilothouse—enclosed deck in which the wheel and map room are located. The upper-most deck on a ship

poop deck (or boat deck)—highest deck at the stern, on which lifeboats are stored

port—left side of a ship when you are facing the bow

screw—a ship's propeller

shoal—shallow area of water, usually marked by a sandbar, reef, or area of rising lake floor

shoaling—striking, or bottoming out, against the bottom of a shallow area of water

spar deck (or weather deck)—deck where the hatches are located

starboard—right side of a ship when you are facing the bow

stern—back or after section of a ship

steward—ship's cook

superstructure—structures and cabins built above the hull of a ship

taconite—low-grade iron, usually processed and formed into small, marble-sized pellets

wheelsman—crew member who steers the ship

working—a ship's twisting, springing, and flexing in heavy seas

NOTES

Abbreviations

MBT (Marine Board transcripts): U.S. Coast Guard, "In the Matter of the Sinking of the SS Edmund Fitzgerald on Lake Superior, 10 November 1975."

CGR (Coast Guard Report): U.S. Department of Transportation, Marine Board of Investigation, "SS Edmund Fitzgerald, Sinking in Lake Superior, 10 November 1975, with Loss of Life, U.S. Coast Guard Marine Board of Investigation and Commandant's Report."

Preface

2 "turn minutes to hours": Gordon Lightfoot, "The Wreck of the *Edmund Fitzgerald*," Moose Music, Ltd., 1976.

3 "Of all the dives": MacInnis, *Fitzgerald's Storm,* p. 2.

6 "Give it a tug": ibid., p. 111.

Chapter One

12 "an older man": Clarence Dennis, MBT, p. 1702.

19 "Every captain knew": Bishop, *The Night the Fitz Went Down,* p. 74.

20 "I remember Captain Lambert": author interview with Eddie Chaput.

21 "I still get letters": "Boat's Demise Uncertain," *Daily Northwestern,* November 11, 1976.

22 "He kept to himself": Thomas Garcia, MBT, p. 2746.

22 "He was a quiet guy": Bishop, *The Night the Fitz Went Down,* p. 74.

23 "prudent mariner": Delmore Webster, MBT, p. 2451.

23 "When he came": ibid., p. 2520.

23 "a very good man": Andrew Rajner, MBT, p. 2270.

23 "The sea was his life": "Captain Eyed Retirement," *Fond du Lac Reporter,* November 12, 1975.

25 "May be home": author interview with Pam Johnson.

28 "So long, boys": Clarence Dennis, MBT, p. 1728.

Chapter Two

31 "It was a beautiful": Cooper, transcript of speech.

31 "At the time": Jesse B. Cooper, MBT, p. 452.

37 "We were having": ibid.

37 *Fitz* storm: SEE Kirk Lombardy, "Great Lakes Storm November 9–11, 1988: *Edmund Fitzgerald* Remembered," *Mariners Weather Log,* Spring/Summer 2002, pp. 1–7.

38 "Actual weather conditions": U.S. Department of Transportation, Marine Board of Investigation, "Foundering of SS Henry Steinbrenner," p. 3.

38 "sluggish": ibid., p. 8.

39 "Seventeen crew members": ibid., p. 4.

39 "the cause of the *Steinbrenner*'s": ibid., p. 1.

46 "When you are in a heavy sea": Delmore Webster, MBT, p. 2490.

46 "considerably": Richard Orgel, MBT, p. 2217.

46 "When you are standing": ibid.

46 "It seems that when the sea": ibid., pp. 2217–18.

46 "It is a funny feeling": Andrew Rajner, MBT, p. 2340.

47 "I asked him": Richard Orgel, MBT, pp. 2218–19.

47 "Oh, this thing": ibid., p. 2219.

47 "He told me": ibid.

47 "I have walked": Peter Pulcer, MBT, p. 255.

47 "I have seen her roll": ibid., p. 239.

48 "She handled like": ibid.

50 "This boat is getting": Ratigan, *Great Lakes Shipwrecks,* p. 18.

52 "excessive hogging": U.S. Department of Transportation, Marine Board of Investigation, "Foundering of the SS Carl D. Bradley," p. 12.

52 "This casualty has emphasized": ibid., p. 3.

53 "The National Transportation": letter, Joseph J. O'Connell, Jr., to Willard J. Smith, February 8, 1968.

55 "tremendous": U.S. Department of Transportation, Marine Board of Investigation, "SS Daniel J. Morrell Sinking with Loss of Life," p. 10.

55 "I'll call you back": ibid.

57 "The main deck": LaLonde, "Sole Survivor Dennis Hale . . ."

58 "spurting water": U.S. Department of Transportation, Marine Board of Investigation, "SS Daniel J. Morrell Sinking," p. 15.

58 "high load due to": ibid., p. 27.

58 "The free surface": ibid.

58 "Had the two screen bulkheads": ibid., p. 32.

60 "rolling some": Jesse B. Cooper, MBT, p. 2104.

64 "Look at this, Morgan": Hemming, *Gales of November,* p. 141. The rest of the conversation is also from this source.

64 "I've got problems": Cooper, transcript of speech.

65 "I went down": Stonehouse, *Edmund Fitzgerald,* p. 10.

67 "I've lost both radars": Marshall, *Shipwrecks of Lake Superior,* p. 55.

68 "Stand by": Hemming, *Gales of November,* p. 169.

68 "Who is this": Cedric Woodard, MBT, p. 1953.

68 "I didn't recognize": ibid., pp. 1953–54.

69 "Okay, thanks": Gary Wigen, MBT, p. 2181.

69 "After we heard": ibid., p. 2196.

69 "I'm very glad": Cedric Woodard, MBT, p. 1973. The rest of this conversation is from this source.

Chapter Three

72 "He gave no indication": Jesse B. Cooper, MBT, p. 460.

73 "Silence is the usual": Bishop, *The Night the Fitz Went Down,* p. 78.

73 "You don't get": Hemming, *Gales of November,* pp. 167–68.

74 "I had a hatch crane": Cooper, transcript of speech.

74 "I don't know": ibid.

75 "There is a target": Morgan Clark, MBT, pp. 647–48. All citations in this conversation are from this source.

77 "Where's the *Fitzgerald*?": Cooper, transcript of speech.

78 "just a fraction" and "When you are staring": Robert May, MBT, p. 700.

78 "We should [have been] able": Morgan Clark, MBT, p. 659.

78 "We had something": ibid., pp. 650–51.

78 "We tried everything": Jesse B. Cooper, MBT, p. 531.

79 "Everything told us": Hemming, *Gales of November,* p. 6.

80 "This is the *Anderson*": Philip Branch, MBT, pp. 2975–76.

Chapter Four

82 "If there had been": author interview with Gary Rosenau.

82 "I've seen": ibid.

83 "I considered it": Philip Branch, MBT, p. 2976.

83 "a conspiracy of ineptitude": Stonehouse, *The Wreck of the Edmund Fitzgerald,* p. 97.

83 "When the *Fitzgerald* was lost": ibid.

84 "an uncertainty": CGR, p. 34.

85 "Do you know": author interview with Charles Millradt.

85 "You've got one": author interview with Don Erickson.

85 "I don't know": Hemming, *Gales of November,* pp. 197–98.

86 "You'll have to make": ibid., p. 197.

86 "gung-ho sailor" and "He was informed": Cooper, transcript of speech.

87 "In my opinion": Albert Jacovetti, MBT, p. 1051.

87 "I don't know": ibid., p. 1052.

87 "There was nothing": Cedric Woodard, MBT, p. 1980.

87 "At the time": ibid., p. 1967.

89 "Bernie, I'm thinking": author interview with Don Erickson.

89 "They think you can just": author interview with Dale Lindstrom.

89 "I'll go to my grave": ibid.

89 "Everybody said no": author interview with Don Erickson.

90 "I don't know": author interview with Dale Lindstrom.

90 "They were out there": author interview with Don Erickson.

91 "Thank God it was": author interview with Jimmie Hobaugh.

91 "When the wind": ibid.

91 "In the ocean": author interview with Jimmie Hobaugh.

94 "There's trouble": author interview with Bishop Richard Ingalls.

94 "Both of us": ibid.

95 "English country Gothic": St. John, "Church Bells to Toll Again."

96 "That morning": ibid.

98 "Call home": author interview with Deborah (Champeau) Gomez-Felder. All direct quotations in this passage are from this source.

98 "Are you okay?" Keefe, "Edmund Fitzgerald Gravesite Consecrated." All direct quotations in this passage are from this source.

100 "He went in": Jesse B. Cooper, MBT, p. 2104.

100 "When we put down": ibid., p. 2110.

100 "I think we want": ibid., pp. 2110–11.

102 "We were under way": Lucci, *Reservist*.

103 "poor sonic trace quality": CGR, p. 48.

103 "sonically rough area": ibid.

104 "probably": CGR, p. 49.

104 "very probably": ibid.

105 "This investigation": Winifred W. Barrow, MBT, p. 6.

105 "He was the straightest": author interview with C. S. Loosmore.

106 "We didn't know": author interview with James A. Wilson.

108 "a free-for-all": ibid.

109 "Everybody'd been thinking": ibid.

110 "We were not plotting": Jesse B. Cooper MBT, pp. 2147– 48.

110 "You are talking": ibid., p. 2097.

110 "there are two or three": ibid., p. 490.

111 "You say": ibid., p. 604.

111 "I would consider": ibid., p. 594.

111 "I firmly believe": ibid., p. 2155.

111 "a hogging situation": ibid., p. 566.

111 "I watched him": ibid., p. 474.

111 "I believe that she was cracked": ibid., pp. 565–66.

112 "At no time": ibid., p. 619.

113 "If you were taking": Andrew Rajner, MBT, p. 2328.

114 "In my opinion": Charles Lindberg, MBT, p. 2738.

114 "If you had such": Gerald Lange, MBT, p. 2568.

114 "I don't believe": John Larson, MBT, p. 2832.

114 "I would have been heading": Harry Hilgemann, MBT, p. 716.

114 "After it is blown up": John Larson, MBT, p. 2832.

115 "In rough weather": Jesse B. Cooper, MBT, p. 541.

115 "We had weekly drills": Gerald Lange, MBT, p. 2567.

115 "We have conflicts": John Larson, MBT, p. 2880.

116 "Mr. Hilsen": Donald Hilsen, MBT, pp. 2858 –59.

117 "There were 29 people": ibid., p. 2859.

117 "All these lifeboat drills": Richard Orgel, MBT, p. 2250.

117 "The problems": ibid.

118 "No doubt that they": Andrew Rajner, MBT, p. 2356.

118 "When you are in": Delmore Webster, MBT, p. 2490.

119 "Captain McSorley was a professional": Gerald Lange, MBT, p. 2559.

119 "First, I will say": ibid., pp. 2559–60.

120 "To my knowledge": Thomas Garcia, MBT, p. 2780.

121 "The survey that we have": Winifred W. Barrow, MBT, p. 2999.

121 "I have been fascinated": Sangiacomo, "Rite Marks 20 Years."

122 "When the *Edmund Fitzgerald*": ibid.

122 "Shipwrecks are different": "Lightfoot Immortalized *Edmund Fitzgerald* Wreck."

122 "According to a legend": "The Cruelest Month," *Newsweek,* November 24, 1975.

Chapter Five

124 "We spent all": author interview with Jimmie Hobaugh.

126 "We hooked up": ibid.

127 "The bow section": author interview with C. S. Loosmore.

128 "He was the youngest": author interview with James A. Wilson.

128 "This casualty presented": CGR, p. i.

129 "The most probable cause": ibid., p. ii.

131 "Not only did": p. 93.

132 "If such extensive damage": ibid., p. 96.

133 "It is concluded": ibid., p. 93.

133 "only a few": ibid., p. 94.

133 "In the opinion": ibid., pp. 93–94.

134 "It was a simple matter": author interview with C. S. Loosmore.

134 "Who would have noticed?": ibid.

135 "Nobody was reporting": ibid.

135 "The topside damage": ibid., p. 96.

135 "When we looked": author interview with James A. Wilson.

136 "If she had hit": ibid.

136 "A long time ago": ibid.

137 "If you look": author interview with C. S. Loosmore.

137 "Where's the edge": ibid.

138 "They knew they had": ibid.

138 "The lake shipping industry": letter, Paul Trimble to Webster B. Todd, Jr., September 16, 1977.

139 "Within the time frame": ibid.

139 "This verified shoal": ibid.

140 "might have been observed": ibid.

140 "The probable cause": National Transportation Safety Board, "Marine Accident Report: S.S. Edmund Fitzgerald Sinking in Lake Superior."

141 "The hatch cover failure": ibid.

142 "The most probable cause": ibid.

142 "On page 2140": ibid.

144 "Don't say anything": *In the Matter of: The Complaint of Oglebay Norton Co.*, Discovery Deposition of George H. Burgner, December 13, 1977.

144 "It's a good place": ibid.

144 "They said they'd do it": ibid.

145 "Go ahead and deliver": ibid.

145 "The steamship company": Larry Oakes, "The Mystery of the Fitzgerald," *Minneapolis Star Tribune,* November 10, 1997.

145 "Captain Pulcer": Burgner deposition, supra.

146 "She had an awful lot": ibid.

146 "He didn't make": ibid.

Chapter Six

150 "there was more": Stonehouse, *The Wreck of the Edmund Fitzgerald,* p. 52.

155 "Storms create excitement": Woutat, "Stirring Up Memories."

155 "The water was": ibid.

156 "When the first flickering": Stonehouse, *Wreck of Fitzgerald,* op.cit., p. 206.

157 "like tin foil": n.a., "Sunken ship shown to be largely intact," *Houston Chronicle,* August 24, 1989.

157 "It got everyone's attention . . ." Donald Woutat, "View of *Edmund Fitzgerald* shows surprising hole in bow," *Minneapolis Star Tribune,* August 25, 1989.

157 "I find that . . ." Paige St. John, "Shipwreck: Clear Photos Fail to Explain Great Lakes Sinking," *Seattle Times,* August 25, 1989.

158 "The mystery . . ." Woutat, "View of *Edmund Fitzgerald,*" op. cit.

159 "Law enforcement officials": author interview with Tom Farnquist.

160 "Frankly, people are not . . ." John Flesher, "Titanic of the Great Lakes," *Grand Rapids Press,* July 3, 1994.

160 "In many ways . . ." MacInnis, *Fitzgerald's Storm,* p. 2.

160 "We're hoping . . ." John Flesher, "Depths of Research," *Grand Rapids Press,* July 10, 1994.

161 "The size is incredible . . ." Jim Reilly. "Diver Explored the Wreck of the *Edmund Fitzgerald,*" *Syracuse Herald Journal,* April 23, 1997.

161 "This thing . . ." Anne Swardson, "How the *Edmund Fitzgerald* Went Down, Down, Down," *Washington Post,* July 5, 1994.

161 "It struck . . ." J. R. Clairborne, "Shedding Light on *Fitzgerald's* Mysterious Fate," *Chicago Sun-Times,* July 6, 1994.

162 "It really looked . . ." "*Edmund Fitzgerald* damage shocks explorers in mini-sub," *Toronto Star,* July 5, 1994.

162 "We still can't say . . ." "*Fitzgerald* Went Down in Seconds," *Cleveland Plain Dealer,* July 6, 1994.

162 "We think . . ." Clairborne, "Shedding Light," op. cit.

164 "All former theories . . ." "Latest *Edmund Fitzgerald* Theory: Structural Failure," *Chicago Tribune,* November 5, 1994.

164 "overworked and hadn't . . ." ibid.

165 "We were not looking": von Sternberg, "A Grim Sight."

165 Remains: It is possible that the remains found outside the *Edmund Fitzgerald* were not those of a crew member. Fred Stonehouse, for one, was skeptical. The body, he pointed out, was not actually inside the wreckage, and the advanced state of decomposition wasn't consistent with the relative recency of the wreck: normally, the icy cold waters of Lake Superior preserved dead bodies for a very long time. Even the positioning of the body was questionable: if the *Fitz* hit bottom as violently as believed, the men in the pilothouse would have been blown backward toward the stern, and probably wouldn't have been found so close to the bow.

167 "This is the most": "Diver Wants to Sink Plans to Remove Ship's Bell."

167 "a last-ditch effort": "Suit Aims to Block Salvaging Bell from Fabled Shipwreck."

168 "historical, educational": ibid.

168 "a right to see": ibid.

169 "He sees": MacInnis, *Fitzgerald's Storm,* p. 104.

170 "On the night": "Bell Rings Loud and Clear."

170 "More than anything": "Bell Recovered from *Edmund Fitzgerald* Wreck."

170 "The *Fitzgerald* isn't": "A Bell for the *Fitzgerald.*"

171 "donated to": [Richard W. Ingalls, Jr.], "Instrument of Donation for the Custodianship and Conservatorship of the Bell of the S.S.*Edmund Fitzgerald*," July 7, 1995.

172 "We restored an artifact": Poulson, "No Peace for Dead's Bell."

172 "The *Edmund Fitzgerald* bell": ibid.

173 "traveling trophy": Borg, "Ship's Bell Won't Be Put on Display."

173 "We thought": Sangiacomo, "*Fitzgerald* Bell Won't Visit Festival."

174 "If I could talk": Sangiacomo, "Dive Irks Families of *Fitzgerald* Victims."

174 "The main thing": ibid.

175 "There are two flaws": "Danger in Shipwreck Bill."

175 "The legislature": "Michigan Law Limits Photos of Remains."

175 "We already have": Flesher, "Bill Would Ban Photos of Bodies on Sunken Ships."

176 "We don't want": "Legislature Consider Shipwreck Photo Law."

179 "contemptuous rogue waves": Richard W. Ingalls, "Remarks by the Rector: The Consecration of the Gravesite of the Crew of the *S.S. Edmund Fitzgerald*." Remarks given at consecration ceremony, reprinted in program.

179 "Hope deferred": ibid.

179 "May we all": ibid.

POSTSCRIPT

183 "I didn't think": author interview with Timothy McCall.

184 "a mess": ibid.

184 "My age": ibid.

184 "We're looking": author interview with John O'Brien.

185 "I know your dad": ibid.

185 "I've been very blessed": ibid.

186 "It made me stay": ibid.

186 "We never went": ibid.

186 "I'm really sorry": ibid.

BIBLIOGRAPHY

Books

Bishop, Hugh E. *The Night the Fitz Went Down*. Duluth: Lake Superior Port Cities, 2000.

Boyer, Dwight. *Ships and Men of the Great Lakes*. New York: Dodd, Mead, 1977.

Bree, Marlin. *In the Teeth of the Northeaster*. St. Paul, Minn.: Maylor Press, 1993.

Brown, David G. *White Hurricane*. Camden, Me.: International Marine/McGraw-Hill, 2002.

Created for the Ages: Mariners' Church of Detroit. Detroit, Mariners' Church of Detroit, 2001.

Havighurst, Walter. *The Long Ships Passing*. New York: Macmillan, 1942 (revised edition, Minneapolis: University of Minnesota Press, 2002).

Hemming, Robert J. *Gales of November*. Holt, Mich.: Thunder Bay Press, 1981 (revised edition, 1997).

Hertel, Captain Robert. *The Edmund Fitzgerald: Lost with All Hands*. Spring Lake, Mich.: River Road Publications, 1999.

Junger, Sebastian. *The Perfect Storm*. New York: HarperCollins, 1997.

Kantar, Andres. *29 Missing: The True and Tragic Story of the Disappearance of the S.S. Edmund Fitzgerald*. East Lansing: Michigan State University Press, 1998.

Lee, Robert E. *Edmund Fitzgerald 1958–1975*. Detroit: Great Lakes Maritime Institute, 1977 (revised edition, 1997).

MacInnis, Dr. Joseph. *Fitzgerald's Storm*. Holt, Mich.: Thunder Bay Press, 1998.

Marshall, James R. *Shipwrecks of Lake Superior*. Duluth: Lake Superior Port Cities, 1987.

Ratigan, William. *Great Lakes Shipwrecks and Survivals*. Grand Rapids: Eerdmans, 1977.

Stonehouse, Frederick. *Lake Superior's Shipwreck Coast*. Marquette, Mich.: Avery Color Studios, 1985.

————. *The Wreck of the Edmund Fitzgerald*. Marquette, Mich.: Avery Color Studios, 1977 (revised edition, 1996).

Wargin, Kathy-Jo, and Gilbert Van Frankenhuyzen (illustrator). *The Edmund Fitzgerald: Song of the Bell*. Chelsea, Mich.: Sleeping Bear Press, 2003.

Wolff, Julius F., Jr. *Lake Superior Shipwrecks*. Duluth: Lake Superior Port Cities, 1990.

Documents and Reports

Cooper, Jesse B. Transcript of speech on the sinking of the *Edmund Fitzgerald*. Given before the Wisconsin Marine Historical Society, November 7, 1986.

In the Matter of the Complaint of Oglebay Norton Co., as Bareboat Charterer, Etcetera. U.S. Court for the Northern District of Ohio, Eastern Division. C-75-1036. DISCOVERY DEPOSITION OF GEORGE H. BURGNER, December 13, 1977.

U.S. Department of Transportation, Marine Board of Investigation. "Foundering of the SS Carl D. Bradley, Lake Michigan, 18 November 1958, with Loss of Life, U.S. Coast Guard Marine Board of Investigation Report and Commandant's Action," July 7, 1959.

U.S. Department of Transportation, Marine Board of Investigation. "SS Daniel J. Morrell Sinking with Loss of Life, Lake Huron, 29 November 1966, U.S. Coast Guard Marine Board of Investigation Report and Commandant's Action," March 4, 1968.

U.S. Department of Transportation, Marine Board of Investigation, "SS Edmund Fitzgerald:

Sinking in Lake Superior on 10 November 1975 with Loss of Life, U.S. Coast Guard Marine Board of Investigation and Commandant's Report," July 26, 1977.

U.S. Department of Transportation, Marine Board of Investigation. "Foundering of SS Henry Steinbrenner, off Passage Island, Lake Superior, on 11 May 1953, with Loss of Life, U.S. Coast Guard Marine Board of Investigation and Commandant's Report," July 10, 1953.

U.S. Department of Transportation, U.S. Coast Guard. "In the Matter of Marine Board Board of Investigation, Sinking of the SS Edmund Fitzgerald on Lake Superior, 10 November 1975." [Complete, unpublished transcripts of witness testimony before the Marine Board of Investigation.]

U.S. National Transportation Safety Board. "Marine Accident Report: SS Edmund Fitzgerald Sinking in Lake Superior, November 10, 1975," May 4, 1978.

Newspaper and Magazine Articles

Articles with no byline appear first.

"A Bell for the Dead." *Orlando* (Fla.) *Sentinel,* July 6, 1995.

"A Bell for the Fitzgerald." *Cleveland Plain Dealer,* July 4, 1995.

"Abyss Gives Up a Ghost Robot: Photos of Legendary Wreck." *Newsday,* August 25, 1989.

"All Hands on Ship Seem Lost." *Washington Post,* November 12, 1975.

"A Proper Remembrance." *Salt Lake Tribune,* July 12, 1995.

"A Raised Bell Recalls the Sunken Fitzgerald." *New York Times,* July 9, 1995.

"Ban on Disaster Photos in Great Lakes criticized." *Las Vegas Review-Journal,* October 4, 1997.

"Bell from Wrecked Freighter Raised." *Patriot Ledger* (Quincy, Mass.), July 6, 1995.

"Bell of Edmund Fitzgerald Is Raised from Lake Superior." *Buffalo* (New York) *News,* July 5, 1995.

"Bell Raised from Edmund Fitzgerald." *Chicago Tribune,* July 5, 1995.

"Bell Raised off Famous Shipwreck." *Cincinnati Post,* July 5, 1995.

"Bell Recovered from Edmund Fitzgerald Wreck." *Milwaukee Journal Sentinel,* July 5, 1995.

"Bell Rings Loud and Clear." *Cleveland Plain Dealer,* July 5, 1995.

"Bells Sound Out Goodbye to the Edmund Fitzgerald." *Orlando* (Fla.) *Sentinel,* July 19, 1999.

"Bells Still Toll for Lost Crewmen." *Detroit News,* November 9, 1998.

"Bell Symbolizes Closure for Survivors." *Milwaukee Journal Sentinel,* July 8, 1995.

"Bell Tolls 'Call to the Last Watch' for Crew of Lost Ore Carrier." *Orlando County Register,* July 8, 1995.

"Bell tolls for Edmund Fitzgerald." *Cincinnati Post,* July 20, 1999.

"Bill May Keep Gawkers from Fitzgerald Site." *Milwaukee Journal Sentinel,* December 30, 1996.

"Bill Would Outlaw Showing Lake Disaster Photos." *Grand Rapids Press,* May 3, 1996.

"Board of Inquiry to Probe Sinking of Freighter." *Fond du Lac Reporter,* November 13, 1975.

"Board Orders Radar Search in Area of Sunken Fitzgerald." *Lima* (Ohio) *News,* November 19, 1975.

"Board Rules on Cause of Sinking." *New York Times,* May 7, 1978.

"Body at Fitzgerald Site May Be Removed." *Minneapolis Star-Tribune,* July 30, 1994.

"Canada May Try to Recover Body Found at Edmund Fitzgerald Wreck." *Chicago Tribune,* July 31, 1994.

"Captain Eyed Retirement." *Fond du Lac Reporter,* November 12, 1975.

"Captain Testifies Ship Sank Quickly." *Advocate* (Newark, N. J.), November 21, 1975.

"Chronology of Disasters." *Fond du Lac Reporter,* November 12, 1975.

"Church Bell Chimed Till It Rang 29 Times." *Chicago Sun-Times,* November 8, 2004.

"Church Remembers Crew of the Edmund Fitzgerald." *Chicago Tribune,* November 13, 1995.

"Cite Condition of Fitzgerald." *Journal-Tribune* (Marysville, Ohio), November 13, 1975.

"Crewmen Families Are Awaiting Word." *Herald-Times-Reporter,* (Manitowoc, Wisc.), November 12, 1975.

"Crewmen's Families Say Last Goodbye." *Detroit News,* July 8, 1999.

"Crew Search Is Hampered by Weather." *Herald-Times-Reporter* (Manitowoc, Wisc.), November 12, 1975.

"Danger in Shipwreck Bill." *Grand Rapids Times,* June 11, 1997.

"Dead Defiled: Relatives of Edmund Fitzgerald Victims Want Dives Stopped." *Grand Rapids Press,* December 22, 1994.

"Debris, Empty Lifeboats Only Sign of Freighter Sunk in Lake with 29." *Chicago Tribune,* November 12, 1975.

"Deep-Water Robot Filming Edmund Fitzgerald Wreck." *Austin American Statesman,* August 25, 1989.

"Dive Finds Corpse by Wreck of the Edmund Fitzgerald." *Toronto Star,* July 28, 1994.

"Dive Team Prepared to Get Edmund Fitzgerald's Bell." *Grand Rapids Press,* June 29, 1995.

"Diver Brings Up Bell of Famed Shipwreck Edmund Fitzgerald." *Greensboro* (N.C.) *News Record,* July 5, 1995.

"Diver Retrieves Bell of Wrecked Edmund Fitzgerald." *Dayton* (Ohio) *Daily News,* July 5, 1995.

"Diver Wants to Sink Plan to Remove Ship's Bell." *Grand Rapids Press,* February 26, 1995.

"Dive to Sunken Freighter Still on Hold." *Grand Rapids Press,* August 14, 1995.

"Early Season Blast of Winter Recalls Some Chilling Memories." *Dallas Morning News,* November 13, 1998.

"Edmund Fitzgerald." *San Francisco Chronicle,* January 10, 1986.

"Edmund Fitzgerald Damage Shocks Explorers in Mini-sub." *Toronto Star,* July 5, 1994.

"Edmund Fitzgerald Divers Must Respect the Grieving." *Minneapolis Star Tribune,* November 10, 2000.

"Edmund Fitzgerald Honored." *Grand Rapids Press,* November 10, 1997.

"Edmund Fitzgerald Intact Until It Crashed on Lake's Bottom." *Pantagraph* (Bloomington, Ill.), July 6, 1994.

"Edmund Fitzgerald's Bell Pulled from Wreck." *Austin American Statesman,* July 5, 1995.

"Edmund Fitzgerald's Bell to Go on Display." *Milwaukee Journal Sentinel,* February 18, 1996.

"Edmund Fitzgerald Sank 1 Year Ago Today in Lake Superior Storm." *Fond du Lac Reporter,* November 10, 1976.

"Edmund Fitzgerald: Ship was Named After Him" (obituary of Edmund Fitzgerald). *Boston Globe,* January 10, 1986.

"Edmund Fitzgerald Wreck Proves to Be a Strong Draw." *Houston Chronicle,* July 31, 1994.

"Edmund Fitzgerald Wreck Remains a Mystery." *Times-Bulletin* (Van Wert, Ohio), November 10, 1976.

"Face of Dead Sailor Isn't Shown." *Milwaukee Journal Sentinel,* November 4, 1995.

"Families Leave Flowers to Mark Lost Sailors' Grave." *Milwaukee Journal Sentinel,* July 19, 1999.

"Families of Fitzgerald Crew Angry About Money Made from Wreck." *Grand Rapids Press,* October 30, 2000.

"Families Plan Final Salute to Freighter's Crew." *Toronto Star,* July 3, 1999.

"Family Objects to Displaying Bell from Edmund Fitzgerald." *Minneapolis Star Tribune,* March 14, 1996.

"Fitzgerald Bell Tolls for Lost Crew." *San Antonio Express-News,* July 8, 1995.

"Fitzgerald Crew Remembered." *Dayton* (Ohio) *Daily News,* November 19, 1997.

"Fitzgerald in Tip-top Shape." *Herald-Times-Reporter* (Manitowoc, Wisc.), November 13, 1975.

"Fitzgerald Researcher Defends Video." *Grand Rapids Press,* November 12, 1995.

"Fitzgerald Sinking Is Still a Mystery." *Detroit News,* November 11, 1998.

"Fitzgerald Service Still Popular." *Detroit Free Press,* November 10, 1997.

"Fitzgerald 'Went Down in Seconds': Probers of Tragedy in Lake Superior Find Crumpled Bow." *Cleveland Plain Dealer,* July 6, 1994.

"For Whom the Bell Tolls." *Traverse City Record-Eagle,* November 10, 1997.

"Freighter Bodies May Not Be Found." *Fond du Lac Reporter,* November 13, 1975.

"Freighter's Crew Gets Final Tribute." *Cleveland Plain Dealer,* July 3, 1999.

"Great Lakes' Biggest Ship to Be Launched Tomorrow." *New York Times,* June 6, 1958.

"Greatest Single-Day Disaster Struck Great Lakes Storm 62 Years Ago." *Fond du Lac Reporter,* November 12, 1975.

"High-tech Tools Fast Unlocking Sunken Secrets." *Toronto Star,* July 19, 1994.

"Hurricanelike Storm Hammers Nation, State." *Detroit News,* November 11, 1998.

"In Service on Calm Waters, Fitz Remembered." *Minneapolis Star Tribune,* July 19, 1999.

"Interactive CD-ROM Dives into 1975 Shipwreck on Lake Superior." *Detroit News,* November 10, 1996.

"Lakes' Safety Plan Tied to '75 Tragedy." *Chicago Tribune,* November 10, 1985.

"Lakes Treacherous in November." *Milwaukee Journal,* November 11, 1975.

"Lake Superior Ship Sinks; 29 Lost." *Daily Tribune* (Wisconsin Rapids, Wisc.), November 11, 1975.

"Lake Superior Ship with 30–35 Missing." *New York Times,* November 11, 1975.

"Last Words from Ship." *Post-Crescent* (Appleton, Wisc.), November 13, 1975.

"Latest Edmund Fitzgerald Theory: Structural Failure." *Chicago Tribune,* November 5, 1994.

"Legend Lives On." *Vancouver Columbian,* November 17, 1995.

"Legislature Consider Shipwreck Photo Law." *Grand Rapids Press,* May 15, 1996.

"Lightfoot Tolls Bell for Fitzgerald." *Milwaukee Journal Sentinel,* November 11, 1995.

"Memorial Service Is Held for Lost Freighter's Crew." *New York Times,* July 19, 1999.

"Michigan Law Limits Photos of Remains." *New York Times,* October 5, 1997.

"Michigan View." *Grand Rapids Press,* May 3, 1992.

"MSU Team Rings in a New Assignment." *Grand Rapids Press,* July 11, 1995.

"No Survivors." *Milwaukee Journal,* November 12, 1975.

"November Ship Disasters." *Holland Evening Sentinel,* November 11, 1975.

"November 'Witch' Has Deadly History." *Cincinnati Post,* November 13, 1998.

"Ore Carrier Sinks in Lake Storm." *Holland Evening Sentinel,* November 11, 1975.

"Photos in Book on Shipwreck Upset Families of the Victims." *New York Times,* November 5, 1995.

"Pictures Shot of 'Edmund Fitzgerald.'" *Fort Lauderdale Sun-Sentinel,* August 25, 1989.

"Plane Sights Wreckage of a Ship." *Milwaukee Journal,* November 14, 1975.

"Plaque Honors Ore Carrier Dead." *Holland Sentinel,* September 3, 1976.

"Plundering the Edmund Fitzgerald." *Chicago Tribune,* November 10, 2000.

"Poor Hatch Coverings Caused Ship's Sinking." *Syracuse* (N.Y.) *Herald-Journal,* August 3, 1977.

"Poor Hatch Closures Blamed in a Sinking." *New York Times,* August 3, 1977.

"Program on Fitzgerald on Tap." *Cleveland Plain Dealer,* November 9, 2000.

"Recovery of 29 Crewmen Doubtful." *Lima* (Ohio) *News,* November 12, 1975.

"Remains Found at Shipwreck." *St. Petersburg* (Fla.) *Times,* July 28, 1994.

"Reports Last Words of Freighter's Captain." *Journal-Tribune* (Marysville, Ohio), November 13, 1975.

"Robot Camera Snaps Sunken Ship." *Chicago Sun-Times,* August 25, 1989.

"Robot Plunges Deep to Transmit Pictures of Edmund Fitzgerald." *Orange County Register,* August 24, 1989.

"Robot Relays Startling Images of Wreck of the Edmund Fitzgerald." *Los Angeles Times,* August 25, 1989.

"Robot to Probe Wreck of Edmund Fitzgerald." *Boston Globe,* August 23, 1989.

"Robot to View Wreckage of Fitzgerald." *Chicago Tribune,* August 23, 1989.

"Robot Views Fitzgerald Hulk." *San Francisco Chronicle,* August 25, 1989.

"Salvaged Bell Rings for Sailors Lost in '76." *Houston Chronicle,* July 8, 1995.

"Saved Bell Tolls for Lost Crew of Ore Carrier." *Roanoke* (Va.) *Times & World News*, July 9, 1995.

"Search Finds Ship Debris but No Sign of 29 Men." *Milwaukee Journal*, November 11, 1975.

"Ship Intact at Lake Bottom: TV Cameras View Edmund Fitzgerald 14 Years After Disaster." *Chicago Tribune*, August 25, 1989.

"Ship Sinking Called Weird." *Fond du Lac Reporter*, November 13, 1975.

"Shipwreck Buffs Flock to Mystery of Fitzgerald." *Seattle Times*, July 31, 1994.

"Shipwreck Photos Anger Relatives." *Grand Rapids Press*, November 4, 1995.

"Shipwreck Society Begins Fund Raising for Museum." *Milwaukee Journal Sentinel*, July 5, 1998.

"Singer Joins Families at Fitzgerald Service." *Grand Rapids Press*, November 13, 2000.

"Sinking Ends a Special Era." *Milwaukee Journal*, November 12, 1975.

"6-Year-Old Freighter Sets Cargo High at Canada Lock." *New York Times*, November 29, 1964.

"Sonar Shows Pieces of 'Fitz'?" *Chronicle-Telegram*, November 19, 1975.

"Storm Rips Great Lakes Ore Boat; Fear 30 Lost." *Chicago Tribune*, November 11, 1975.

"Storm Sinks Ore Carrier." *News* (Port Arthur, Tex.), November 11, 1975.

"Suit Aims to Block Salvaging Bell from Fabled Shipwreck." *Grand Rapids Press*, May 3, 1995.

"Sunken Freighter Edmund Fitzgerald Goal of Dive Teams." *Pentagraph* (Bloomington, Ill.), July 5, 1994.

"Sunken Ore Boat Leaking Heavy Oil; Spill No Problem." *New York Times*, November 13, 1975.

"Sunken Ship Quiz Continues." *Sheboygan* (Wisc.) *Press*, November 20, 1975.

"Sunken Ship Shown to Be Largely Intact." *Houston Chronicle*, August 24, 1989.

"Team Sets Out to Study Great Lakes Wreck." *New York Times*, August 23, 1989.

"Team to Probe Wreck of Edmund Fitzgerald." *Minneapolis Star Tribune,* August 22, 1989.

"The Legend of the Fitz." *Blade* (Toledo, Ohio), November 10, 2000.

"The Wreck Edmund Fitzgerald Should Lie in Peace." *Tulsa* (Okla.) *World,* November 24, 2000.

"Tragedy Becoming a Cash Cow for Many." *Holland Sentinel,* November 9, 2000.

"Twenty-five Years After Its Sinking, Edmund Fitzgerald Remembered." *Dubuque Herald,* November 11, 2000.

"Union Protests Coast Guard Probe on Fitzgerald." *Fond du Lac Reporter,* November 18, 1975.

"Two Decades Ago Today, a Monstrous Lake Superior Storm Killed." *Cincinnati Post,* November 10, 1995.

"Victims' Relatives Worried Edmund Fitzgerald Wreck Will Become Diving Mecca." *Commercial Appeal* (Memphis, Tenn.), November 5, 2000.

"Video of Shipwreck Opens Old Wounds." *Chicago Tribune,* August 28, 1989.

"Waves Astonished Missing Skipper." *Milwaukee Journal,* November 13, 1975.

"Wicked Wind Whips Sank Superior Ship." *Madison* (Wisc.) *Capital Times,* November 14, 1996.

"Worries About Intruders at Wreck of Edmund Fitzgerald." *New York Times,* November 5, 2000.

"Wreckage Is Eyed by Sonar." *Herald-Times-Reporter* (Manitowoc, Wisc.), November 15, 1975.

"Wreckage of Ore Carrier Found in at Least 2 Pieces." *New York Times,* November 27, 1975.

Aig, Marlene. "Singer Avoids 'Wreck' of Lightfoot." *Chicago Sun-Times,* September 19, 1987.

Albrecht, Brian. "Lectures to Discuss Edmund Fitzgerald." *Cleveland Plain Dealer,* November 11, 1999.

Ammeson, Jane. "For Some, Ship's Sinking Remains Personal Matter." *South Bend* (Ind.) *Tribune,* November 5, 2000.

Armstrong, Robert. "Captain Speculates About Sinking of the 'Fitz.'" *Minneapolis Star Tribune,* March 18, 2001.

Atkins, Harry. "Ships, Aircraft Scour Lake for Lost Ore Ship." *Sheboygan* (Wisc.) *Press,* November 11, 1975.

Barth, Janis. "N. Country Man Was Skipper of Ill-fated Edmund Fitzgerald." *Syracuse* (N.Y.) *Post-Standard,* June 27, 1984.

Basheda, Valerie. "Divers Finally Bring Up What Fitzgerald Left Behind." *Detroit News,* July 21, 1992.

Batz, Bob. "Sister Has Made Peace with Sinking of Freighter." *Dayton* (Ohio) *Daily News,* August 8, 1994.

Behm, Don. "Crew Had Little Notice in Wreck." *Milwaukee Journal Sentinel,* November 12, 1992.

Borg, Gary. "Ship's Bell Won't Be Put on Display." *Chicago Tribune,* March 14, 1996.

Bratt, Heidi Mae. "Service Honors Fitzgerald Dead." *Detroit News,* November 12, 1990.

Brennan, Pat. "Sailors on Lake Superior Ships Shun Talk of Edmund Fitzgerald." *Toronto Star,* November 10, 1990.

Brochu, Ron. "Only a Song Remains of the Edmund Fitzgerald." *Albany* (N.Y.) *Times Union,* November 12, 2000.

Catlin, Roger. "Gordon Lightfoot Is Haunted by 'Wreck' Even on the Road." *Chicago Sun-Times,* October 18, 1989.

———. "Lightfoot Still Sings of Lost Ship but Hopes It Is Left Alone." *Minneapolis Star-Tribune,* November 3, 1989.

Champeau, Jack. "'I'll Bring You Back.'" *Guideposts,* March 2002.

Chapman, Chip. "Church Rector Worked Undercover in Pacific After the War." *Grosse Pointe* (Mich.) *News,* March 3, 1984.

Christiansen, Richard. "'Ten November' Comes Crashing as Story's Emotion Is Washed Out." *Chicago Tribune,* September 18, 1987.

Clairborne J. R., and Tenisha White. "Shedding Light on Fitzgerald's Mysterious Fate." *Chicago Sun-Times,* July 6, 1994.

Clark, Del. "Diver Targets 1958 Shipwreck." *Grand Rapids Press,* August 7, 1995.

———. "Researcher Sinks Some Theories About 'Fitz.'" *Grand Rapids Press,* November 10, 1994.

Crump, Sarah. "Lawyer's New Book Explores Tragedy of Edmund Fitzgerald." *Cleveland Plain Dealer,* January 30, 2003.

Donnelly, Francis X. "Fitzgerald Memories for Sale." *Detroit News,* October 29, 2000.

———. "Rector Maintains Faith for Families." *Detroit News and Free Press,* October 29, 2000.

Drake, Sylvie. "Steven Dietz: A Playwright, Sink or Swim." *Los Angeles Times,* June 11, 1989.

Drummond, Dee. "Edmund Fitzgerald Sailors' Families Get Closure." *Madison* (Wisc.) *Capital Times,* July 19, 1999.

———. "25 Years Later, 600 Mourn Edmund Fitzgerald Victims." *Blade* (Toledo, Ohio), November 13, 2000.

Dugas, Joseph H. "Fate of Fitzgerald Remains Overboard." *Grand Rapids Press,* July 12, 1998.

Dybas, Cheryl Lyn. "For Sale: Soul of the *Edmund Fitzgerald.*" *Traverse,* November 2000.

Eddy, Kristin. "Great Lakes Taps More Beers to Go." *Cleveland Plain Dealer,* January 20, 1993.

Farnquist, Tom. "New Clues Are Sought to Fitzgerald Disaster." *Cleveland Plain Dealer,* August 23, 1989.

Farnquist, Thomas L. "Requiem for the Edmund Fitzgerald." *National Geographic,* January 1996.

Finnerty, John. "Valley Man's Work Took Him to Famous Shipwreck." *Daily Item,* November 30, 2003.

Flesher, John. "Bill Would Ban Photos of Bodies on Sunken Ships." *Wisconsin State Journal,* May 3, 1995.

———. "Body Discovered Near Sunken Ore Carrier; Divers Examine 19-Year-Old Wreckage of the Edmund Fitzgerald." *Buffalo News,* July 29, 1994.

———. "Canada OKs Dive to Recover Edmund Fitzgerald's Bell." *Detroit Free News and Detroit Free Press,* May 27, 1995.

———. "Crew Examines Sunken Ship, Submarine Carries Explorers to Edmund Fitzgerald." *Buffalo News,* July 4, 1994.

———. "Depths of Research: Scientists Visit the Edmund Fitzgerald Wreck, Then Diagnose the Health of the Great Lakes." *Grand Rapids Press,* July 10, 1994.

———. "Diving into Painful Memories: Explorer of '74 Shipwreck Discovers Kin's Resentment." *Cleveland Plain Dealer,* December 25, 1994.

———. "Edmund Fitzgerald Families Plan 'Graveside service.'" *Milwaukee Journal Sentinel,* July 4, 1999.

———. "Explorers Say Edmund Fitzgerald Blew Apart When It Hit Bottom." *Minneapolis Star-Tribune,* July 5, 1994.

———. "'Feast Your Eyes': Submarine Gives Researchers Unprecedented View of Famous Shipwreck." *Grand Rapids Press,* July 6, 1994.

———. "Fitzgerald Legend Still Lives On." *Holland Sentinel,* November 9, 2000.

———. "'It's Time to Leave It Alone,' Families Say of Gravesite." *Grand Rapids Press,* November 5, 2000.

———. "Lakes Explorer Sues to Overturn Law Against Photographing Victims." *Detroit News,* November 14, 1997.

———. "New Law Bans Photos of Lake Disaster Victims." *Wisconsin State Journal,* October 4, 1997.

———. "Noted Lake Freighter Capsized, Then Broke Up." *Orange County Register,* July 6, 1994.

———. "Scientists Plan to Probe Sinking of the Fitzgerald." *Buffalo News,* July 3, 1994.

———. "Shipwreck Photos Upset Crew Families." *Pittsburgh Post-Gazette,* November 5, 1995.

———. "Titanic of the Great Lakes." *Grand Rapids Press,* July 3, 1994.

———. "U.P. Memorial Honors 6,000 Shipwrecks." *Grand Rapids Press,* July 1, 1998.

——. "Waves Turn Minutes to Hours." *Houston Chronicle,* November 6, 2000.

Goodman, David. "Minister, Singer Help Honor Crew of Edmund Fitzgerald." *Oakland Press,* November 13, 2000.

Graczyk, Michael L. "November Is Most Treacherous Period of Year for Ships Plying Great Lakes." *Fond du Lac Reporter,* November 12, 1975.

Greenwood, Tom. "Anchor Raising Revives Memories of 2 Ex-Crewmen." *Detroit News,* July 14, 1992.

——. "Fitzgerald's Anchor May Be Rescued." *Detroit News,* April 28, 1992.

Hanlon, Michael. "In 1975, Ship Sank in Lake Within Minutes." *Toronto Star,* November 11, 1998.

Haugen, Peter. "A Sinking Feeling on Stage." *Sacramento Bee,* October 13, 1996.

Heglin, Mark. "Fitzgerald Sank Year Ago Tuesday." *Manitowoc* (Wisc.) *Herald-Times-Reporter,* November 10, 1976.

Heinlein, Gary. "Questions of Ethics Surface Along with Bell." *Detroit News,* July 10, 1995.

Hindes, Martha. "The Bell Tolls." *Detroit News,* November 10, 1983.

Hodgson, Cindy. "Large Crowd Turns Out to Remember the Edmund Fitzgerald." *Lakeshore Chronicle* (Manitowoc, Wisc.), November 9, 2003.

Hornbeck, Mark. "Families Hope for Clues to Ship's Sinking." *Detroit News,* August 25, 1989.

Houlihan-Skilton, Mary. "In-Depth Look at Baffling Shipwreck." *Chicago Sun-Times,* December 21, 1993.

Jensen, Brenda. "Searchers Find Body in Fitzgerald Shipwreck." *Grand Rapids Press,* July 28, 1994.

Jones, Meg. "Museum Recalls Lakes' Wrecks." *Milwaukee Journal Sentinel,* March 11, 2001.

Joseph, Paul. "Gales of November Guarantee to Keep Us Guessing on Weather." *Milwaukee Journal Sentinel,* November 2, 2001.

——. "Windy Storm Today Brings Reminder of Edmund Fitzgerald." *Milwaukee Journal Sentinel,* November 10, 1996.

Judd, Terry. "Edmund Fitzgerald Story Is Re-examined." *Grand Rapids Press,* December 23, 1997.

———. "New Video Explores Demise of Edmund Fitzgerald." *Grand Rapids Press,* November 8, 2003.

Kampert, Patrick. "Gordon Lightfoot Has More to Sing About These Days." *Chicago Tribune,* July 7, 1991.

Keefe, Bill. "Rev. Richard W. Ingalls: Honoring the Memory of Mariners Lost at Sea." *Lakeland Boating,* March 1997.

Keefe, William F. "Edmund Fitzgerald Gravesite Consecrated." *Beacher* (Michigan City, Ind.), September 2, 1999.

Keen, Judy. "Ballad May Get Final Verse: Edmund Fitzgerald Still Holds Secrets," *USA Today,* August 24, 1989.

Kerwin, James L. "Great Lakes Sailors Observe Freighter Loss." *Detroit News,* November 24, 1985.

Kilpatrick, Ken. "Edmund Fitzgerald Lives On in Song." *Toronto Star,* August 18, 2001.

Ko, Michael. "The Big Blowout." *Chicago Tribune,* November 11, 1998.

LaLonde, Pati. "Sole Survivor Dennis Hale Was the Only Man to Survive the Wreck of the Daniel J. Morrell." *Bay City Times,* November 18, 2004.

Leavitt, Paul. "Nationline." *USA Today,* August 23, 1989.

Loohaus, Jackie. "28 Years Later." *Milwaukee Journal Sentinel,* November 9, 2003.

Lubenow, Thomas G. "Little Hope Seen for Ship's Crew." *Milwaukee Journal,* November 12, 1975.

Lucci, Mike. "25th Commemoration of the Wreck of the Edmund Fitzgerald." *United States Coast Guard Commandant's Bulletin,* November 1982. Reprinted and updated in *Reservist,* November 1995.

Madsen, Joyce Styron. "Disaster of the Great Lakes: The Mystery of the Edmund Fitzgerald." *Boys' Quest,* December 2001–January 2002.

Malan, John. "Fast-Moving Storm Doomed Ship 22 Years Ago Today." *Milwaukee Journal Sentinel,* November 10, 1997.

———. "November Is Month of Big Low Pressure Systems." *Milwaukee Journal Sentinel,* November 7, 1996.

———. "Ship Was on Collision Course with Low Pressure System." *Milwaukee Journal Sentinel,* November 11, 1996.

———. "Storm Team 4: Low Pressure Can Stir Wicked Storms." *Milwaukee Journal Sentinel,* November 8, 2004.

———. "Surprise Storm Sank the Edmund Fitzgerald 21 Years Ago Today." *Milwaukee Journal Sentinel,* November 10, 1996.

Mauro, Lucia. "A Murky Look at Tragedy." *Chicago Sun-Times,* October 13, 1997.

Michaelson, Mike. "Finding the 'Edmund Fitzgerald.' " *Post-Tribune* (Gary, Ind.), October 6, 2002.

———. "UP Visitors Race the Fate of the Edmund Fitzgerald." *Daily Herald* (Arlington Heights, Ill.), October 6, 2002.

Mietkiewicz, Henry. "Tragedy Still Mystifies 19 Years On." *Toronto Star,* November 6, 1996.

Miller, Geralda. "Edmund Fitzgerald Bell Rings 29 Times." *Grand Rapids Press,* November 11, 2002.

Mitchell, Bob. "Lake Shipwreck's Secrets Exposed." *Toronto Star,* August 25, 1989.

Moe, Doug. "Lore of the Edmund Fitzgerald." *Madison* (Wisc.) *Capital Times,* November 11, 2002.

Moore, Glynn. "Sad Song Keeps Sad Story Alive for 25 Years." *Augusta* (Ga.) *Chronicle,* November 16, 2000.

Oakes, Larry. "A Tragedy That Stirs the Heart and Imagination." *Minneapolis Star Tribune,* November 10, 2000.

———. "Remembering the Edmund Fitzgerald: 'Pirates' vs. Privacy." *Minneapolis Star Tribune,* November 10, 1995.

———. "The Mystery of the Fitzgerald." *Minneapolis Star Tribune,* November 10, 1997.

Phillips, Don. "After 15 Years, Mystery Still Shrouds Fitzgerald." *Washington Post,* November 10, 1990.

————. "Great Lakes Shipping Rides Wave of Popularity Transportation." *Los Angeles Times,* February 3, 1991.

Potter, Sean. "November 10, 1975." *Weatherwise,* November/December 2004.

Poulson, David. "No Peace for Dead's Bell." *Grand Rapids Press,* March 17, 1996.

Powers Ann. "Sailing Far from the Edmund Fitzgerald." *New York Times,* August 12, 2000.

Rasmussen, Frederick N. "The Vanishing Fitzgerald." *Baltimore Sun,* November 11, 2000.

Reilly, Jim. "Diver Explores the Wreck of the Edmund Fitzgerald." *Syracuse* (N.Y.) *Herald Journal,* April 23, 1997.

Rouvalis, Cristina. "Guiding Light: Lighthouse to Shine for 25th Anniversary of Wreck of Edmund Fitzgerald." *Pittsburgh Post-Gazette,* November 5, 2000.

Sales, Randy A. "Edmund Fitzgerald DVD Renews the Fascination." *Minneapolis Star Tribune,* November 10, 2003.

Sangiacomo, Michael. "Dive Irks Families of Fitzgerald Victims." *Cleveland Plain Dealer,* September 9, 1995.

————. "Families Ring Bell to Honor Lost Crew." *Cleveland Plain Dealer,* November 11, 2000.

————. "Fitzgerald Bell Won't Visit Festival." *Cleveland Plain Dealer,* March 15, 1996.

————. "Rite Marks 20 Years Since Ship Went Down." *Cleveland Plain Dealer,* November 11, 1995.

————. "Tragedy of Shipwreck May Find Its Final Rest." *Cleveland Plain Dealer,* June 28, 1995.

————. "Tribute Honors Sailors." *Cleveland Plain Dealer,* November 7, 1992.

Schmid, Randolph E. "November Witches Wreak Havoc with Deadly Weather." *Columbian* (Vancouver), November 16, 1998.

Scott, Gerald. "Church Honors Memory of Freighter." *Renaissance Times,* November 1, 1999.

———. "Detroit's Mariners' Church Hosts Ship Decommissioning." *Renaissance Times,* May 4, 1998.

Sepkowski, Karl. "Sunken Ship's Bell Will Honor 29 Who Died." *Toronto Star,* May 28, 1995.

———. "Crew of Edmund Fitzgerald Honored at Bell's Dedication." *Toronto Star,* November 11, 1995.

———. "Tears Flow as Edmund Fitzgerald's Bell Raised." *Toronto Star,* July 5, 1995.

Simonson, Mike. "Judge Allows Dive for Shipwreck's Bell." *Milwaukee Journal Sentinel,* May 19, 1995.

Smith, Whitney. "10 Nov. Plumbs the Depths of Boredom." *Commercial Appeal* (Memphis, Tenn.), October 5, 1996.

Stermer, Paul A. "Shipwrecks Dot the Great Lakes." *South Bend Tribune,* November 8, 2001.

St. John, Paige. "Church Bell to Toll Again for 29 Lost on Edmund Fitzgerald." *Grand Rapids Press,* November 11, 1990.

———. "Divers Looting Great Lakes Antiquities." *Fort Lauderdale Sun-Sentinel,* December 9, 1990.

———. "'Fitzgerald' Families Now Relive Tragedy." *St. Petersburg* (Fla.) *Times,* August 28, 1989.

———. "Shipwreck: Clear Photos Fail to Explain Great Lakes Sinking." *Seattle Times,* August 25, 1989.

Suhr, Jim. "Bells Again Toll for the Crew of the Fitzgerald at Ceremonies." *Wisconsin State Journal,* November 11, 2000.

Svoboda, Sandra W. "Church Service Honors Edmund Fitzgerald's Lost Crewmen." *Wisconsin State Journal,* November 13, 1995.

Swardson, Anne. "How the Edmund Fitzgerald Went Down, Down, Down; Sub Probes Wreck of Fabled Vessel." *Washington Post,* July 5, 1994.

Tiede, Tom. "Fitz Wreck Remains a Mystery." *Post* (Frederick, Md.), May 21, 1979.

Tomaszewski, Deidre S. "Paints Putting Edmund Fitzgerald to the Fore." *Detroit News,* December 23, 1992.

Velkely, Gina. "Fascination with Ships, Lakes Spurs Kids' Book About 'Fitzgerald.'" *Grand Rapids Press,* March 18, 1999.

Volgenau, Gerry. "Mich.'s Whitefish Point Offers a Big Lake and Great Birdwatching." Knight Ridder Tribune News Service, June 17, 2002.

Von Sternberg, Bob. "A Grim Sight: Body of Crewman Spotted Near Wreck of the Edmund Fitzgerald." *Minneapolis Star Tribune,* July 28, 1994.

Weeks, Don. "Interactive CD-ROM Dives into 1975 Shipwreck on Lake Superior." *Detroit News and Free Press,* November 10, 1996.

Wharton, Tom. "Lightfoot Says Much in Memorable Songs." *Salt Lake City Tribune,* November 12, 1990.

Woutat, Donald. "Stirring Up Memories: Edmund Fitzgerald Haunts Michigan Town." *Minneapolis Star Tribune,* August 27, 1989.

———. "View of Edmund Fitzgerald Shows Surprising Hole in Bow." *Minneapolis Star Tribune,* August 25, 1989.

Zacharias, Pat. "Detroit, Michigan, at the Millennium: 29 Lost Their Lives in Sinking of Fitzgerald." *Detroit News,* November 10, 1999.

ACKNOWLEDGMENTS

IF I'VE LEARNED ONE LESSON IN WRITING EIGHT BOOKS, IT'S THAT THE process of writing a nonfiction book is, in every respect, a collaborative adventure. The writer is only as strong as the information he or she receives, and in the process of obtaining important information, the writer depends on the trust and honesty of strangers. At times, researching the *Edmund Fitzgerald* was a walk through a minefield: I had to deal with turf wars, people who had been burned by the press in the past, family members weary from talking about the tragedy over the course of three decades, and individuals with their own private agendas. Fortunately, these times paled in comparison to the hours I spent with people who were generous with their time and memories. Others were helpful in other ways. I always feel blessed at the end of a book, and this one is no exception.

While researching the book, I attempted to contact relatives of the lost crewmen. Some were willing to talk, others weren't. Every family member has his or her individual way of honoring and preserving the memory of a loved one, and I tried not to infringe on that. I'd like to thank Pam Johnson, Deborah (Champeau)

Gomez-Felder, John O'Brien, Jon Soyring, and Mary Soyring for sharing some of their memories for this book. Janice Armagost and Cheryl Rozman, though reluctant to be formally interviewed for the record, were kind enough to provide me with critical details about their loved ones.

My gratitude to those whose memories and insights helped, in both large and small ways, in adding depth and color to the *Fitzgerald* story: Brent Biehl, Eddie Chaput, Robert N. Dunn, Don Erickson, Jimmie Hobaugh, Thom Holden, Bishop Richard W. Ingalls, Reverend Richard W. Ingalls, Jr., Sean Ley, Dale Lindstrom, C. S. Loosmore, Charles Millradt, Lee Radzik, Gary Rosenau, Christiana Sams, Mal Sillars, and James A. Wilson. Tom Farnquist, director of the Great Lakes Shipwreck Historical Society in Whitefish Point, Michigan, was gracious and candid in answering my questions and assisting with many of the facts and details, even though he knew that there were bound to be parts of the book that made him uncomfortable. Tim McCall not only helped via his *Edmund Fitzgerald* Web site (*www.ssefo.com*), he also sat for an interview and assisted with arranging a couple of critical interviews with family members.

The Historian's Office at the United States Coast Guard headquarters in Washington, D.C., allowed me to review its *Edmund Fitzgerald* file and photocopy the transcripts of the Marine Board of Investigation hearings. Thanks to Dr. Robert Browning and Scott Price for their assistance.

I am grateful to Doris Sampson for permission to use her beautiful painting on the title page, and to David Conklin, Tom Farnquist, and the Great Lakes Shipwreck Historical Society for use of Conklin's painting of the *Fitzgerald*'s wreckage, reprinted on the back cover.

Like so many people, I first heard about the *Edmund Fitzgerald* through Gordon Lightfoot's song "The Wreck of the *Edmund Fitzgerald*." I'd heard of the *Fitz* immediately after its loss—its home port, Milwaukee, is less than a half-hour from my home, and the tragedy was covered extensively in that city's papers— but I really didn't feel any strong connection to the story until I'd heard Lightfoot's haunting lyrics and melody. So I owe a true debt of gratitude to the troubadour who reported the news. I'm also grateful for his permission to reprint the lyrics to his song in this book, and to Barry Harvey of Early Morning Productions, for helping with the arrangements.

While researching the *Fitzgerald* story, I read and looked over hundreds of books, newspaper and magazine articles, television documentaries, official reports, and court documents. Many of these sources are cited in the Notes and Bibliography sections of this book, but I feel that I should make additional mention of three previously published books that were especially helpful in the early goings, when I was initially piecing together the events described in my account. Frederick Stonehouse's *The Wreck of the Edmund Fitzgerald* was the first substantial volume published on the tragedy, and it remains invaluable for its straightforward telling of the story and its frank, detailed analysis of the different theories about the causes of the loss of the ship and crew. Robert J. Hemming's *Gales of November* was especially useful when I was researching the backgrounds of the *Fitzgerald* crew members. Dr. Joseph MacInnis's *Fitzgerald's Storm,* a dramatic rendering of the *Fitzgerald* story, is well worth reading.

Special thanks to Greg Bonofiglio and Jim Novy, who were helpful beyond the call of duty or friendship.

Thanks to the staff of Bloomsbury, especially to Kathy Belden, who edited this book, and Karen Rinaldi, who was so instrumental in getting it added to the publisher's list. At a time when publishing is becoming alarmingly impersonal and bottom line oriented, Bloomsbury remains decisively writer friendly.

I am grateful to the staff at Inkwell Management, particularly Kim Witherspoon and David Forrer, for help and guidance. I'm lucky to have them in my corner.

Finally, my deepest thanks to Susan, who carried my career longer than she should have, and to my children—Adam, Emily Joy, and Jack Henry—who are constant reminders of what's important in life.

INDEX

A NOTE ON THE AUTHOR

Michael Schumacher is the author of six books, including biographies of Allen Ginsberg (*Dharma Lion*), Eric Clapton (*Crossroads*), Phil Ochs (*There but for Fortune*), and Francis Ford Coppola (*Francis Ford Coppola*). He edited the selected correspondence of Allen and Louis Ginsberg and has written scripts for twenty-five documentaries about Great Lakes shipwrecks. He lives in Wisconsin.